THERE IS AN ISLE

Published in 1998 by Mercier Press
PO Box 5 5 French Church Street Cork
Tel: (021) 275040; Fax: (021) 274969
e.mail: books@mercier.ie
16 Hume Street Dublin 2
Tel: (01) 661 5299; Fax: (01) 661 8583
e.mail: books@marino.ie

Trade enquiries to CMD Distribution
55A Spruce Avenue
Stillorgan Industrial Park
Blackrock County Dublin
Tel: (01) 294 2556; Fax: (01) 294 2564

© Criostoir O'Flynn

ISBN 1 85635 219 6
10 9 8 7 6 5 4 3 2

A CIP record for this title is available
from the British Library

Cover design by
Penhouse Design Group
Printed in Ireland by ColourBooks
Baldoyle Industrial Estate, Dublin 13

Published in the US and Canada by
the Irish American Book Company
6309 Monarch Park Place, Niwot,
Colorado, 80503
Tel: (303) 530-1352, (800) 452-7115
Fax: (303) 530-4488, (800) 401-9705

THERE IS AN ISLE

A LIMERICK BOYHOOD

CRIOSTOIR O'FLYNN

MERCIER PRESS

IRISH AMERICAN BOOK COMPANY (IABC)
Boulder, Colorado

There is an isle, a bonny isle,
Stands proudly from the sea,
And dearer far than all this world
Is that dear isle to me.
It is not that alone it stands
Where all around is fresh and fair,
But because it is my native land
And my home, my home is there.

Farewell, farewell! Though lands may meet
My gaze where'er I roam,
I shall not find a spot so fair
As that dear isle to me.
It is not that alone it stands
Where all around is fresh and fair,
But because it is my native land
And my home, my home is there.

CONTENTS

1

ISLANDMAN

'This is my island in the sun . . .'

I was born on an island. My island is not as obvious as those offshore islands in the Atlantic, the Great Blasket Island about which Tomás Ó Criomhthain wrote his famous autobiography *An tOileánach* (*The Islandman*) (1929) or the Aran Islands of Liam O'Flaherty. In fact, my island is not even marked on the map of Ireland; so let me guide you to it.

Consider the map of Ireland and follow the course of the river Shannon from its source in County Cavan south through the centre of the country until it turns west to flow for another sixty miles to its meeting with the Atlantic Ocean. At the point where the river turns to the west, a small island formed. That is my island. The reason it is not marked on the map is that it is now only a very small part of the modern city of Limerick.

On this island in the Shannon, protected by the natural moat made by the narrow loop of the branching river, the city of Limerick began as a settlement in prehistoric times. Because the river was fordable at that point, this settlement became the commercial link between the south and the west of Ireland, and also a crucial strategic factor in the frequent cattle-raids and other hostilities between the kings and chiefs of the provinces of Connacht and Munster. When Saint Patrick returned to Ireland as a missionary bishop, having spent six years of his youth as a slave herding pigs in Antrim, and incidentally being prepared for his life's work by learning the language and culture of the Irish people, he eventually arrived at Limerick and converted the local chief and his people to Christianity – an event commemorated in the name of the nearby village, *Tobar Phádraig* (Patrickswell), as proudly proclaimed on their jerseys every time the hurlers of that famous GAA club take the field. Patrick left one of his monks to organize the building of the first church and the consolidation of the new faith. That first bishop of Limerick must have had a Latin name unpronounceable by the natives, for he has come down in history and folklore only by the name Mainchín (from *manach*, a monk, and *ín*, the mark of the diminutive), a name barbarously anglicised as Munchin. In spite of a local legend to the contrary, historians tell us that the first Christian church was built on the island, on the site of the now disused Protestant church of Saint Munchin (I must use that meaningless solecism until the people of Limerick decide to revert to the real name of our first bishop and patron of our diocese).

When the Vikings sailed up the Shannon they must have thanked Thor and Odin when they saw the island, with its church and other rich pickings, and its potential as a base from which to launch further raids into the countryside on both sides of the river, raids which eventually brought their marauding longships as far as Ireland's most famous monastic settlement and school at Clonmacnoise near Athlone. With his older brother, Mahon, that valiant Clareman, Brian Boru, burned the Norse settlement of Limerick before going on finally to break the Viking power in Ireland at the Battle of Clontarf in 1014.

Next to arrive with evil intent at the island in the Shannon were the Normans, a more formidable enemy than the haphazardly raiding Norsemen, and more fortunate in that the O'Brien descendants of the great Brian were willing to bow the knee to the king of England for what they saw as political and military advantage over rival Irish chieftains. King John curbed the ambition of those first Normans in Limerick by retaining the whole island as his personal property – it is still known as the King's Island. By order of King John a castle was built on the island, together with a bridge connecting the castle, with its strategic drawbridge, to the northern bank of the river in County Clare. Even today the remaining towers of King John's Castle are awesome; so we can imagine what it must have seemed like to the natives of Limerick and the surrounding countryside as it rose, stone by stone, on the island in the Shannon, a menacing symbol of the foreign power that had come to stay. From the time the first Norman garrison took up residence in the new castle until 1922, when the British finally withdrew from twenty-six of the thirty-two counties of Ireland, it was occupied as a military stronghold. Recently restored, the castle is now the main historical attraction for tourists in Limerick. For me, King John's Castle, the adjacent Thomond Bridge and the Treaty Stone on its pedestal on the opposite bank of the river, have a more personal significance and symbolism. The house in which I was born and reared is literally only a stone's throw from the castle. As a child I played King of the Castle on the steps leading up to the gate of the then unoccupied castle. And the first words I heard that made me aware of the world outside the front door of our house were 'street', 'castle', 'bridge', 'river', 'island'.

Soon after the castle was built in the early part of the thirteenth century, the island town was enclosed by a defensive wall. The native Irish were not allowed to live within the walled town, but set up shanty dwellings outside it, just as the native Africans did outside the white-controlled cities of South Africa while the policy of apartheid was in force. Thus arose the names Englishtown for the walled settlement on the island and Irishtown for the adjacent unofficial settlement where the Irish could grow vegetables and keep pigs and poultry. These were a source of sustenance for themselves and of trade when the gates were opened in the morning and they could cross the bridge on the Abbey River (the origin of its name, Baal's Bridge, is unclear) and enter the walled town. The names Irishtown and English-town were the common appellations in my boyhood, although not so frequently used now by the younger generation in the modern much-extended city. Limerick is not unique, of course, in having a district known as the Irishtown but I have met many natives of Dublin who were unaware of the significance of the existence of such an area near Ringsend, an area which was originally outside the city walls, just as Trinity College was when it was built on College Green.

When the inevitable intermingling of the races had occurred, and with the building of better houses in the Irishtown, the city wall was extended to enclose that area also, so that Limerick then assumed the outline of a somewhat misshapen hourglass, with the bridge across the narrow loop of the Shannon (the Abbey River) as its link. The tradition of gardens outside the walls continued, however, and in later times one such garden, *Garrdha Eoin* ('Owen's Garden') became a favourite resort for the citizens. In its anglicised form, Garryowen, the name was to become known worldwide. A similar settlement of the native Irish was established on the Clare bank of the Shannon, at the northern end of Thomond Bridge, and from the gate at that point it acquired the name it has kept to this day, Thomond-gate (that word Thomond, by the way, should be pronounced 'Thoo-mond', deriving as it does from the Irish *Tuadhmhumhan*, meaning North Munster, as opposed to *Deasmhumhan*, anglicised as Desmond, meaning South Munster). Here there was an area similar to *Garrdha Eoin* called *Fearann Seoin* ('John's Land') which has become Farranshone. The inhabitants of the Thomondgate area were traditionally known as Soda Cakes. The origin of the name is not documented, but my father told us that an old man who lived in Thomondgate told him that it derived from the second siege of Limerick in 1691 when the army of the Dutch General Ginkel attacked the city from the Clare side. (In the previous year, William III launched his unsuccessful attack from the Garryowen or southern side.) The garrison of a small outpost on the Clare side of Thomond Bridge were supplied at their posts with soda bread baked by the natives of that area. 'That's a good story anyway!' my mother used to comment.

When the walls of Limerick were almost totally demolished in the eighteenth century, the city was developed on land largely reclaimed from the tidal swamps along by the river. These new streets were laid out on a grid pattern. One of the most significant developments was made by a wealthy family named Arthur, who also built a quay for their ships near the point where the Abbey River rejoins the Shannon below Curragour Falls (which are not really falls, by the way, but churning rapids caused at low tide by an irregular shelf of rock). Beside the quay they built a row of tall townhouses, such as were also built in the new streets of the expanding city. When, as happened in Dublin and other cities, a still newer area around the Crescent became fashionable in the nineteenth century, the houses at Arthur's Quay were abandoned by their wealthy owners and turned into rented accommodation for the working class. It was into downgraded mansions like these that were crowded not only the poor natives but also the crowds of country folk who converged on the city from the three adjoining counties of Limerick, Clare and Tipperary, seeking work in the new factories or hoping to survive the Famine of 1845–7. In a two-room apartment in one of those houses my mother was born in 1894, and her childhood playground was the riverside at Arthur's Quay, where turf-boats still unloaded cargoes from Kilrush and other points down-river. The new suburbs of the second half of this century have seen Limerick expand so much that the old Island Parish is now only a very small part of the city. But it remains the historic and symbolic heart of Limerick, and the anthem adopted by the natives of St Mary's Island Parish, 'There Is an Isle', can serve by extension for the whole city of Limerick. And why not for the whole green island of Ireland?

2

THE BELLS OF ST MARY'S

I was born a week before Christmas Day in 1927. I was the sixth child of my parents, Richard O'Flynn and Elizabeth Connolly, known to their relations and friends as Richie and Lily. Their first children were two girls, Mary and Lily, then came six boys, Tom, Joe, Dick, Christy (me!), Maurice and Paddy. As was the custom then, all of us were named with reference to religious, family or seasonal connections. My mother often said that the Christmas when I was born was the best in her life, because everyone was attending to her instead of the normal Christmas situation when the mother is working even harder than usual in attending to everyone else. She also told me often that, although I was christened twice, I was given only one of the two nice Christmas names she had chosen for me, Christopher and Stephen.

In those days the Church still taught that babies who died unbaptised were consigned for all eternity to a place called Limbo; hence, babies were taken to the church to be baptised as soon as possible, usually only a few days after birth. This meant that the mother could not be present, nor sometimes even the father (taking a day, or even an hour, off work was not as easy then as it seems to be nowadays). The new baby was usually taken to the church by a grandmother or aunt, and other uncles or aunts were drafted in as godparents. Our mother's mother, Granny Connolly, who lived in Crosby Row just up the street from us, relished this role, as did all the good women of her honoured status. But it so happened that one of the ways from our house near the castle to St Mary's Parish Church led past a certain grocery-cum-pub. The proprietor of this establishment was an old friend of Granny Connolly's and the snug was a regular conference centre for herself and her cronies. It was her custom when bearing the new baby cradled in her black shawl along to the baptismal font, to drop in to the grocery-cum-pub in order proudly to display the latest addition to her growing flock of grandchildren. With me the celebrations were apparently more spirited than usual, with the result that at my ecclesiastical christening in St Mary's shortly after, Granny Connolly could not recollect the second name she had been instructed to convey to the officiating priest. Consequently I came back to my mother's arms deprived forever of the special patronage of St Stephen and named only for the legendary warrior who carried the Christchild across a river and thus became the patron saint of all travellers.

Like my Granny Connolly's house in the little riverside street of Crosby Row, and the houses in Arthur's Quay and Watergate where my mother and father, respectively, were born, St Mary's Church in which I was baptised and where I was brought as a child to my first Mass, exists no more. It was in itself a 'sermon in stone', reminding the people of the parish of the Penal Days when the law of the land forbade Catholics to have a 'Mass-house' within the city walls. The church was actually built on a small plot of land between the city wall and that narrow looping branch of the Shannon which is called the Abbey River (because of the Franciscan abbey which once stood on its bank). It was built only a little over fifty years after the ill-fated Treaty of Limerick, which treacherously guaranteed civil and religious liberty to

16

the native Catholic population, was signed on the historic Treaty Stone on the Clare side of Thomond Bridge in 1691. The first Mass was celebrated on 10 December 1749 (only three years after the defeat of Bonnie Prince Charlie at Culloden). The parish registers date back to that year, and I am indebted to an article by Liam Bartlett (who served as sacristan in St Mary's from 1929 to 1981 and who taught my brothers and myself, as well as hundreds of other young natives of the parish, the ritual of serving the priest at Mass) for the information that among the notable entries in those registers are the following:

19 December 1803: Dr O'Flynn baptised Gerald, son to Patrick Griffin and Ellen Geary.

[This was the child who was to become known as poet and novelist, author of *The Collegians* (1829) on which Boucicault based his play, *The Colleen Bawn* (1860) and Sir Jules Benedict his opera, *The Lily of Killarney* (1862).]

29 December 1820: Rev. M. Enright baptised Bryan, son to Michael Ryan and Catherine Merriman.

[This child was a grandson of the Clare poet Brian Merriman (*c*.1745–1805) who, probably to escape from the notoriety achieved by his masterpiece, *Cúirt an Mheán Oíche* (*The Midnight Court*), had moved from the village of Feakle to Limerick where he abandoned poetry to set up in the more respectable business of teaching mathematics in a room in Clare Street while living, perhaps, with his married daughter in Mary Street near St Mary's Cathedral.]

My earliest memory of attending Mass in that historic Penal-Days church, old St Mary's, is of holding on to my mother's hand as we climbed the stairs to one of the two galleries, from which grandstand perch I had a clear view of the priest's hands at the consecration of the host and the wine, a view most people at Mass did not have until after the Vatican Council when the ritual was altered so that the celebrant faced the congregation.

Some months before my Granny Connolly brought me to the baptismal font in the old St Mary's, a new parish priest, Fr Michael Hannan, had been appointed, and he, despairing of repairing the old church, decided to build a new one. So, while we went to Mass every Sunday in the old church, we watched the creation, stone by stone, of the beautiful new Hiberno-Romanesque church beside it. When it opened on 31 July 1932, the year of the Eucharistic Congress in Dublin, my eldest brother, Tom, was one of the altar boys, and it was in the new church that I made my First Holy Communion in 1934. In these days when every diocese in Ireland seems to be deeply in debt to the banks, it is proudly recalled by the old residents of St Mary's Parish on the King's Island that the total cost of the new church, £47,000, was met by the donations of the parishioners, at home or in exile, through collections and other activities.

Because St Mary's Parish was the oldest in the modern city, and as it was coterminous with the King's Island which had been the historic nucleus of Limerick, the words 'Island' and 'Parish' came to be synonymous; so, when a native of the Island in the Shannon is asked which part of Limerick City he comes from, he will reply simply that he comes from 'the Parish'. Modern conditions of life, when people move house or county, or even country, with such frequency, have done much to weaken that feeling of local pride, but in my youth all the older areas of Limerick City - Garryowen, Irishtown, the village of the Thomondgate Soda Cakes on the Clare side of Thomond Bridge, Boherbuoy (*An Bóthar Buí*, 'The Yellow Road') with its famous band, Park (outside the line of the old city walls and reputed to have been a settlement of Danes, a name then still applied to the inhabitants), the area around Wolfe Tone Street known as 'the back of the Monument' after the statue of the 'Liberator' of Ireland was erected there in 1857, Carey's Road and the neighbourhood of the railway station – each of these was like a little republic in itself, so far as sporting and other allegiances went, and the natives of each area were just as proud of their quarter as were the inhabitants of the Island Parish.

There is a story in the folklore of the parish that illustrates how much loyalty to one's own area was a part of our life. In the mid-1930s the Corporation decided to clear the worst slums of the city by building over five hundred houses in that part of the King's Island known as the Island Field, where the garrison of nearby King John's Castle had for centuries practised their drilling and shooting – and buried their dead in the small military cemetery which can still be seen there. One fine summer's day a gang of workmen, natives of the Island Parish, were labouring at the preparatory blasting and other work for the scheme when the bell of St Munchin's church across the river in Thomondgate began to sound the noonday Angelus. As was the custom everywhere then, the men stopped work and removed their caps to say the Angelus privately. Whereupon the foreman immediately reprimanded his gang thus: 'Wait now, lads, we'll wait for our own.' The men replaced their caps and resumed work until, a few seconds later, our sacristan, Liam Bartlett, began to ring out the noonday Angelus from our brand-new St Mary's. 'Right now, lads,' said the foreman, 'there's the blessed Angelus!' Whereupon the caps were duly doffed and those devout Catholic (St Mary's) workmen acknowledged, like the humble peasants in that ubiquitous picture by Millet, that the Creator himself became a workman in Palestine long ago.

3

'I REMEMBER, I REMEMBER'

Thus began one of the poems we learned in school:

> I remember, I remember,
> The house where I was born,
> The little window where the sun
> Came creeping in at morn.

Our house, as I have mentioned, was only a stone's throw from King John's Castle, but the stone would have to be thrown, not northwards towards Thomond Bridge and the Shannon River, but west along the narrow side-street called Old Church Street which is actually the continuation, in a straight line, of Mary Street–Nicholas Street, the original main street of the island city. The house was one in a terrace of four, three of them identical two-storey houses, the fourth a three-storey mansion with an impressive central doorway, hall and stairs. The mansion and its three adjacent houses are all built of cut stone and they date back to around 1700 shortly after the two sieges of Limerick. The mansion beside our house was built as the palace or official residence of the Protestant Bishop of Limerick – ancient maps show a large building on the site – and the three adjacent houses appear to have been for the use of lesser clergy. A strange feature of the terrace is the large wooden gate between the ground floors of the first and second of the three two-storey houses. This opens into a wide passage which allowed the bishop's coach to go right through the building into an area behind the houses where stables and coach-houses were situated (accommodation for servants would probably have been over the stables). Above this coach entrance were two extra rooms, forming, in effect, an extension of the upper storey of the first house, a point which was to become of serious importance in the life of our family, as will be seen.

Next to the Bishop's Palace and its three adjoining houses, the Protestant church of St Munchin with its extensive churchyard occupied the land down to the river, and to complete what was obviously an ecclesiastical enclave in this corner of the King's Island, the church grounds extended to include an almshouse for Protestant widows and a Villiers School. The old building behind our houses and the Bishop's Palace was in our time a parish hall for the Protestant congregation of the nearby St Munchin's Church, none of whom lived in our area except the caretaker-sexton and the old ladies in the almshouses beside the Villiers School. Occasionally, the Protestant ladies' committee put on a jumble sale in the hall, selling clothes and footwear, books, pictures, household utensils, ornaments and bric-à-brac, and while the Catholic Church at that time forbade its members to attend any kind of Protestant service – even the funeral of a close friend or business colleague – there was no law against going to a Protestant jumble sale; indeed, most of the customers were the Catholic mothers from our streets, and many a good secondhand Protestant boot or shirt became a regular attender at Sunday Mass in St Mary's in our parish or in the Catholic St Munchin's across Thomond Bridge. I remember hearing my father joking as he struggled with a shirt-stud one Sunday morning that this fine Protestant shirt he was wearing for the first time might jump off his back and fly out the door of the church when he went to Mass!

The Protestant bishops resided in the mansion on the island until 1784, when a new official residence was built in Henry Street ('up the town', to use our island parlance) in the fashionable newly-developed area of the expanding city. In my childhood, the erstwhile palace was let out in flats – 'cottered', my mother called it – and it was occupied by about twelve families. Its open doorway resulted in the unlit hall and stairs sometimes providing a night's shelter from the elements for some poor homeless beggarman or woman, so that the residents often had to step over bodies as they made their way to their own apartments. On dark winter nights, a child who lived on the top floor would stand in the hallway and shout, 'Ma, throw me down a lightin' paper!' The mother would wind up a piece of newspaper, light it in the fire and drop it from the landing down to the hall; the child would pick it up and dash up the stairs carrying this improvised and potentially dangerous torch. By the 1970s, when I had occasion to revisit the scenes of my childhood to make a programme about Limerick with Donncha Ó Dúlaing for RTÉ, the old mansion was abandoned and derelict, as was the house next door where I had spent the first eleven years of my life. Happily, both are now restored, the mansion by the Limerick Civic Trust and the house by Martin Finnin, a local builder, who, with his wife Anne, welcomed me cordially when I was again revisiting the scenes of my childhood in order to write this chronicle.

The old Bishop's Palace next door to our house was the source of one of the first stories we heard at the fireside as children, from our Granny Connolly as well as from our parents, the story of the Bishop's Lady, and a terrifying story it was, especially when heard on a winter's night with the wind from the river howling around the castle and our old houses. Apparently, among the Protestant bishops who resided in the palace during the eighteenth century, there was one unfortunate prelate who must often have envied the celibate state of the Catholic clergy, whatever inconveniences they might have been suffering as a result of the Penal Laws. This bishop had a wife who was, as the poet Michael Hogan, the self-styled Bard of Thomond (1829–99), was to write in his masterpiece, 'Drunken Thady and the Bishop's Lady':

> In love with suppers, cards and balls,
> And luxurious sin of festive halls,
> Where flaming hearts, and flaming wine,
> Invite the passions all to dine.

Such a harum-scarum was that Bishop's Lady that when she died she was sentenced to atone for her sins by haunting Thomond Bridge and the River Shannon. She even terrorised the garrison of King John's Castle and paid an unwelcome visit to the bishop himself:

> She knock'd two drunken soldiers dead,
> Two more, with batter'd foreheads fled;
> She broke the sentry-box in staves,
> And dashed the fragments in the waves.
> She pitched her reverend Lord downstairs
> And burned the house about his ears . . .

Anyone daring to cross Thomond Bridge on a dark night was in danger of being thrown into the river by 'this unruly, rampant she-ghost'. Every child in our castle area of the island could point out what were said to be the actual marks of the Bishop's Lady's fingers on the stone parapet of Thomond Bridge, and so convinced were we that she haunted the old mansion next door that we would not dare to go into the dark hallway or up the stairs after dark, even to visit some of our pals who lived in the apartments.

When my parents married in 1918, having postponed their wedding from the previous year because of the death in Flanders of my father's young brother, Tom, they returned from their honeymoon in Cork to settle into married bliss

23

in a little room in Rutland Street, on the top floor of one of the old nineteenth-century houses opposite the Custom House. On the ground floor of that building was one of the most popular shops in the area, The Cosy, one of the first fish-and-chip shops in Limerick. The newlyweds were thus compensated for the hardship of having to drag buckets of water up several flights of stairs by having only to go down the same stairs to buy their supper. My mother told us that the poor people were ashamed at first to be seen buying fish-and-chips, feeling that the neighbours would deduce that they had nothing to eat at home!

Another item from her early days of married life throws an interesting light on the superstitions, or 'pishrogues' as they were called (one of the many Irish words then in use in the Limerick dialect of Hiberno-English) which were part of life in the early part of this century when people still believed in fairies. Even in the early 1930s, when I was growing up, some people would return home if the first person they met in the morning was a red-haired woman; our Granny told us of a certain old woman who had only a cat for companion and was reputed to be a witch; and a morose bachelor in a street not far from ours was said to have the 'evil eye' that would ensure bad luck for anyone who met him on the street. Even after the Second World War, workmen refused to demolish a 'fairy' mound and tree in the fields where the Ballynanty houses now stand near Thomond Park rugby grounds.

My mother's own story was that, on their first night in their cosy one-room home, when it came time to go to bed, they knelt and said the Rosary, as most people did in those days; then 'himself' carefully swept the hearth, poked up the dying embers of the fire, carefully arranged the only two chairs in position at the fireside, and placed two cups of water on the table. When his puzzled young bride asked him why he was going through this ceremony, he told her that the ritual was always observed in his family home in

Watergate, and that it was to ensure that if any of Them came to visit during the night, they would find a welcome and rest by the family fireside. When she asked who he meant by 'Them', he explained that any of their dead relatives might be spending some of their Purgatory revisiting the scenes of their life (shades of the Bishop's Lady!). My mother assured us that she could not sleep that night with the terror of peeping at the glowing embers in the fireplace and the two empty waiting chairs. She tolerated her new husband's practice of his family's traditional reverence for the dead for a few nights, but eventually issued the ultimatum – she would not get into bed unless he desisted; which, being more in love with his lovely living young wife than with his dead ancestors, he promptly did. My mother, of course, had her own share of pishrogues, and one of her expressions, when asserting that something or other was sure to happen, was 'Burn me for a witch!' if her prophecy did not come true.

My parents did not have to stay long in their upper room in Rutland Street before a girl with whom my mother had worked in Cleeve's caramel factory on Charlotte's Quay – now the site of a car park by the Abbey River – told her of a house in the parish, near the castle, in the letting of which the girl's brother had some function, he being the rent-collector for those houses on behalf of Nash's office up the town. This was the house next door to the old 'cottered' Bishop's Palace, a house that was actually a house-and-a-half because of those two extra bedrooms over the coach entrance as described earlier. Because of this factor, the house was let as two apartments, to my parents and to another young married couple, Jack and Mary Anne Sheehan. On the ground floor, the front room facing the street (what should have been the parlour or sitting-room) became the kitchen-cum-living-room for the O'Flynn couple, the Sheehans getting the back room looking out on the small yard. The reverse obtained upstairs, the Sheehans having the two front bedrooms, the O'Flynns the back pair (a peculiar feature of those bedrooms was that the smaller one was reached through the main one; this was a crucial factor in one of our fireside stories, to be narrated later).

The fact that they would have a common front door, hallway and stairs, and share the small yard with its single toilet and one tap on the wall, did not diminish the happiness of those two young couples as they settled into this shared house-and-a-half. They thought themselves extremely fortunate in comparison with the many thousands of people who were then living in appalling conditions in overcrowded tenements or cramped cottages, and not only in Limerick but in every city in Ireland, Britain and Europe. To have merely to walk out to the backyard to fill a bucket of water, instead of having to carry it up many flights of stairs, to have a toilet shared by only four people instead of several families, to have space in the yard for a small shed and a clothes-line for each couple, and finally to have the red gas-meter in the kitchen-cum-living-room into which one slotted a penny to fuel a gas-lamp and a gas-ring, all this must have seemed like heaven on earth for my parents and for that other young couple as they happily took shared possession of the house shortly after the end of the First World War. And each couple probably hoped that the other couple would soon find another place and move out, leaving the entire house-and-a-half in their possession.

They would not have been so happy and optimistic if an angel from heaven had revealed to them that they would still be sharing that house almost up to the outbreak of another world war nearly twenty years later; by which time the O'Flynns had a family of eight, two girls and six boys, ranging in age from eighteen to two years, and the Sheehans had a grown-up family of four daughters and one son.

4

A ROOM WITH A VIEW

Now that I have described the social and domestic conditions into which I was deposited when I became a member of the human race, the Irish nation, and the Catholic Church – three organisations in which I am still happily listed – the academic sociologist might be inclined to focus on that single room, combined kitchen, sitting-room and living-room, on the floor of which I crawled while my mother washed clothes or cooked on the shiny black range. In this room all the domestic life, apart from sleep, of our entire family was concentrated. The sociologist would deduce logically that a child growing up in such conditions must have been underprivileged, and was probably undernourished also, given the fact that the early 1930s were a period of economic depression all over Europe and America, when Ireland was suffering the added effects of the economic war with the ever-bullying John Bull who was still demanding annual payments for the land he had stolen from the people of Ireland and only grudgingly returned after using it as a cattle ranch for centuries.

Perhaps, then, the social psychologist will diagnose nostalgic eclecticism when I assert that my most strenuous efforts can dredge up very little that savours of pervasive discontent, recurrent unhappiness or real deprivation connected with that room which was the centre of my childhood. And as for being undernourished, we were certainly not overfed as many children in premier league countries are nowadays, but I only wish that the children of the prosperous Ireland of the latter decades of this century could be fed the unadulterated natural food on which we grew up.

Not that there was not extreme poverty and material deprivation in many homes in Limerick at that time, even in our own little area of the King's Island. An image that remains in my memory symbolises the hardship endured by many parents in trying to rear the large family that was the average in those times: on a summer's evening a little lad from a house not far from ours came dancing up the street, chanting happily at the top of his voice, 'I got two cuts o' bread for my sup-per!' His declaration and his happiness were quickly cut short as he was followed and retrieved by his irate mother, who dragged him home while boxing his ears in the approved fashion. The incident became a tragicomic item in our folklore, in what the poet Thomas Gray (1716–71) in his 'Elegy' called 'the short and simple annals of the poor'. But we all understood only too well the innocent elation of that child and the embarrassment of his poor mother. Long before the outbreak of the Second World War brought official bread-rationing to Ireland, there were days in every working-class home when the mother had to ration the final slices of a loaf, whether home-baked or from the bakery – and often it was the mother herself who drank her cup of tea breadless. Another such item, related in the general folklore of the Parish and of other areas in the city, was of the mother who stuck her head out the window of the upper room which was her home and called loudly to her son playing in the street, 'Johnny, come in for your blue duck egg what no one in the lane has!'

Our home was no exception, and if it makes the professional sociologist any happier, he or she can rest assured that there were days when the three standard meals of the working-class, breakfast, dinner and supper, were just about sufficient, in our own phrase, 'to keep body and soul together', and when we went to bed, not exactly hungry, but still capable of polishing off 'a good feed' of any description. We knew from what some of our schoolmates or neighbours told us that there were families where actual hunger was a constant factor in life and where, even in winter, sometimes there was not enough fuel in any form for fire or cooking. And one of the warnings we got from older brothers and sisters was to keep a close eye on the few slices of bread-and-butter we brought to the convent school; otherwise, when lunchtime came round we might find that our lunch had disappeared. In the small provision shops that were a feature of every street, it was a common sight to see customers buying an ounce of tea, which the shopkeeper weighed out from a packet into a paper twisted into a cone, or a quarter pound of butter or sugar; some local shops also kept coal for sale by the stone.

In the small room that was our home and castle, the essential furniture consisted of a table, a dresser, a corner press, some chairs and the big black range, that last item installed, they told me, the year before I was born, replacing the open fire-grate. There would not have been space for sufficient chairs even if they could have been bought. A few small stools provided seating for some of the younger ones to read or learn lessons, and in winter we preferred to sit on the floor around the fire for our storytelling. Money had to be spent on priorities – food, rent, clothes, gas (coal for the range came free in our house, paid for only by our father's sweat). Since replacing a broken cup was not in that category, in large families like ours a younger child sometimes had to stand at the table at tea-time and drink tea from a jam-jar, from which container it tasted just the same as from any cup, and much better, at any rate, than from the tin mugs we bought from the tinkers. It should be noted that the term 'tinker' was still a respectable professional appellation in those times, as manifested in the old rhyme, 'Tinker, tailor, soldier, sailor, butcher, baker, candlestick-maker', and we distinguished between the garrulous tinkers who hawked their pots and pans from door to door and those stranger and more sinister wanderers, the gipsies, who occasionally came across Thomond Bridge in their colourful caravans and caused us to abandon our games near the castle and run back to the safety of our own street until they had passed on their unending way.

Our room looked out on the street, and the street in those times was very different from what an urban street is today. In a locality like ours, the street was the playground of all the local children, and we were more fortunate than most in having, just around the corner, another and more open street that sloped down beside King John's Castle to Thomond Bridge. Traffic on our street was almost non-existent, except for a few men on bicycles going to and returning from work – most people walked to work. Even on nearby Castle Street, a farmer's cart coming in across Thomond Bridge from County Clare was a more frequent sight than a car, and the children rolled their hoops or whipped their tops up and down beside the ancient towers of the castle.

Whenever it was that I was first put in a position where I could look out the window of our one room downstairs, I would have seen, across from our house, a wide lane, called appropriately, as I would learn later, Broad Lane. To the left of this, a terrace of red-brick two-storey houses with front and back gardens, to the right a big yellow-washed house, then the big gate of a yard, and then further tall houses and a few small shops. I would not have been able to see that the last shop was Halpin's public house, around the corner of which there was a very wide street leading straight down to the gates of St Mary's Convent of Mercy. Broad Lane opposite us went down to the wall of the convent gardens, with cottages at both sides. The road continued along by the convent wall, with cottages on the left side, until it met the end of our street at the Villiers School; then it branched on down between other houses to the part of the island known as the Island Field, beyond which was the river. Thus, from outside our door, down Broad Lane, left by the convent wall, and back up by the Villiers School and the churchyard of St Munchin, constituted our local 'block'. In every area, the block was important both as a social unit larger than the street but less than the parish, and also as being the sports-track around which very competitive races were run – a race 'around the block' could be a sprint of one lap or a mini-marathon.

I have given the precise layout of our street and the nearby streets in our area of the King's Island, as they were when my wondering infant eyes stared out at them for the first time, because that scene and that block have been radically altered in recent years. While our side of the street – except for a house and shop that stood at the corner beyond the Bishop's Palace – and the terrace of red-brick houses opposite, remain intact, the rest of our block has been demolished to make way for a new road that cuts through what used to be the hallowed gardens of St Mary's Convent. So, what used to be our traffic-free street playground has been transmogrified into a main artery linking the road from Ennis and Shannon Airport to the Dublin road on the other side of the city. Why the Corporation of Limerick allowed this polluting juggernaut highway to tear through the very heart of the island that is the historic nucleus of the city, instead of imitating the builders of the railway in the last century who brought their iron road away from the city altogether and across the new Metal Bridge, is a political mystery much discussed by the ordinary citizens of the old city by the Shannon. When those same local politicians approved the restoration of King John's Castle, they vitiated that excellent renovation by allowing the construction, in

31

what should have been the ancient castle courtyard, of a cluttering and incongruous modern structure in glass and steel. And by a strange paradox, during the same period the Corporation and public officials of Limerick have done more to embellish our ancient city by the Shannon than their counterparts in any city or town in Ireland.

When my infant eyes looked out through the window of that room on Old Church Street, they saw my older brothers and sisters playing with the other children of the area; but they also recorded three images that made such a lasting impression that I see them now on the screen of memory. I see the gutter between the footpath and the road, just outside the window, flowing with water on which shiny bubbles are sailing along like little glass globes. I see, on a summer's evening, a small black horse and its cart halted outside our door, the horse wearing a feedbag on its head, the cart half-loaded with sacks of coal. I see a huge fire blazing in the middle of the road between our footpath and the opening of the broad lane opposite our house. As I grew from baby to toddler, I would learn that that rush of water with its bright bubbles was simply good old Irish rain, I would be told that my father owned the little black horse and the cart, and I would sit with all the children and adults of our street around a similar blazing May Eve bonefire ('Not bonfire,' says Douglas Hyde in *A Literary History of Ireland* (1899) of which more later).

5

INTERIOR DESIGN

I turn in memory from the view of the street outside that window to consider the interior view. My first pictures of life in that very much lived-in room of ours are of my mother working – and singing, forever singing, while she worked. The life of the mother of a young family in those days was one of almost continuous drudgery. Without electricity or any of the machines and gadgets that are common equipment in every kitchen nowadays, the daily household chores of cooking, baking, washing and ironing clothes, scrubbing, sewing, knitting, darning, patching and mending, as well as breast-feeding the latest arrival and attending to older children, ensured that the mother was working literally from morning to night. Every drop of water had to be brought in a bucket from the tap in the yard (I have noted how fortunate we were in this regard, in comparison with people in tenements who had to carry water up several flights of stairs). Every pot of water had to be heated on the range or on the single gas-ring before clothes could be washed and scrubbed in a zinc bath or a wooden tub which was placed on two chairs.

Drying clothes was another huge problem. At least in summer they could be hung out somehow in the confined space of our shared yard, but in winter they were hanging on several lines across the room near the range. Ironing was done with what was literally only a shaped lump of iron with a handle; this had to be heated on the range (or in the fire by the mother who did not have a range) and anyone who is old enough to have seen the mother using such an iron will remember the effective method of testing if it was hot enough – by spitting on it! A basin sufficed for washing what my mother called 'the salutin' part' – face, ears, neck, hands – while the zinc bath or wooden tub was used for more complete ablutions. Many children, especially in the tenements, did not even get the morning 'cat's lick', a rub of the face with a damp cloth.

It was not just the drying of clothes but all other chores that were made more difficult in winter when the light in the room consisted of the single gas-mantle and an oil lamp on the table around which the children were gathered to labour at their 'ekers' (school homework or exercises) or to play cards and other games. My father, like every man-of-the-house in those times, had his own family chores to attend to after his daily grind as breadwinner; he was cobbler and barber and general handyman, so that on a typical night in winter he might be cutting our hair or repairing shoes at one side of the range, while my mother darned socks or stitched or patched a torn garment at the other side, and at the table the children laboured over schoolbooks and exercise copies, occasionally asking each other, or the patient mother or father, to 'examine me in my poem' or catechism or any of the other lessons that had to be memorised for the next day.

Unless they have seen one in period films or television plays, younger readers of this chronicle will not even know what a range was. It was a large iron fitting combining fireplace, oven and hot-plates. The fire was contained in one section, behind a grill of vertical bars; the oven, divided into two sections, occupied the rest of the structure, with several hot-plates on the surface, including one over the fire which could be removed with a hook in order to add coal. With this contraption the housewife could have loaves or other items baking in the oven, pots and a kettle or a frying-pan on the hot-plates, and even, for the 'cup o' tay' in winter, make toast at the fire with the extending fork devised for that task.

The only machine at my mother's disposal was a Singer sewing-machine, worked by the foot-pedal. My father bought this when they still had only the first two children, my mother having learned to use one as a young girl when attending, with her workmates from the caramel factory, evening classes organised by Sinn Féin and Cumann na mBan. These were held at the Gaelic League Hall, Halla Íde in Thomas Street, where benevolent ladies of the 'quality' instructed working-class girls in home economics and useful crafts. She also attended a few Irish classes conducted by a teacher they all knew as 'Seoirse'. This was Seoirse Mac Fhlannchadha, George Clancy, who had been a fellow-student and close friend of James Joyce at University College Dublin, and whose life was to end tragically on the night of 7 March 1921, when, as Mayor of Limerick, he was assassinated in front of his wife by a murder gang of the British forces.

Besides being a skilled machinist, my mother was a diligent and talented knitter; she could also do crochet work and when we became altar boys (or acolytes as we said in those days) in St Mary's Parish Church and subsequently in the local Convent of Mercy, it was she who made our surplices with their fancy crochet borders – borders modestly restrained in size and style to suit our status as mere acolytes; some of our fellow-servers had surplices with lacework borders so deep that my mother said they would be more suitable for the bishop! As the two eldest children were girls, they were soon learning all those skills from her – girls in those days, being uninhibited by the sexist dicta of feminism, took pride in being able to emulate their mother in her housekeeping, as boys felt proud to follow their father as a natural matter-of-course into a trade or a job in docks or mill or factory, and also into the local rugby club or band if they had sporting or musical talent.

We were fortunate in having a mother, and eventually two big sisters, who could knit and sew so well. We never wore a single item from a shop that could be knitted – jerseys, stockings, gloves, scarves, woolly headgear – unlike some of our friends and schoolmates who were often attired in flimsy cotton products from the factories of Birmingham or Manchester. And although our hand-me-down trousers usually had one or more large patches – which we considered sound protection against the cold, the boot of an opponent, or the swishing cane or leather strap in school – we were never exposed *a posteriori*, or, to use the cruder phrase, we were never seen with our arse out through our trousers. Having a mother who was a skilful knitter meant also, of course, that we had to give a hand – two hands, in fact – when the skeins of wool had to be wound into balls for knitting; sometimes, when some other chore occupied my mother, instead of standing with the skein of wool stretched between our hands, we had to put it over the backs of two chairs and wind it from there.

Our boots, like our trousers and schoolbooks, were handed down from an older brother to the next in line, repaired when required by my father on the three-footed last which was a standard item of equipment in homes fortunate enough to have a dutiful father like ours – and that, in spite of unfortunate exceptions, meant the average home in most areas of Limerick at that time. As children we never wore shoes except the new pair for First Communion. The black suit and frilly white shirt for a boy, the white dress and veil for a girl, were carefully preserved from one first communicant to the next in line (the poorest families were discreetly clothed by the St Vincent de Paul Society or by the local nuns). In winter we wore boots and thick woollen stockings (on the very cold days, my mother supplemented even those with newspaper wrapped around our toes). In summer we had leather sandals or what we called 'sandshoes' (white tennis shoes) but we preferred to go barefoot all day long when possible – and most of the day in summer was spent on the bank of the Shannon or in the river itself or in the fields and streams of adjacent County Clare.

When I say that we sometimes went to school barefoot, our academic sociologist will be wary now of making false deductions. Certainly there were some children in our classrooms who did not have adequate footwear even in winter; but to see a child barefoot in the classroom or on the street in summer did not mean that his parents could not afford to buy him sandals or sandshoes. The street pavements were made of wide flags of limestone, and the summer sun warmed them nicely – 'the sun is crackin' the flags' was the standard description of a hot summer's day. In our classrooms, the floors were of wood, and this, like the pavements, made going barefoot a pleasure, and the wearing of stockings and shoes in summer an unbearable ordeal.

So far, I have only described the activity in that micro-cosmic room under the aspect of work and survival. There was, of course, another element to our life. One of the proverbs we heard repeatedly from our Granny and other elders was to the effect that 'all work and no play makes Jack a dull boy', and in the home as well as on the local streets we had fun and games and recreation of a kind that might seem very strange, if not dull and boring, to the children who now sit for hours frenetically pressing buttons in the playing of electronic games on the television set.

As soon as we could count up to six, and our fingers could move a coloured marker, we were enlisted to make up the numbers in a foursome at Ludo, a game that must have been Job's favourite as a child, or to enjoy the thrill of shooting up a ladder or sliding down a sinuous serpent in Snakes and Ladders. These and many other such games were of more educational value, and a better preparation for the ups and downs of life, than any of the multiplicity of expensive educational toys being marketed today. They were also of such a leisurely nature – you had to wait your turn to throw the dice and move your counter – that they allowed for conversation; they allowed also, of course, for occasions of disagreement and argument, sometimes even for accusations and vehement denials of cheating. When the rare violent altercation occurred, board and counters could be upended and the intervention of a parent or older sibling might be required to restore peace. Card games – beginning with beggar-my-neighbour, matchers and old maid, progressing through pontoon to the real skills of forty-five – and the age-old draughts came at a later stage, and these were no less beneficial and entertaining, nor were they less fraught with the consequences of the frailties of human nature.

6

'TELL ME A STORY'

In those days when television had not yet been heard of, and radio was so new that it was still unknown in most working-class homes, including our own – even our wind-up box gramophone with its steel needles and heavy wax records was a luxury many people could not afford – another of our favourite ways of entertaining ourselves, one that is almost unknown to children today, was the telling of stories and jokes. The latter included, as a basic component, the traditional repertoire of Paddy-the-Irishman anecdotes.

The first stories we heard were the bedtime stories told by my mother. These were the age-old, universal fairytales, 'Jack and the Beanstalk', 'Beauty and the Beast', 'The Sleeping Beauty', 'Hansel and Gretel', 'Cinderella', 'Little Red Riding Hood', 'The Three Little Pigs', and so on (whatever stories our ancestors told their children were lost with our ancestral language). We had none of the fancy coloured books or records of those stories that can be used by the modern parent; the storytelling was really traditional and oral. When, like Christopher Robin in the song, we had knelt in our nightshirts and said our bedtime prayers, my mother would lie on the edge of the bed with the current audience all curled up 'as snug as a bug in a rug' as she used to say. When the story for the night was decided on, she would commence with the traditional opening: 'Once upon a time, and a very good time it was . . . ' Then on to the tale: 'There was this poor widow-woman and she had only the one son, and his name was Jack.'

Unfortunately for our enjoyment of my mother's bedtime storytelling, there was a big problem that tended to crop up regularly. From what I have written about the daily workload of the mother in those times, it will be easily understood that by the time she lay on the bed with us, my poor mother was much more ready to fall asleep than we were – and fall asleep she often did, gradually dozing off as her voice became more and more of an unintelligible drone. Whereupon her two or three listeners would rouse her with cries and pushes: 'Ma! Ma! Wake up! Tell us the rest of the story!' She would start up from her incipient sleep and say, 'Oh! Ah! Where was I?' 'Jack was just at the top of the beanstalk and he saw the giant's castle.' And so it went on until we got the full story, by hook or by crook, and then poor Mother was free to go back downstairs to that front room and take up her knitting, darning, washing, ironing or any of the other labours of love she performed daily for the children she had brought into the world. Meanwhile, above in the bed, we would be reliving the story, and – in spite of the fact that all the stories ended with the reassuring and optimistic 'And they lived happy ever after – puff-puff, long enough!' (even our storyteller did not know the provenance of her signing-off phrase: 'That's how we always heard it,' she said) – we would be hiding our heads from the beast or the wolf, or especially from that terrible giant who roared, 'Fee-fo-fum! I smell the blood of an Irishman! His liver and lights for my supper tonight, and his blood for my morning drink!'

When we got to the DIY age, we used to lie in bed on a summer's night telling stories and singing songs, each one having to contribute in turn. And it is with true filial regret that I must record how we were a source of annoyance to my poor mother who, having issued a few warnings for silence and sleep, would eventually, as a last resort, come rushing up to the bedroom armed with the sweeping-brush, with the handle of which she walloped every bump in the bedclothes – we having disappeared under cover. 'Did I tell ye to go to sleep, did I? God give me patience with ye! And I having to get up in the morning at cockcrow!' (She had to set her alarm-clock for 6.30 a.m. in order to get the current Mass-server up and off to the convent for Mass at 7 a.m.) To that heartsore lament of our mother the little blaguards under the bedclothes responded with roaring and bawling: 'Oh, me head! Oh, me arm, me arm! Oh God, me back is broke! Oh, Ma, me leg, me leg!'

Having distributed a generous quantity of light blows to the moving bulges in the bedclothes, the poor woman would go back downstairs, still calling on God and his Holy Mother to give her the patience she needed, and we would surface unharmed but pretending to be sorely damaged. Nobody ever suffered much pain from those brush-handle ad-monitions, but they were effective in shutting us up at last, by which time we were sleepy anyway. That was the only form of physical punishment we ever knew. I cannot recall either of our parents 'raising a hand to us' and we knew how lucky we were – from some of our neighbours and classmates we heard how their fathers belted and thumped them regularly, and how their mothers used a stick or the wooden spoon, on both boys and girls.

When we sat on the floor at the fireside in winter, we had ghost stories that made us dread all the more the eventual trip up the stairs, candlestick in hand, into bedrooms that were, to use the Limerick term, 'freezing cold' and that looked out, as I have indicated, on the nearby ghost-producing churchyard of St Munchin's Protestant church. From our parents and grandparents we also heard the traditional stories of Limerick, of that first *ad hoc* mayor of Limerick, Seán na Scuab, the poor broommaker whose mother, brought in from the hills of Clare to meet her son all dressed up in his mayoral robes, exclaimed, 'Wisha, Seán, *a stór*, sure I hardly know you!' To which the first mayor of Limerick replied, 'Wisha, mother, *a ghrá*, sure I hardly know myself!' And we heard how the first appointee to the see of Limerick, Mainchín, cursed the men of Limerick who refused to build him a church as per the instructions of his boss, Pádraig – 'May the native perish in you,' the irate little monk roared at that Celtic settlement on the island in the Shannon, 'and may the stranger flourish in you!' From my own experience and observation, I am inclined to believe that the curse of Mainchín is still effective.

Among other traditional stories told at our fireside, and told often, there was the one about the Wise Women of Mungret – how the resourceful Limerick monks dressed up as Greek-spouting washerwomen to bamboozle their opponents from Cork – and the legend of the Silver Bells of St Mary's Cathedral, and of course our favourite, because of that old cottered mansion next door, the tale of Drunken Thady and the Bishop's Lady (this was always illustrated, especially by our Granny Connolly who had known the poet personally, with apt quotations from the comic poem by Michael Hogan, the Bard of Thomond). Apart from legends and folktales, we had the history of Limerick itself, and especially that of the grim castle in whose shadow we played on the long evenings of summer. We never tired of hearing the story of the sieges of Limerick, with Sarsfield's ride to Ballyneety to destroy King Billy's guns as the highlight. We fancied Sarsfield and his five hundred horsemen, with their horses' hooves muffled, moving out silently by night from their base in our Island Field, across Thomond Bridge and off towards Killaloe and Keeper Hill. We had the remains of part of the walls of Limerick adjoining our convent school in Peter's Cell, another section just across the road from our Granda Flynn's house in Watergate, with further sections and even some preserved cannonballs to be seen in the paradisial gardens of the convent. And at the northern end of Thomond Bridge, the Treaty Stone on its modern pedestal was a daily reminder to us of how the garrison marched out of Limerick, most of them to depart for France with Sarsfield and to become the 'Wild Geese' of history, adopting as their battle-cry when they charged the English on the battlefields of France and Flanders, '*Cuimhnígí ar Luimneach agus ar fheall na Sasanach!*' ('Remember Limerick and the treachery of the English!')

From more recent times we had the stories of the Easter Rising of 1916, the subsequent Black-and-Tan war, the fatal treaty that allowed Britain to cut off six of the thirty-two counties of Ireland for the benefit of the unionists in the North, and the consequent tragic civil war that divided the men who had risked their lives in the fight for freedom in 1916 and 1920-21. These latter tales were no dead items in a book, but the vivid narration of our parents, relatives and neighbours who had lived through the dangers and atrocities of the recent euphemistically-named Troubles. The civil war ended in 1923, only four years before I was born. We knew that my mother's younger brother, Joe Connolly, who was now the distant American source of parcels of clothes and bundles of comics, had been arrested by Free State troops and imprisoned for two years in Gormanston camp (where his Republican OC, Seán T. O'Kelly, had further aggravated his young life by sentencing himself and two pals to a fortnight of cleaning the latrines because, on a freezing cold night in winter, they had broken up one of the latrine doors to make a little fire). We knew also that my mother's sister, Cissie Connolly, had been a member of Cumann na mBan and had met her future husband, Joe O'Connor, while she was helping to cook for and nurse the Republicans in the New (now Sarsfield) Barracks when the Free State forces were attacking Limerick. They also were in exile in New York as a reward for their devotion to the concept of an Irish Republic 'free from the centre to the sea' and their refusal to recognise the right of any British government to partition the island of Ireland for the benefit of the descendants of the Ulster planters of the seventeenth century.

My mother told us of the night when, long after the hour of curfew imposed by the British occupation forces, they heard a drunken man from a neighbouring street singing and shouting his way homeward. In spite of her fearful pleas, my father went out and tried to hurry the man home. Having got him safely to the corner of his own street, my father hurried back home; but only a short while later, they heard gunfire in the distance, and later they heard that the man had been shot dead by a lorry-load of Black-and-Tans cruising, as was their wont, around the city streets in search of a victim. The civil war of 1922–23 brought death to our streets again. My mother often related how she and other women performed what was literally a corporal work of mercy when they washed the bullet-riddled body of a young man from one of the houses in the lane opposite our house. He was Captain Michael Danford, a Republican, one of the many who, having fought the Black-and-Tans, regarded the Treaty signed by Michael Collins and the others as a betrayal of the cause of Emmet, Tone, Pearse and Connolly, as well as a callous desertion of the Catholic Nationalist people in the six-county puppet state set up by the partition of Ireland. He was captured by the Free State troops in Limerick and his body was found on the side of the road at Ballysimon, outside the city. He was, of course, 'shot while trying to escape', the newly-recruited Free State troops being as adept as the Black-and-Tans at prodding their prisoner with bayonets and forcing him off the lorry so that he could be officially described as above. My mother's vivid description always made us shudder: 'His poor body,' she said, 'was black and blue from the beating they gave him, and he was all swollen and covered in dried blood.'

Some dents in the old grey stones of our own house my father at first told us were made by bullets during the Siege of Limerick! Later he said they were made by the guns of the Black-and-Tans. Another story of which we got two versions was about the raid on our own house. Version A, as told by my father to the younger open-mouthed listener, told how a party of savage and drunken Black-and-Tans came battering on the hall-door one dark night in 1921 when the two families were in bed, each young couple with their two very young children. Jack Sheehan went down and opened the front door, whereupon the Tans rushed past him and up the stairs; but at the top of the stairs they were met by Richie Flynn, who, just like our namesake Errol Flynn, as Robin Hood in the film, or James Cagney in gangster films, knocked each one of the English blaguards over the banisters down to the hall, where Jack Sheehan caught them, one by one, and kicked them out the door! As we reached the stage or age when doubt and incredulity sets in, and you don't really believe any more that your Da is the bravest and strongest man in the world, we got Version B of this adventure from my mother. In this version, it was a party of Irish Free State troops who paid a late night call to the ancient house on Old Church Street. Not being blessed with the tape-recorder memory from which other chroniclers can give verbatim accounts of conversations, sermons, and things they read in childhood, I offer my mother's version in her own words from a real tape-recording made some years before her death.

The night they raided us your father, as usual, instead of being in bed, was sitting up writing out music or cutting out things out of the paper. He was always at that; he had a big trunk inside in the small bedroom that was empty at that time, and it was packed with stuff that he said would be very interesting in years to come; the children would want to read it, all about the Troubles. He had all the papers they used to bring out, ones like the *Bottom Dog* and *Scissors and Paste* and – what was that other one? I forget the name of it now. He had piles of stuff too that the Free Staters wouldn't like, papers from the Republican side, and he had things my brother Joe gave him to mind – Joe was in jail in Gormanston at the time – he wouldn't tell me what they were, but I partly guessed from the fact that Joe hid some stuff in the lav out in the yard of my mother's house in Crosby Row. My father used to be givin' out about him, 'God only knows what that fella is bringin' into the house!' – and one day when poor Mrs Phayer was sittin' on the lav in her yard next door, didn't the stuff Joe had hidden blow a hole in the wall and she was nearly blown into Kingdom Come! If the Free Staters found anything like that, they might burn the house down, let alone what they might do to Da himself. And because he was in the Sinn Féin band he had the uniform in a box as well – he joined the Volunteers, you know, after hearing De Valera at some meeting, although his own mother over in Watergate used to curse the Volunteers because her own son, Tom, was after being killed out in Flanders. She said the Volunteers were in league with the Germans – sure she was only saying what all the poor mothers were saying that had sons or husbands killed in the Munster Fusiliers. When your Da joined up he was going mad to get a rifle and to be a fighter but what did they do but order him into their band because he was a musician and used to play with the Sarsfield band in Irishtown.

Anyway, there was I dozing in the bed with the two babies when we heard the lorry first, and then when we heard the battering on the hall-door, we knew it was a raid. The first thing your Da did was to shake the Holy Water on us, he nearly drownded us in the bed with it! Everyone had a bottle of Holy Water handy in the house in those days. Jack Sheehan opened the door to them and they charged in. They searched the rooms below first, our front room and the Sheehans' back room; then they came up the stairs. The officer had a flashlamp and he had something written on a piece of paper, I suppose our name and the number of the house. He was asking Da why he wasn't in bed, was he just after running in home, and so on; and questions about the Republicans he knew. Somebody must have told them about our Joe and that I was his sister. Da said he didn't know any Republicans – if you said that to the Tans you'd most likely get a belt of a revolver in the face, but this Free State officer seemed a decent man; he even told me not to be upset – of course, I was crying thinkin' they might shoot my husband and leave me with two little orphans! When he noticed the opening leading from our bedroom into the small bedroom inside, with no door, only a step up to the room inside – he said, 'What's in there?' Da told him it was only an empty bedroom, we only had the two young babies and we never used the small room. I was praying to the Sacred Heart and Our Lady that they wouldn't go in there; but the officer ordered one of the soldiers to go and take a look. The soldier was cute enough though, he must have been an old stager from the Great War. He knew if there was any gunman hiding in that dark room, he'd be likely to get the first bullet; so, he just stood near the doorway and lit a match and moved it around a bit, and then he said, 'Nothin' there, sir, just an empty room like he said.'

They didn't bother much with the Sheehans, but even so we all went downstairs when they were gone and we made a big pot of tea and toast, and we all sat around trying to console one another, and thanking God they didn't wreck the house or shoot anyone. Anyway, your Da spent the rest of the night tearing up all the papers he was saving for ye to read – wasn't it an awful pity! He lit a fire and he burned every one of them; he even cut up his band uniform in little bits and burned that too, he got such a fright, though he had another uniform for the Sarsfield band over in his father's house in Watergate. And he put the other things, the stuff Joe gave him to mind, into a coal sack and he took it down to the river and dumped it.

All things considered, my memory is that, given the respective ages of the listener, we enjoyed my father's heroic Version A better than the true story. Anyway, it will be seen that the ancient art of the *seanchaí* (storyteller), as old as the prehistoric cave-dwellers, was still alive and well in the days of my Limerick childhood, and was practised not only at the fireside or at bedtime but also, as will be told, as a social pastime on the street.

7

MY TWO FATHERS

Even before I was old enough to be told by my mother that
I had been christened twice and still had been deprived of
one of the two lovely names she had chosen for me, I began
to form the notion that I had two fathers, and a very
contrasting pair they were.

One of these men would sometimes arrive outside the
window where I was observing the street; he came on that
horse and cart I mentioned earlier, with sometimes many,
sometimes only a few, sacks of coal standing behind him on
the cart. He wore a peaked cap, and when it was raining he
had a sack pinned around his shoulders like a short cloak.
When he came into the room I was frightened of his
blackened face; but then he would chat with my mother, say
nice things to me, pick me up from the floor or tickle my
face if I were in the pram by the window. After having a cup
of tea, he would talk to me again, say goodbye to my mother,
and go off on his cart with the lovely little black horse. At
other times, he came late in the evening when all the family
were at home, and then he never had the little black horse
and the cart, but his face was even blacker, and my mother
would be fussing around looking sad and saying things like,
'Oh, wisha, God help you, you're frozen and famished; a
dog wouldn't be out in this weather. Get them things off

49

you before you get your death! I have a nice bit o' dinner steaming hot for you.'

The other man, my second Da, spoke with the same gentle voice and tickled me just like the black-faced man, but he was dressed in what I would have called style if I could talk and knew the word. His face was clean like my mother's, his black hair was sleeked back and shiny, and he was wearing a black suit, a white shirt, and what I would later learn to call a dickie-bow. This man used to say goodbye to my mother and to everyone else in the room, then he would pick up a big black box and go away. He always went away when it was night-time and I was feeling sleepy in the pram or in my mother's arms, and I never ever saw that shiny clean man coming home.

What puzzled me most about my two fathers – I could hear my mother and all the others calling the two men Da – was that I never saw them together. Some nights the tired, wet, black-faced Da came home and after a while I couldn't see him anywhere. Then later on the stylish Da appeared, put on his overcoat, took his big black box, said his goodbyes, patted my face and went off out the door.

As I added days and weeks and months to my account on this planet, and was allowed to stay awake and observing in that room for longer periods, I sometimes saw the clean and shiny Da standing over in the corner, dressed in an ordinary shirt and trousers like all the other men in the street, and blowing into a big silvery thing to make lovely sounds. To my incipient vocabulary, the word 'sax' would soon be added; that was what the clean Da had over in the corner, his sax, and that was what he carried away some nights in his big black box. Add a few more years and I was boasting to other toddlers on the street that my father was better than theirs, because he had two jobs; he sold coal during the day and he played the saxophone in a danceband sometimes at night when their fathers were sitting at home doing nothing.

In order to explain how my father had two such contrasting occupations, coal-beller and saxophonist, I must go back to his father, whose name, Richard, he had been given. My Grandfather O'Flynn lived, as I have said, in Watergate, an area in the Irishtown, that second globe of the hourglass-shaped medieval city. When I was a child he was an old man with a white moustache and weak, bleary eyes who sat by the fire drinking a mug of tea or smoking his pipe. In the house with him lived the eldest of his four sons, Daniel, a bachelor, known to us as our Uncle Danny, and the younger of his two daughters, Brigid, a spinster (when I first visited that house as a toddler, Daniel would have been about forty and Brigid thirty-three). The elder daughter, Mary, and the youngest son, Michael, were in New York. The third son was our Uncle Tom who had enlisted in the Munster Fusiliers at the age of eighteen and died at Passchendaele in 1917. My father was the second of the four sons.

My father's mother died some years before I was born. He told us that she was always called *Bríd Bhán* (the Irish for 'Fair Brigid') because as a young girl she had been as lovely as the famous blonde immortalised in that most beautiful of Irish songs, *An Chúilfhionn* ('The Fair One'). Her pet name is an indication that the Irish language was still fairly widely spoken among the common people in Limerick City when my paternal grandmother was born, about 1860. Our Aunt Brigid, like many of her neighbours, kept two pigs in a shed in the backyard and sometimes they were allowed to roam on the common cowle behind the houses. My sister Mary, the eldest in our family, told me that when she was a child my mother, as well as other women in our streets, had a few pigs roaming on a similar cowle opposite our house, where the row of red-bricked houses was subsequently built. Our Granny Connolly kept hens in Crosby Row, but no pigs. In my childhood only one woman in our street, Mrs Murray, kept pigs in her backyard and the children in all the other houses took turns to bring the after-dinner 'skins' to the Murray house, gaining a penny or a halfpenny according to the quantity delivered. It was one of the great days in our street when the low cart from the 'store' (as the bacon factories were called) came to collect the fattened pigs from Mrs Murray. The screeching of the pigs as the men dragged them out the lane beside the house was enough to raise the dead in nearby St Munchin's churchyard; they seemed naturally reluctant to be turned into bacon and ham for the rich and into the multifarious offal, from pig's head to pig's tail and crubeens, that was part of the staple diet of the poorer majority. The pigs in Aunt Brigid's yard were in a shed with a small area outside it enclosed by a low wall. We were warned to keep away from them, an unnecessary admonition since the stink was sufficient to disgust us. Another item of interest in the yard was the big barrel under the rainspout. Aunt Brigid told us that rainwater was the best for washing hair or clothes – she herself had a lovely head of long black hair – but we did not like the look of the green slime on the sides of the barrel.

In the big kitchen-living-room of Granda Flynn's house, there were two old pictures, each of them showing a man who was posing as if he thought he was a very important person. My father told us who they were: Daniel O'Connell (in his pose as Liberator of Ireland, complete with Round Tower, Irish Greyhound, and Maid of Erin with harp and shamrock), the man who got justice for the Catholics of Ireland; and Robert Emmet, who was hanged, drawn and quartered in the public street in Dublin because he tried to get freedom for Ireland from England. (Poor Robert Emmet seemed to me to be dressed for the hunt but had lost his cap and horse, which might explain, I thought, the way his arms were folded and the cross look on his long face with its glib or quiff pasted back on his big forehead.)

I learned later that it was because my Granda Flynn went away to sea as a young man that I, as a child, seemed to have two fathers, the black-faced man in the peaked cap with the horse and cart, and the stylish man with the sleeked-back hair who played lovely tunes on the saxophone.

As a young married man, our Granda Flynn was working in the docks unloading cargoes of grain, coal, timber and anything else that gave a day's work. That is the significant phrase, 'a day's work', because the system prevailing in those pre-trade union days meant that men had to hope to be selected by the stevedore who had been contracted by the company to unload a ship's cargo. The stevedores added to their fee from the company by taking a cut from the wages of the men they selected, and it was this immoral levy that brought about the cataclysmic change in the life of young Richard O'Flynn from Watergate – and also, of course, in the lives of his wife and young children.

At the end of one particular job, when a certain stevedore was paying his men, O'Flynn objected to the size of the deduction. Words led to a fistfight, in which the stevedore, an older man, was laid flat on his back on the dockside. But the consequences were more serious for the young docker; he found himself being passed over, day after day, no matter what line-up he stood in. A man left standing unselected on the dockside at daybreak had more than his wounded pride to endure. He had to turn around and go home to tell his wife or mother that there would be no money that week. (The dole had not yet been invented by governments to alleviate the social effects of the invention of engines and machines.) When he was passed over yet once more, and realised that he would not be able to feed his wife and children, O'Flynn took a drastic step, physically and metaphorically: he signed on as a crew member with a ship that was just about to leave Limerick for Liverpool, and whose captain was desperately trying to replace a local man who had sent word that he was unwell and could not sail. The captain agreed on an advance of pay, which was entrusted to a neighbour from Mungret Street in the Irishtown (they had not yet settled in Watergate) who had also been passed over in the stevedore's selection. This man brought the money to the young Bríd Bhán O'Flynn (née O'Donohue) together with the news that she would not be seeing her husband, Richie, for some time to come as he was gone on a ship to Liverpool.

And so the docker became a sailor. Many young Limerickmen went to sea in those days when the docks were constantly busy and there was not much formality about signing on as a deckhand or stoker. It was a way of escape from the misery and grinding poverty of the slums, an alternative to joining the British Army as my other grandfather, Maurice Connolly, and his pals in Arthur's Quay did about the same time that Richie Flynn of Watergate sailed down the Shannon on his first voyage.

8

A Life on the Ocean Wave

When that first impromptu voyage gave him a taste for the sea and a feeling of independence, the hot-headed young Richard O'Flynn from Mungret Street in Limerick's Irishtown made several more voyages, graduating to bigger ships and farther shores. Many of these longer voyages began and ended in Liverpool, thus necessitating extra travel by ship and train for him to get home to Limerick or back to Liverpool. It was only natural, then, that he should consider moving his family to Liverpool, a move resisted by Bríd Bhán until she agreed that it would mean a saving of money. In 1901 the big move was made, with the result that my father, then aged seven, and his older brother, Danny, found themselves in a school in Liverpool where they could hardly understand what their classmates were saying. Many of them had Irish surnames and were probably descended from the survivors of those hundreds of thousands of desperate emigrants who had fled from the famine-stricken Ireland of 1847 only for many of them to die in dockside cellars in Liverpool where they were rackrented more than they had ever been by landlord or agent in Ireland. And so Bríd Bhán found herself living in a dockland tenement in Liverpool more overcrowded than the one she had left in Mungret Street.

My father and his brother soon realised, and it helped them to survive, that the education they had already received in Limerick from the Sisters of Mercy and lay teachers in St John's, and in the lower classes of the Christian Brothers' school in John Street, put them far ahead of their Liverpudlian classmates. And it was this positive fact that brought about the negative and sad aspect of my father's personal story of 'the leaving of Liverpool'. It seems (as my mother would say) that some big occasion was coming up in their area in Liverpool. What it was did not register in my father's childhood memory but it may have had something to do with education, because, in connection with the event, academic tests were held in the schools and the top pupil in each class was to be presented with a prize by a member of the Royal Family who would be visiting Liverpool for the ceremonies. The name of young Richard O'Flynn from Limerick, Ireland, was duly entered on the list of prizewinners (he told us that Danny could have won out easily in his own class but for the fact that on the day of the test, as on many other days, he was mitching in the labyrinthine docks of Liverpool). But young O'Flynn never got his prize – which is why we used to lament retrospectively for our poor deprived Dad – because by the time the royal person came to shake hands with the bright sparks of Liverpool and give them their prizes, Bríd Bhán and her young family, including a new baby, Michael, born in Liverpool – were back in Limerick. This time they settled in that house in Watergate where I would one day come with my father to visit the old retired sailor, our Granda O'Flynn.

From the moment when she stepped off the ship on arrival at Liverpool, Bríd Bhán O'Flynn, pregnant with the child who was to be the last of her family, conceived a dislike for the place, and the fact that her husband went off on a long voyage soon after establishing his wife and children in a single room in a dockside tenement, had done nothing to lessen her nostalgia and loneliness. Just as my own mother issued an ultimatum to my father in their first home in Limerick, resulting in the abandonment of his ancestral ritual of the hearth, so Bríd Bhán gave her seafaring husband the choice of living on his own in Liverpool – even if that involved the danger that he might eventually set up a second family there – or returning to his lawful wedded wife in Limerick after each voyage. So, back they all went to Watergate and the Irishtown, and 'they lived happy ever after – puff, puff, long enough!'

I often regret not having come into the world until some years after my paternal grandmother went in the other direction. Her version of the family history would have been worth listening to. Apparently she was a woman who could give the rough edge of her tongue to anyone who provoked her. There was a story about her encounter with a local shopkeeper after the outbreak of the 1914–18 war when, as would happen again when Hitler's war began in 1939, many shopkeepers transferred much of their stock from the open to the black market. This dodge was more serious for the common customer in 1914, because Britain was still using Ireland as a cattle ranch and a recruiting ground, and many more ordinary items were imported from Britain and the Continent. When she went doing her usual shopping, and was told by the shopkeeper about some item she requested, 'Oh, I'm sorry but we have none of that now – that's made in Germany,' and the same about a second item, and yet again a third time the same sad story, Bríd Bhán shook up her shawl and let fly: 'Well, aren't you the lucky man that your shite isn't made in Germany!'

It was my mother who often entertained us with one of our favourite stories about our old sailor Granda, perhaps because it concerned his long-suffering wife as much as himself. This was the story about one of the times when his ship was torpedoed during the First World War. There were two or three other Limerickmen on the ship with him, and when the ship was ominously overdue on a voyage from

Liverpool to America, the wives went together every day to the church to light votive candles and pray for the safe return of their husbands. But as day followed day, with no news, and even the owners of the ship accepted that she was gone down somewhere in the Atlantic, one by one the sorrowing wives began to resign themselves to the grim fact that they were now widows. The day came when only Bríd Bhán herself was going to the church to light a candle, and when kind neighbours remonstrated with her, she declared that she knew her husband was alive somewhere, 'Because,' she said, 'there's no hope of Richie Flynn ever getting into heaven and the devil isn't ready for him yet!' The neighbours naturally thought that she was gone a bit soft in the head, and that she would eventually give up her ritual of lighting a candle. When she did give it up, it was because news came from the shipping company that the crew were safe and well in Newfoundland, having spent weeks rowing their lifeboats in the Atlantic before being picked up by another ship.

Having told two of the stories in which his wife figured as much as himself, I must round off this brief account of my Granda Flynn's seafaring with one of his yarns in which Bríd Bhán had 'neither hand, act nor part', as my mother would say. He told us that after the Easter Rising in 1916 there was a lot of bad blood between English and Irish sailors, not so much on the same ship where they had to pull together but when they met with the crews of other ships in foreign ports. On one occasion, when they were drinking in a bar somewhere in the West Indies, Richie Flynn and the other Limerickmen from his crew, together with a few other Irish sailors from other ships, got into a big randyboo with some English sailors who said the Irish rebels in Dublin were 'stabbing England in the back' and helping the Germans to win the war. ('Randyboo', a Limerick word for a big row or commotion, from the French, *rendezvous*, was one of the words picked up by the Munster Fusiliers during spells of leave behind the frontline.) We could easily imagine our Granda O'Flynn, a man whose son was just then in the frontline in Flanders, replying in colourful Limerick idiom to those English seamen. But hot words in such circumstances always led to blows and soon that tavern in a West Indies port was the scene of a symbolic battle between the forces of Dark Rosaleen and John Bull. In the thick of the fight, the drunken Irish sailors realised that a huge black man had joined in on their side and was throwing the drunken English sailors out the door as if they were babies.

When order was restored the Paddies naturally began to pour the best of drink into their black ally and to ask him why he had joined in on their side. 'Because I am Irish too!' he told them proudly. 'My name is McCarthy! My people came from Ireland long ago.' And when we heard that story, we knew from our history classes at school that many Irish people were shipped to the West Indies long ago, and indeed many of them from our own seaport town of Limerick. The sword-and-Bible-wielding Oliver Cromwell gave the Irish people in the good lands he confiscated the grim choice, 'to Hell or to Connacht', but he gave no choice to the hundreds of priests and thousands of young boys and girls who were rounded up by his troops and sent as slaves to the English plantations in the West Indies, where they were destined to intermarry with their African companions in slavery.

[While I was writing this chapter, in August 1997, television newscasts were showing scenes of the devastation caused on the island of Montserrat by the eruption of a volcano. Among some of the natives being interviewed one night there was a black woman named Mary Irish.]

9

'THE BEST-LAID SCHEMES O' MICE AN' MEN . . .'

I don't know if my sailor grandfather ever heard one of his Scottish shipmates recite Robert Burns's poem, 'To a Mouse (on turning her up in her nest with the plow, November, 1785)'. Even if he had heard it, I doubt if a man so headstrong and independent would have taken very much notice of the poet's doleful warning that the most logically thought out plans can prove difficult to put into operation.

Even as a deckhand or stoker – he eventually graduated to donkey-man, the academically-unqualified but practically-experienced engineer who could do things with a ship's engine that no textbook writer ever envisaged – the young sailor from Limerick must have had ample time on his long voyages to contemplate life in general and his own in particular. And from brooding on the way in which he and other men were treated on the dockside in Limerick, he resolved that none of his own children would ever work for anyone but themselves. To put this resolution into effect required planning and his plan evolved from his own experience of life, as a docker and as a sailor. He conceived the idea of setting up a firm of his own, which would import coal and other cargoes directly. He could establish contacts in Liverpool and other English ports, and with his four sons growing up strongly into manhood, it was easy for him to imagine his new firm competing with the established importers on Limerick's docks.

Knowing that there would be periods when either ships or cargoes might be difficult to contract and that coal, the main item he had in mind, would be less in demand in summer, in addition to investing his accumulating seafaring wages in stables, horses and carts, he decided to add some jaunting-cars to his plans. These were the taxis of the time, of which there were still some in use in Limerick in my childhood. They can still be seen in Killarney where they are a novelty for the tourists and a lucrative source of income for the jarveys.

Most of us who dream dreams and conjure up schemes to achieve fame and fortune never get beyond the dreaming and planning stage. Fair dues to my sailor Grandad, he tried to put his plan into effect. In between voyages, he set up stables in Watergate, just down the street from the house where Bríd Bhán was engaged in the daily struggle of rearing four sons and two daughters while their father was sailing the seven seas and dreaming his dreams of how to make them all independent for life. He invested in four horses, one for each of his sons, and bought carts and jaunting cars. And he began to make the necessary contacts in Liverpool and elsewhere to ensure that he would be able to set up as an independent importer.

It was nothing so catastrophic as the ploughshare that wrecked the nest of Burns's 'wee, sleekit, cow'rin', tim'rous beastie' that ruined my Granda Flynn's great scheme for the setting up of an importing company called O'Flynn and Sons. It was something much more unpredictable, and yet something that has been around as long as the story of Adam and Eve: human nature. The scheming sailor forgot that each of his children was just as much an individual as himself, and even if he didn't know the word genes, he knew well enough the expression 'a chip off the ould block', also 'like father, like son'. During those years while he was staring at the Atlantic or the Pacific with eagle eyes, like Keats's 'stout Cortez', his sons and daughters were growing up with minds of their own. And the qualities of character that had caused the father so impulsively to leave his wife and children and go to sea were equally strong in the children – together with whatever traits came to them from Bríd Bhán and her forebears.

Another flaw in the scheme developed in its originator himself. The sea is conducive to meditation and the conception of plans but the salt sea air is also productive of thirst. Anyone who has seen dockers unloading a cargo of coal from the hold of a ship, as I did in my childhood, or seen any other aspect of the back-breaking physical labour involved in the life of a docker in those days, will appreciate that after such a day's labour any man could do with a few pints; so, even before he went to sea, I imagine my sailor grandfather was well able to down the black stuff. Even on his spells at home between voyages, he was one of the most supportive patrons of Martin Clohessy's pub, now de-molished, which stood at the corner of the Irishtown and Charlotte's Quay beside Baal's Bridge on the Abbey River. So much so that, after allowing a reasonable time for the relaxation the man needed, but with growing concern for the finances of the family – the homecoming sailor with his flush funds and need of an audience for his yarns was an obvious mark for the bums – Bríd Bhán would sally forth from the house in Watergate accompanied by the family terrier. This lively little pet she would slip in the door of Martin Clohessy's pub, and wait. If the terrier came out, she had to continue the search in other pubs in the Irishtown; if he failed to reappear, she made her own vigorous entry to the pub, where she would find her furious husband kicking at and cursing the family pet who was snapping playfully at his boots; but rather than suffer the disgrace of his wife's tongue-lashing, he would go peacefully home with her.

About the time when the Welshman, Lloyd George, was killing two birds with the one stone by sending the demobbed and unemployed debris of 1914-18, along with the scum of Britain's slums and jails, across to terrorise the Irish people into submission to Britannia's rule – it was in Limerick that his force of thugs, in their makeshift uniforms of soldier's khaki and policeman's black, were given the name Black-and-Tans, with no offence intended to the famous County Limerick hunting pack, the Scarteen Black-and-Tans – my Granda O'Flynn came home to Watergate from his last voyage. By that time his elder daughter Mary had emigrated to America and sent for his youngest son Michael. Some years previously, in 1917, the second youngest son Thomas had become a statistic in the casualty lists of the Battle of Ypres. That left only the two eldest of his four sons, Daniel and Richard, and his youngest child, the second daughter Brigid. Unfortunately, while the father was still at sea, those two remaining sons had become seriously infected with a disease for which medical science did not have, and never will have, a cure, viz. music. Nor did the planning father's personal handicap disappear overnight. Casting anchor on the home hearth did nothing to diminish the ex-sailor's thirst, and he continued his contributions to the wealth of Martin Clohessy and other publicans, although his diminished funds deprived him now of a ready audience for his seafaring tales. And so the result of the great scheme was that his workforce was reduced to two, my father and his older brother, our Uncle Danny, both of them under the spell of Orpheus and therefore unfit for any kind of practical business in life but condemned to earn their living by coal-belling, i.e. buying coal a ton at a time, twenty sacks, in one of the big coal-yards on the docks, then hawking it around the city to customers who bought one or more bags, too often on credit.

My father, having learned as a youth to play the piccolo and the flute in the local Sarsfield band, found when he married that his musical talent could provide a second source of financial support for his wife and children, perhaps eventually even an escape from the physical drudgery of the occupation his own father's well-intentioned scheme had forced him into. With the advent of the jazz era in the 1920s, he bought a saxophone in Savin's music shop (on the 'weekly system') and taught himself to play it. And being eventually the father of two girls and six boys and himself the son of a man who thought up a great scheme for his children – need I say it? – he saw the personnel for a danceband of his own growing up there in that room in Old Church Street; all that was needed – this is how planners plan – was to teach all of us to read music and to play the various instruments. There was also, of course, the small problem of buying the instruments. He found time and patience, in spite of his two occupations, to teach us all in turn how to read music, and his sons acquired some skill in playing the piccolo and the flute, the only instruments to hand. His first setback came when the eldest child, my sister Mary, showed more interest in her mother's Singer sewing-machine than in the secondhand violin her father had bought for her. Not surprising, perhaps, when he was trying to teach her himself while keeping a step ahead of her in *First Steps in Violin* or something similar. Ironically, he could not afford to send her across the road to that yellow-washed house at the corner of Broad Lane, opposite the Bishop's Palace, where our good neighbours, Tom and Nan Glynn, a genteel and courteous elderly brother and sister, took pupils for piano and violin. Incidentally, we boys thought that any lad learning the violin was a sissy, an attitude that cost me some mental anguish because a good friend and classmate of mine, whose people had a small shop in nearby Nicholas Street, had to endure the jibes of my street pals when they saw him going into Glynn's with his violin case.

The next setback, a more permanent and cumulative one, to the plans of the second Richard O'Flynn for his family, came with the realisation that, what with the bad debts from his coal business and the irregularity of the one-night stands in the dancehalls, whether in Limerick or farther afield, he was being put to the pin of his collar to feed and clothe his increasing family and to keep the rented roof over our heads. In the meantime, the frustrations of life caused our Uncle Danny to frequent Martin Clohessy's almost as often as his ex-sailor father. The result was that from a handicapped start the coal business – in which the originator had now lost all interest – went from bad to worse, and even if the advent of the Second World War had not put an end to it, there is no doubt that it would have died a natural death from other causes.

When I first visited the stables in Watergate as a child there were only two horses left in the stalls: my father's Peggy, the little black horse I used to see outside the window when I sat in my pram, and Uncle Danny's big white horse, Billy; and there were two coal-carts in the adjacent shed. There was also one dilapidated jaunting-car, tilted on its shafts and covered in cobwebs. I knew nothing at that time of the great plan my old Granda Flynn, who sat by the fire in the house up the road from the stables, had conceived while away at sea, but as I grew older and heard the history of the stables and the plan, that mouldering jaunting-car became symbolic of the failed hopes and unrealised dreams of our sailor grandfather. And I knew now that I did not really have two fathers, just the one good Da who broke his back by day lifting bags of coal, often up several flights of stairs in the old tenements, and blew his guts out at night playing the saxophone in dancehalls (often in faraway country towns from which he came home in the small hours) so that Ma, who worked just as hard all day at home, could have enough money to get us food and clothes, and to pay for the rent and the gas and everything else.

At the risk of causing some readers to wonder if I might not be descended from an inferior botching branch of the planners of the Great Pyramid, I must revert briefly to my other grandfather, Maurice Connolly. Believe it or not, he also, if on a smaller scale, conceived a plan to set himself and his family up in business. Maybe it had something to do with the social conditions of the time or perhaps it is something innate in the human spirit that makes many of us wish to do our own thing and not be dependent on others for a living. Considering the disastrous outcome in both cases – maybe it had something to do with the curse of that vengeful little monk, Mainchín – it is obvious that both my grandfathers were afflicted with the ambition to be personally independent and 'beholden to nobody'. In fact, that idea was enshrined in one of our Granny Connolly's favourite dicta and it became something of a family motto with us, even if only as a joke when we mimicked that good woman in her absence.

Anyway, having done his bit for the British Empire in the Boer War by eating lots of oranges and grapes, and on the side giving bread and sugar from the military stores to the starving women and children of the Boers who had been herded into camps by the British 'for their own safety', my soldier grandfather came home from South Africa to his wife and young family in their two-room apartment in a tenement on Arthur's Quay in Limerick just about the time when my sailor grandfather was moving his wife and young family from Mungret Street in Limerick to a tenement in Liverpool's dockland. Granny Connolly's account of her husband's part in the Boer campaign was succinct and graphic: 'Shur he never even saw a Boer!' she told us. 'When the Boers saw them comin' in their red coats they skedaddled off up into the hills – that's why they changed into the khaki uniforms in the end. The poor soldiers spent all their time marchin' and marchin', and some of them droppin' dead with the thirst and the fever.'

The returned soldier, hopefully a sadder and a wiser man like the poor ex-soldier in the ballad, Patrick Sheehan from the Glen of Aherlow, found employment as a packer in Kivlehan's Catholic repository, a shop that sold statues and other religious items, beside Cruise's Hotel in Patrick Street. He didn't have far to go to his job, just around the corner from Arthur's Quay. But the man who came safely home from the Boer War was to 'meet his Waterloo', as his wife, our Granny, said, in the apparently safe occupation of packing and unpacking statues and holy pictures. One day, when bending over a box to unpack some item, he was startled by a sudden call from his employer. In turning with his arms full of straw he was jabbed in the eye by a straw. He subsequently lost the sight of the eye. As my mother told it to us:

> He got a big action out of it. Gaffney, the solicitor, got him a big action, and with that he got us the house in Crosby Row and we moved from Arthur's Quay. And because myself and my sisters used often mind Miss Anne's shop in the quay while she'd be at Mass or if she had to go anywhere, he decided to start up a shop for us in Crosby Row. The shop was to be just like Miss Anne's, selling bread and tea and sugar and everything; he used even go out and buy timber boxes, orange boxes and the like, and chop them up to make bundles of firewood for sale. All the small shops used to sell them for people to start the fire.

They still did in Limerick when she was telling us the story, and some people hawked them from door to door in a boxcar. 'But we never did any good with the shop,' my mother would conclude, 'because the fishermen robbed us!'

That final succinct statement needs elucidation. It was not that there were violent gangs of fishermen in Limerick going around holding up the proprietors of small local shops but that the same credit system which was such a negative factor in my father's coal business was operative in many other areas. Together with the pawnshops, it was a crucial factor in the day-to-day survival of many poor families, even if it caused serious problems for the families of the shop-keepers and others who were involved in that risky financial gamble. Between the Connolly house in Crosby Row and the nearby Shannon River there were two rows of houses which were mainly inhabited by fishermen and their families. These naturally became customers of the new local shop in the Connolly house. In this era of supermarkets and cars, refrigerators and freezers, it should be noted that opening a small shop in your own house was a very common venture in those days when people had to walk everywhere and when provisions were bought on a daily basis. The problem for the proprietor of a small shop was that the customers often bought their goods on tick, to be paid off when the weekly wage packet came in on Friday night. Even then the account might be only partially settled, leaving the shopkeeper in that classic position 'between the devil and the deep blue sea'.

With his army *esprit de corps* and code of honour still ingrained in his soul, my ex-soldier grandfather found it very difficult to understand that some of his customers seemed to have no standards of honour or self-respect. And when he eventually pointed out that their credit was going 'beyond the beyonds' in his shop, they would simply go elsewhere, to whatever other small shop would open an account for them and give them goods on the 'Kathleen Mavourneen' system ('it may be for years, and it may be forever!'). Like those fishermen on the Sea of Galilee long ago, I suppose the Crosby Row fishermen too often 'laboured all night and caught nothing', but there was no miracle-worker waiting on the slip to take them out again on the Shannon and fill their nets to breaking point.

I never knew my grandfather Connolly but from what my mother told us of him I don't think he would have objected when, visiting our Granny Connolly with my mother, we played beside the river with our first cousins, the Brommels who lived in her house, and the children of the fishermen. Our uncle Maurice Connolly, who was unmarried at that time, sometimes went out with the fishermen in the evenings if someone was sick or they needed an extra hand, and he rowed with many of them in the local Curragour Rowing Club. One summer's day when I was about four years old, along with other children from our street I was paddling at the river's edge on the Island Bank while our mothers sat on the bank, knitting and chatting. Uncle Maurice came along in a boat with another man and when he spotted us they pulled in and asked Ma to let us go in the boat for a little trip. They took us all the way around the island, by the loop of the Shannon which we call the Abbey River. If ever I doubted it, I had a clear demonstration on that glorious summer's day, with the Shannon at full tide, that I did indeed live on an island. And I wouldn't mind at all if the joys of heaven included occasional repeats of that circumnavigation of our Island Parish.

10

ACROSS THE THRESHOLD

I must have been wheeled out in my pram, asleep and totally unaware of the world about me, many times before the summer days came when my mother would position the pram outside the window and leave me, sitting up wide-eyed, to observe life on Old Church Street while she went on with her daily chores in the kitchen.

What remains in my memory from those first observations of life outside our front door is the image of children playing in bright sunshine, children running, singing, jumping, shouting, skipping. Some of those children would have been my own brothers and sisters. And from one of those children, a girl named Philomena Daly who lived in the first house of the red-brick terrace opposite our house, I heard a statement many years later that gave us both a good laugh. 'It's a wonder you ever grew up,' Philly said, 'because I used to eat half of your goody!'

Apparently, when my harassed mother would put me out in the sunshine, she would then go back in and prepare the mug of goody (a mixture of crustless bread, warm milk, butter and sugar, on which babies were fed until they were equipped to tackle tougher food). But as soon as the pram was seen issuing from our doorway, my two sisters, Mary and Lily, would abandon whatever game they were engaged in with the other girls and vanish into the hallway of the Bishop's Palace. In fairness to my loving sisters, it must be noted that they were the eldest in our family, and that I was the fourth boychild, so that by the time my goody days arrived, they were understandably weary of being called away from their play to spoonfeed 'his lordship' in the pram. When my mother reappeared with the mug of goody, she would call their names, and probably add: 'I'm sure I saw them playing on the street; they must be around somewhere.' But help was at hand for my poor mother, in the form of a willing volunteer, a good little girl who was prepared to forego her fun and games in order to feed the lovely little 'boy the Flynns' sitting there hungry and goggle-eyed in his pram. My grateful mother used to wish God's blessing on good little Philly Daly. 'Little did she know,' Philly told me, 'that for every spoon I gave you, I took one myself – oh, but your mother made lovely goody!'

Son-as-bye, as my mother herself would say (I don't know the etymology of that), and as I have often said to my dear friend Philly, although my father and Uncle Danny were both six feet tall, I was always the smallest in my class, a physical fact that could have had serious repercussions in the school yard but for the compensating factor that I had three older brothers; it was only in my mid-teens that I began to shoot up like a giraffe, and then so fast that I got all sorts of what were called 'growing pains', and was threatened for a while by that ever-menacing scourge, tuberculosis, that cut short the lives of my brother Joe and my sister Lily.

By the time my brother Maurice was occupying the pram outside our door, I would be toddling along past the Bishop's Palace to the corner of the street, from where I could see King John's Castle just across the road, and down the short slope of Castle Street to Thomond Bridge and the River Shannon. Soon I would be walked by my mother or my siblings down to the bridge, and be shown the Treaty Stone at the Thomondgate side and also those frightening marks of the Bishop's Lady's fingers on the stone parapet of the bridge! On some fine day in early summer, the toddler would walk for the first time – having previously been pushed in the pram – along by the river to the island bank which was our summer paradise and of which more will be told. And so, gradually, literally *céim ar chéim*, I learned the layout of our locality, first of our own street, then of the neighbouring streets. And by playing with other toddlers, as well as from the instruction of my 'big' brothers and sisters, I became aware of the social community into which I was born, learning names of individual children, their families, their father's occupation, and so on.

The first aspect of that social life I had already learned without crossing the threshold to the street; this was the fact that we were sharing our house with other people who were called a different name from our family. They were the Sheehans, we were the O'Flynns, and although we were using the same front door, hall and stairs, the same single tap and toilet in the backyard, and constantly meeting one another, I was never aware of any friction or discontent between the two families. While they were always ready and willing to help when help was needed, each family respected the privacy and the rights of the other. As my sisters and some of the Sheehan girls were classmates in the local convent school, they sometimes did their homework by communal effort in our kitchen or theirs. But later in life I often wondered what Mrs Sheehan might have thought of the noises emanating from our kitchen-cum-living-room when my father began to teach himself the saxophone some time in the mid-1920s. My mother assured me, however, that in those days before the radio became a common household item, people loved to hear any kind of music, even the beginner's efforts on an instrument – 'And, of course,' she added with pride, 'remember that your Da was no beginner when it came to the music; he took to the sax like a duck to the water. The only problem, he said, was the mouthpiece with the reed being so different from just blowing air into the flute.' I myself recall that sometimes on a summer evening when my father was practising the saxophone, with the window opened as far as it would go, some of the boys and girls used to come and sit on the pavement under the window enjoying the music.

The hall (the old Bishop's Palace) next door remained a forbidding mystery to me for a long time, being such a huge house with so many different families coming and going. But beyond it, at the corner facing King John's Castle, there was a tall house (now demolished) on the ground floor of which was Mrs Griffin's shop selling flour, oatmeal, etc. from big sacks and bins. I used to watch fascinated as she scooped the lovely white flour from a bin on to the big shiny tin dispenser on the scales. On the other side of our house our neighbours were named Nealon and in the third house of our terrace, next to the churchyard of St Munchin's Protestant church, lived the family McCoy. Strangely enough, the father in each of those families was a house-painter, as was also the father in the house directly opposite us, the Dalys'. And in each of those families, all the sons followed the father into his trade, as the custom then was. Eventually our little street seemed to have its own branch of the house-painters' union, there were so many men and youths in paint-stained white overalls going off to work in the morning and coming home late in the evening. Another strange triad of which I became aware early in my street explorations was that there were three families living in our street all with the name O'Flynn, but with no relationship between them, as far as anyone was aware, other than that we were all descended, as I am proud to record, from the same high king, the great Flann Sinna who is buried under the high cross of the scriptures at Clonmacnoise, where, as T. W. Rolleston (1857–1920) put it:

In a quiet water'd land, a land of roses,
Stands Saint Kieran's city fair;
And the warriors of Erin in their famous
        generations
Slumber there.

It is also on record that there was an abbot named Flann in
Clonmacnoise at some stage whose tyranny annoyed the
monks so much that in the end they threw him into the
nearby Shannon. With him, of course, we claim no relationship whatsoever.

On the opposite side of the street, I had to learn that the
big yellow house beside Broad Lane belonged to the
musicians, Tom and Nan Glynn. Then there was the big
wooden gate of the yard where a family named Ryan, who
lived around the corner in Castle Street, kept their horses –
they were in the timber business. Later, after a fire which
resulted in some of the horses having to be put down, they
changed to lorries. Mrs Murray, who kept the pigs, was next;
then more houses, one of them cottered, and two small shops,
one owned by a woman named Chris O'Brien, who sold
groceries, buns, coal and bundles of sticks; the other Nonie
Mack's, our street sweet shop. And finally there was Halpin's
pub at the corner of the New Walk, a street as wide as an
Italian village piazza, that led down to the convent. We
learned soon enough, both from the talk of our elders and
from the sermons in the church, especially at the Lenten
missions, that there was something very dangerous about
the stuff the men drank in the pubs. Still we often stopped
at the open door of Halpin's to sniff the strange smell of the
stout and to watch the men sitting on their stools, smoking
pipes, spitting in the sawdust, until Tom Halpin or his father
came out to chase us away. Old man Halpin was one of our
local heroes, because we knew he had played for Garryowen
and had been capped several times for the Irish rugby team.
Another cause of pride in our street, as I was to hear often

from my mother, was connected with St Mary's lovely new parish church; the young man who was sacristan, William Bartlett, and the young lady who was the talented organist and choir-mistress, Josie Freeman, both lived in our street.

Eventually I would get to know every family in the cottered Bishop's Palace next door, as well as all the families around the whole block and in nearby Castle Street and the New Walk. I can still name them all. I remember them with pride and gratitude, and – did I say it before? I'll say it again! – I thank God that I was privileged to grow up in that community and in those years. That was the kind of society into which children were born in every town and city until the Second World War, and the subsequent progressive substitution of horsepower for horses, rendered the street as a social unit obsolete. But as with life in our own house, so life on our street and around our area was not by any means heaven on earth. Inevitably, because we were thrown together every day of our lives, and because so much of our time was spent on the street, our street games caused squabbles among the girls and many a fistfight among the boys. Even the adults had occasional differences and rows, and sometimes hot words about some disputed football match or politics – it was the era of the Blueshirts and of De Valera's Fianna Fáil coming to power in 1932 – could result in a fistfight between men from the same street or from different areas.

The women could also have the occasional falling-out, usually, as in every street in every village and town from China to Peru, as a result of their children's squabbles. We even had one such day when two women got involved in physical combat on the street, a fight that was an example of what is called in Irish *troid na mbó maol* ('a fight between hornless cows'), consisting more of pushing and hair-pulling than of blows or scratches; but it became memorable in our folklore for the hortatory shouting from the aged mother of one of the contestants, who shrilly advised her battling daughter to: 'Streel her in the gutter! Streel her in the gutter!' The other women, including my own mother, were more interested in restoring peace, much to the disappointment, I must admit, of all of us nippers who were thoroughly enjoying the randyboo. Happily, I can record that the parents learned from the children to let bygones be bygones. Soon after, on Bonefire Night, they were singing together with all the other neighbours around the fire outside our door.

11

RING-A-RING-A-ROSY

The street, as I have noted, was a playground for the children, and usually the boys kept to the roadway, playing ball games, while the girls kept to the wide limestone flags of the pavement (we called it the path, and Americans call it the sidewalk) to play Picky (Hopscotch) or adult-imitation games like House and School and Hospital. Some of the girls' games, like skipping and chanting games such as Wallflowers, saw them move to the road, and in this our little neck of the Island Parish was very fortunate because we had Broad Lane opening from our street and we had Castle Street just around the corner down to Thomond Bridge. Thus there was scope for all and no contention between the boys and the girls. The boys took to the pavement only on summer evenings to play cards – often in the convenient nook provided by the fact that the front wall of our house extended a little from the façade of the Bishop's Palace. The favourite card game was pontoon, in which the 'money' consisted of the picture cards which were published in series by the tobacco companies.

Another and unique play-area available to us was the grassy patch between the castle itself and the iron railings that ran beside the pavement down to Thomond Bridge (both grassy patch and railings have since disappeared, probably thrown into the Shannon by the Bishop's Lady. What a pity she wouldn't throw some of our urban planners into the river some night!). Since the end of the civil war in 1923, the castle was unoccupied, and some of the bars in the railings were distorted enough for us to be able to squeeze through. We used our mothers' household coal-shovels to dig little tunnels, to make castles, and to construct earthworks and trenches for our war-games (from relations who had been in the Munster Fusiliers, we were all well-versed in the history of the mud-and-blood trenches of the Great War). But the ghosts of all the soldiers who had occupied that grim castle towering above our childish games, from the day the first Norman knights and their archers took possession until the day the final shots of the civil war were fired – and especially the ghosts of the Irish soldiers who were killed on old Thomond Bridge or drowned in the river during Ginkel's siege in 1691 – must have appealed to us to go outside the railings and roll our hoops or spin our tops.

As soon as I could walk, I was introduced as a link in the chanting ring:

Ring-a-ring-a-rosy,
A bottle full of posies.
High-sha! High-sha!
We all fall down!

And as soon as I could fill even a passive part, I was drafted into their games of House and School by those same loving sisters who would have let me starve rather than spoonfeed me! As I grew older I realised my good fortune in having two big sisters who not only helped my mother with the knitting, sewing and household work as far as they were able but who went out to work and bring home a wage as soon as the law allowed them to end their formal schooling. I presume the street games of children, before the proliferation of the motor car made the urban street a potential deathtrap, have been well documented by sociologists but both the feminist and the educational theorist of today might be intrigued by the fact that little girls like my sisters and their friends used to spend hours on summer days imagining that an area of the flagstone pavement, marked off into 'rooms' with a piece of chalk (or a chunk of red brick!) was their very own house, with father going to or coming home from work, mother doing the household chores, the children being good or bold or sick, sometimes being sent on messages from one 'house' to another, even being sent to 'school' on another section of the pavement! It was for this pavement house that girls collected 'chainies' (from china), the fragments of broken cups and saucers that were transformed into the shining delph of the imaginary house.

The pavement school had neither blackboard nor books but it had a teacher armed with a stick, and it had the ambience of discipline by which many a toddler got a mild but useful preparation for the corporal punishment that was then an integral part of the school system in all countries. Incidentally, in those times when professional nursery schools were unknown and Madame Montessori would have been thought to be a circus acrobat, the playschool on the pavement served the purpose just as well. The older children used the lessons they were learning in school to conduct their imitation school, and this was supplemented by the learning children picked up inside the home when their older siblings were doing their homework, which usually involved the chanting of tables, poems, catechism. The very first plate from which I began to try to spoon my pandy (mashed potato with butter and salt and a dash of milk) was an enamel one with the alphabet all around the rim, and gradually revealing a clock as I spooned up the grub. The big difference between the pavement playschool and the real thing, of course, was that even the smallest toddler could decide to stand up, defy the 'teacher' (who might even be a big sister) and go home, with only the futile threat of not being allowed back ever again as the sole deterrent.

Before graduating to the full status of participant in the boys' games, I had to pass through the intermediate stage of mixed road games like the basic tig, in which one player chased the rest until she touched someone, who then took over as chaser, or more elaborate games such as Queenie, London Bridge is Falling Down and Wallflowers. Then there were 'cross-the-road' games such as Steps and Numbers. In Steps, the 'leader' called out the number and kind of steps (fairy steps, scissors steps, etc.) to be taken by the children at the other side of the street, a process that often led to accusations of favouritism since whoever reached the other wall first became leader. In Numbers, the leader faced the wall and rattled out the numbers from one to seven, during which counting the others tried to advance; when the counting ended, the leader whirled round and anyone seen moving was sent back to the opposite pavement to start all over again. This also led to disputes as to whether the alleged mover had actually been moving. In Queenie the leader stood in the middle of the road with the others behind her back; she threw the ball over her head and, after a clean catch or a scramble, whoever took the ball hid it behind her back. All then shouted 'Queenie! Who has the ball?' The leader turned round, and saw all the others standing with their hands behind their backs; if she guessed correctly which of them had the ball, she continued as leader; if not, the ball-keeper became the new Queenie.

Two other 'cross-the-road' games that are worth chronicling, since they are all now a part of social history and unknown to the deprived children of this electronic age, were called respectively Trades and Ticky-Ticky-Tack. In the former, the leader sat against the wall and was approached by all the others, who halted at the edge of the pavement. Then a dialogue was chanted as follows:

Group: Here we come to learn our trade.
Leader: What trade?
Group: Any trade.
Leader: Set to work and do it.

The group then began to mimic the action of someone working at the trade which they had agreed upon before approaching. The leader had to guess which trade they were working at. When the right guess was eventually made, all ran off to the other side of the road, chased by the leader. Anyone caught had to join the leader's side and thus it went on until all were caught.

The other game has often come into my mind down through the years because of its strange name and dialogue. Again a group having agreed on a colour approached the leader and a dialogue took place but in this case each member of the group had a small stone which was banged on the pavement to accompany the opening chant:

Group: Ticky-Ticky-Tack-Tu-Mullen!
Leader: Who goes there?
Group: A little divil runnin' down the Abbey Lane.
Leader: What do that little divil want?
Group: He wants a colour.
Leader: What colour?
Group: Any colour.

The leader then began to guess and, as in the previous game, when the right colour was guessed, all ran, the leader chased and anyone caught had to change sides. What I find intriguing in retrospect about that particular game is firstly the opening line (is it a corruption of some old Irish phrase?) with its accompanying banging of stones; secondly, and even more interestingly perhaps, there is still standing in the grounds of the local St Mary's Convent one high and very impressive wall of the thirteenth-century Dominican Abbey.

And from our Old Church Street, from the very pavements where we were playing this game about the devil and his search for colours (souls, perhaps?), there was still in our day a very narrow lane, called 'the Abbey Lane' running right down to the wall of the convent grounds. (Incidentally, that lane ran beside the house of Mrs Murray and from her yard a side door led out on to the lane, so that it was from this lane her fatted pigs made their journey out to the waiting cart that was to take them to their fate.)

In our street, as in every town in those times, the group skipping games of the girls had many rhymes and chants. These did not register for long in the mind of the male of the species who was usually considered a nuisance by the more skilful females and advised to stay out altogether. I recollect a few, such as 'Stop the rope, take the rope, never leave it empty,' and 'Salt, Mustard, Ginger, Pepper'. The girls also had another use for the rope which gave them hours of enjoyment; this was the individual swing around the street poles, sometimes two or three ropes being attached to the same pole. If a big brother were not available, any passing adult would be asked to push the loop high on the pole.

A game in which boys and girls joined, especially in the light of the streetlamps in autumn or winter, was a street version of Forfeits. Each of the group placed some personal token – a stone, a marble, a piece of string – in the hands of the leader held behind his/her back. As each token was picked out, the leader was asked: 'What's the owner of this to do?' The task assigned could be something like three rounds of the block, or knocking at the door of some house and asking a foolish question ('Go and ask Mrs Murray how many black puddings can be made out of one pig'). A task peculiar to our street and one that could cause a nightmare later on, especially if the moon was shining on the tombs and crosses, was to go to the iron gate of the churchyard beside McCoys' house, stand with your hands on the bars of the gate, and call out the 'prayer' we thought the Protestant minister said at the graveside. We had often watched burials from a safe Catholic distance but had never been near enough to hear what the minister actually said. Our innocently unChristian version was: 'Ashes to ashes, and dust to dust, if God won't take you, the devil must!' If you didn't shout loudly enough, you could be sent back to chant the traditional anti-Protestant rhyme – a *multum-in-parvo* couplet that encapsulates in so few words the anguish and bitterness of the starving Catholic population of Ireland who were offered a life-saving bowl of soup by proselytisers on condition that they attend the Protestant religious service:

Proddy-woddy, ring the bell!
All the Soupers down to hell!

This was the rhyme we shouted at the pupils of the Villiers School which was situated at the end of our street, along with the widows' almshouse, in the extension of the grounds of St Munchin's Protestant Church and churchyard. Because our school hours were more or less the same, we did not see the 'Proddies' very often; perhaps only on holydays of obligation, when Catholic schools were closed and we had the day to ourselves after attending the obligatory Mass and were likely to be playing on our street as the pupils from the Villiers School were going home. Incidentally, we used to say – and so did the adults – that you could always know a Protestant from a Catholic because they had a very sallow complexion; we were not aware that in the eighteenth century the Irish poets habitually used the word *buí* (yellow) as a pejorative term for Protestants. I am glad to record that the young lads from the Villiers School were no daws when it came to vituperation. When they were safely at the corner of our street and Castle Street, before turning down towards Thomond Bridge (many of them seemed to live in the Ennis Road area) they would shout back at us:

Hail Mary, full of grace,
The cat fell down and broke his face.

One day, we were momentarily shocked into silence when we heard a Limerick Protestant boy of about twelve shouting what we had been told the barbaric Orangemen shouted at Catholics in Belfast as they were burning them out of their homes. We reported it euphemistically to our parents as 'Eff the Pope!' When we recovered our Catholic spirits, we chased the Prod and his pals, but they had a good start on us, otherwise they would have ended up where the Bishop's Lady threw poor Drunken Thady.

To conclude this chapter, I record my mother's story of how the Protestant boys once deprived the O'Flynn family of part of their dinner. One day, when my eldest brother Tom was about five years old, my mother sent him across to Chris O'Brien's shop, just up the street, to buy a yellow turnip. On his way back with what was to be the vegetable for the family dinner, he encountered some of the Villiers pupils going home from school, lads of up to twelve years of age. They took the turnip from the child and proceeded to run along the street using the turnip for practice as rugby three-quarters. My mother was distracted from her washing-tub or whatever she was slaving at by the entrance of her crying child with his tale of woe, that the Proddies had stolen the turnip! Like ourselves when we heard the fellow cursing the Pope, she ran out and chased the blaguards who were using our turnip as a rugby ball while they ran down towards Thomond Bridge. Of course, they were too fast for her; but to add insult to injury, they threw the turnip into the river! She went down to the Villiers School next day to lodge a complaint, and was sympathetically received, but she was subsequently told that none of the Villiers pupils remembered anything about such an incident. She noticed, however, that from then on the older Villiers lads, like those Wise Men from the East who were warned by an angel, went home by a different route (down by an alleyway we called the 'water passage' to the river, and on up to Thomond Bridge).

12

'TACKLE HIM LOW!'

When a boy was big enough to be initiated into the strictly male road games by his bigger brothers or by his neighbours, he found himself in a much more violent world than that of Ticky-Ticky-Tack or imitation House and School. The road was the playing pitch for our games of rugby, soccer and hurling, especially in the winter months when we could not play in the nearby Island Field because of the seasonal swamping from the Shannon. Our hurling was conditioned by the desire to emulate the great Mick Mackey and his colleagues, whose decade of the 1930s was the golden age of Limerick hurling. Then Limerick won three All-Irelands and five National League titles, the latter being consecutive, a feat that has never been equalled. *Our* chances of ever playing for Limerick in Croke Park were severely hampered by the fact that we could afford neither hurleys nor *sliotar*. The only time we saw these items was when we played for a school hurling team in inter-schools competitions. Our hurley was a crook – the curving branch of a young ash or any other tree; in this, perhaps, we were nearer to what the young Setanta used on his way to Eamhain Macha to join An Chraobh Rua and to start his career as the greatest hero of Irish saga by scoring the greatest hurling goal ever scored when he slotted the ball down the throat of the hound of the king's smith, Culann, and made recompense by taking on the job of guarding the smith's house himself, thus acquiring his soubriquet, Cú Chulainn.

The 'ball' we used was usually made by someone's mother from rags packed tight into an old stocking; when this fell apart and while waiting for somebody's benevolent Ma to find time and materials to make a replacement, we hurled with an empty Cleeve's condensed milk tin. Whenever we happened to come into possession of a worn tennis ball – where they came from we never asked – or a sponge ball, we preferred to keep them for handball or for 'serves', a version of handball played with crooks; both handball and serves we played against the handy side wall of Glynns' house at the corner of Broad Lane across from our house (on dry days only, so as not to mark Tom Glynn's yellow-washed wall) or against the big wooden gate of the old coach entrance beside our house.

In addition to serves we played another strange game against that old coach gate beside our house. This was called 'cat'. We knew nothing of cricket, except that it was played by the Protestant Young Men's Society in their grounds near the Ennis Road, and also by all the chaps in the English comics and library books, where some envious little scut called Smith Minor was always trying to keep the dashing Willoughby or Hamilton-Morton from becoming captain of the first eleven. In fact, our street cat was actually a form of cricket, the ball being a short stick pared to a point at both ends; this was thrown at the player who was defending with a hurling crook a square chalked on the ground at the wall or gate, the object being to land it in the square. The batsman (crooksman in our game) had to hit the cat as far away as he could. If the thrower made a clean catch, they swapped roles; if not, the batsman had to hit the 'cat' back to the square by tapping one of the pointed ends to 'rise' the cat in the air so that he could strike it. His score consisted of the sum of the strokes he piled up until he was eventually caught or 'squared' out.

Soccer was becoming popular in the cities and towns of Ireland during those years, and every parish in Limerick had its amateur club. Compared to the unimaginative mimicking names that are common today, some of our Limerick clubs in the early 1930s had glorious names like Trojans and our own Island Parish Dalcassians. I'm sure both Homer and Brian Boru's poet, Mac Liag, would have appreciated the influence of classical culture and national heritage evinced by those names. I came across a similar example when I came to settle near the port of Dún Laoghaire in the mid-1960s and saw the old bucket-chain dredger at its interminable work in the harbour; it was the dirtiest boat of any kind that I ever laid eyes on, but all its filth and rust and heavy clanking buckets were gloriously compensated for in its name, *Sisyphus*.

Perhaps the names of those two Limerick soccer clubs stuck in my childish memory because the first soccer match I ever saw was played in a field out beyond Hasset's Cross in Thomondgate, what has since become Thomond Park, home of our Island Shannon Rugby Club, and it was between the said Trojans (who were reputed in our Parish to be desperate knackers from the slums up in Palmerstown or Boherbuoy or some other such distant uncivilised area!) and our own Dalcassians (Dals for short) who were probably being described to the children in other parts of Limerick in similar derogatory terms. I was brought to the match by my sister, Lily, then in her early teens, and her friend Madge Danford (a daughter of Captain Michael Danford, the neighbouring man who was killed by the Free State soldiers in 1923) who brought along a nephew of hers. I remember only two things about that event: firstly that I thought we would never get to the field and secondly that the match was abandoned after a fight started and the spectators joined in – our two guardians dragged us away as they ran off with the other non-combatants.

In our summer games in the spacious and grassy Island

Field, we put down sticks for goals and played with the best kind of ball available (whoever owned the ball had to be captain of one of the sides). But in our street version of soccer, there was a rule unknown to the game's administrators in Dublin or London. The teams having been picked by means of the ritual 'Eeny-meeny-miney-mo', stones or ganseys were put down as goalposts, and because of the variety of footwear – sandals, tennis shoes, boots hobnailed, broken, too big or too tight, or even bare feet – the rule was proclaimed: 'No rushin'!' This, being interpreted, meant that no contact between opposing feet or footwear was allowed. Such an *ad hoc* rule was probably conducive to the development of knacky footwork but it often led to disputes and subsequent fisticuffs when a heavy boot came down on the toes protruding from a sandal or a broken shoe.

Just in case the incident of my mother's turnip being turned into an imaginary rugby ball by some lively young blaguards from the Villiers School might leave some readers worried about our relations with Protestants in general, we were very proud of the fact that one of the best soccer referees in Limerick was a Protestant neighbour of ours, George King, who was caretaker of the entire Protestant Church enclave – the Bishop's Palace with our three houses attached, the church and its churchyard, the widows' almshouse and the Villiers School – which constituted that area of the King's Island. As an Englishman, George had a headstart in knowledge and experience when it came to the development of soccer in Limerick. He had an only son known as 'Gu-gu', who was stronger in body than in brain and who was greatly addicted to cowboy films. On summer evenings, he used to invite some of us to play Cowboys-and-Indians with him in the spacious grounds of the almshouse and school, and even in the churchyard if his father was not at home; but, being somewhat witless, he once left one of his fellow cowboys, or an enemy Indian, tied to a tree and went in home to have his tea. As night came on, the cries of the unfortunate prisoner brought George King out to investigate; thereafter, our games of cowboys, like all our other games, had to be strictly confined to the streets.

Our favourite sport was rugby – we found that middle 'g' difficult, so we called the game 'rubby'; apparently, the chaps at English public schools, except, perhaps, at the eponymous school where the game originated, found the word even more difficult, because in all the aforementioned comics and library books they called the game 'rugger'. Again, we only got to handle a real rugby-ball as soon as we were recruited into the clubs by older brothers or relations; so, in our street version, five, six or seven a side, we used the rag ball or the Cleeve's milk tin. The slogan 'Tackle him low!' was an echo from the shouts of our elders at matches, and to be thus tackled and 'hopped off the ground' on the hard street made being tackled on a real field like falling on a cushion. And not for rugby alone, but for any field game, it provided a toughening up that would have been approved of by the Spartans who fought and died at Thermopylæ.

Anyone who is *au fait* with the relationship between society and sport in Ireland will know that Limerick is the only place where sport is truly democratic, and consequently that it is the only place where rugby was – and is still – played by the working-classes as well as by the types who play it anywhere else. In Wales, of course, it was played more by the miners and other workers than by the ex-pupils of the public schools, who were not very numerous in Wales anyway. My father told us that rugby was actually brought to Limerick by the Welsh soldiers in the British Army, just as the music of the flute or brass bands was an unintentional gift, through the garrison regimental bands, from dear Queen Victoria to her disloyal and ungrateful subjects in the cities and towns of Ireland. My father was dead before I came across the autobiography of the poet Robert Graves, *Goodbye to All That* (1929). Having been wounded in the war, Graves was posted to Limerick in 1919 to rejoin the Royal Welsh

Third Battalion stationed in the barracks at King John's Castle. His brief account of Limerick is derogatory but much less so than some accounts of our city and its citizens given in books and in the media by writers who were born and/or reared in Limerick. 'I played my last game of rugger as fullback for the battalion against Limerick City,' he tells us. 'We were all crocks and our opponents seemed bent on showing what fine fighting material England had lost by withholding Home Rule. How jovially they jumped on me and rubbed my face in the mud!'

When I read that reference to 'the fine fighting material' lost by England, I thought of the five thousand men from Limerick City, including my father's younger brother, our Uncle Tom, who willingly became 'fighting material' for England in 1914–18 in the belief that England would honour her promise to give Ireland Home Rule as soon as the war ended. The grandfather of Robert Graves, Dr Charles Graves (1812–99), had been Protestant Bishop of Limerick from 1866, and his father, Alfred Perceval Graves (1846–1931), was an enthusiastic scholar of Celtic literature and tradition, although he was employed as an inspector of schools in England for some years. He was also the author of many poems and songs, the most famous of which is 'Father O'Flynn'.

Whatever its provenance, rugby became the most popular team sport in Limerick. The first rugby match I saw was played in the Markets Field, and it was a schools game between the Christian Brothers School in Sexton Street and a visiting team. I was still in the convent school, and as with my first soccer match, I was 'dragged' along to the match, this time by my big brothers, and probably to get me out of my mother's way. The only thing I remember about that match is the song my older brothers were practising during the days before it (although they were still in the primary school in Quay Lane in our own parish, they were obviously enlisted, with all the other CBS pupils in other parishes, to attend the match and add their vocal power to the occasion). The CBS team were known as 'Christians' and when we were rehearsing the song at home – probably in bed! – I had the notion at first that the other team would be black and pagans, because in the convent school, preparing for my first Holy Communion, I was being told by the nuns about the black babies in Africa who were all pagans but who could become Christians if we brought in our ha'pennies and pennies and put them on the tongue of a little black doll who swallowed them when you pressed his levering arm. My biggest brother, Tom, who was my ever-patient mentor and protector, explained to me that the other team were actually both white and Christian, but they were coming from some college owned by priests and they were what Ma called 'lawdy-daws' and our Christians were going to send them back to their fancy college with their eye in a sling, their nose in a knot, cauliflower ears and generally in such bad shape that they would probably not be able to walk for a week let alone play rugby. In fond remembrance of my brother Tom, who thus gave me my first brief lesson in the elements of rugby, I give the words I remember of the first war-chant I ever sang:

Come on, Christians, win the cup!
Score away, don't get fed up!
That you ever let us down
No one can say.
Get like tigers on the ball,
Bring it with you, one and all,
Come on, Christians boys,
Away, away, away!

That match may have been the last rugby match played by Christians, because the Christian Brothers decided some time before I graduated from the convent school that their schools would comply with the ban imposed by the GAA on 'foreign' (English) games: soccer, rugby, cricket and hockey. For both adults and children in Limerick, this was a very confusing situation; we were rightfully proud of any Limerickman who got his 'All-Ireland cap' in rugby, but we were equally proud of our great Limerick hurlers, the Mackeys, the Clohessys, Mick Kennedy, Gareth Howard, Jackie Power, Paddy Scanlon the great goalie and all the rest of them; in fact, in the democratic language of sport in Limerick, whenever we got a 'split' head in hurling, and had to go to Barrington's Hospital to be stitched and bandaged, the adults' comment was, 'Ah, I see you got your All-Ireland cap!' Once, as a child, I happened to be in a house in the Irishtown with my father and the man of the house let me hold the big silver cup recently won by Richmond, the local rugby club of which he was captain. Another day, I stood in childish boredom at a corner in Patrick Street while my father and another man carried on one of those adult conversations that are literally over the head of the waiting child. But things brightened up considerably for me when the other man, as they finally parted, put his hand in his pocket and gave me a big brown penny, as was the custom on such occasions whenever there was a copper to spare for the child. As the other man went off up Patrick Street, my father pointed him out to me and said, 'That man's name is Sheahan, and he played for Young Munster in the Bateman Cup.' As I grew older, I would read and hear often ('too bloody often!' the supporters of other clubs grumbled) of that glorious day for Limerick rugby in 1928 when the unfancied Young Munster club went up to Dublin and beat the cocky Lansdowne in the final of the Bateman Cup, and I would relish the memory of having met Danaher Sheahan. But on that day, he could have been Moses or Julius Caesar for all I knew, and his real claim to fame in my childish heart was that he had given me a penny.

A year or so after that schools match in the Markets Field, my brothers brought me to another match at the same venue, but this time a senior game between Garryowen and UCC. This match is etched on my memory for two reasons. When we set out we had no money but I was instructed, as we went up the Irishtown and on to Garryowen, that we would all get in 'before a man'. That caused me some puzzlement – who was this man before whom we were all to get in? – until we got near the entrance to the field. There were other young fellows like ourselves hanging around there, and my brother Tom gave me the following instructions: 'Watch out for a man, and ask him to get you in before him. If he says all right, you walk in and pretend he's your father. Then wait inside and we'll all get together again.' I have narrated my childhood mystification on the matter of having two fathers; but here was a situation where I had to let on that some complete stranger was my father! I had no time to worry about the implications of this or whether it might not be hurtful to poor Da back at home, because just then a bus arrived and caused great excitement among all the prospective 'sons' on the lookout for a surrogate father. Tom gave me a push and said, 'They're the Cork team! Go on, go on, ask one of them! We'll all get in with them!' And so I found myself standing in front of what I thought was a giant, looking up at him with my innocent eyes ('saucer eyes' was one of my mother's joking names for me!) and asking him could I go in before him. I can still see that man's dark curly head and his big smile as he patted me on the head. 'Come on, son!' he said and took me by the hand. I was impressed by the fact that he knew I was his 'son' for the day but I was still worried for fear the man at the gate would ask me any questions. But no questions were asked, and 'while a cat would be licking his ear' I was inside and thanking the big man. He gave me another pat on the head and said, 'Enjoy the match.' I thought that man was some kind of an angel in human form who had got me into heaven. But my brothers took a more detached view. 'That fella is one of the UCC forwards,' Tom said, 'and he'll be trying to kick Garryowen all over the field in a minute.'

The second reason why that first senior match lingers in my mind is because of the shock I got when the teams came out on the field. Garryowen's light blue was familiar to us, being also the colour of the Quay Lane CBS jersey, but when University College Cork came out – my eyes popped and my mouth gaped: they had the pirate's flag on their chest! I knew the skull-and-crossbones emblem already, and all about prisoners being made to walk the plank to Davy Jones's locker, from reading stories in the comics. Pirates had given me nightmares since I encountered Long John Silver (*Treasure Island* was one of the few books in our house, and one of the first long books I had read, on my father's recommendation). Like Dante turning to his guide, Virgil, in their journey through Hell and Purgatory, once again I had to ask my mentor for enlightenment. 'They're all in the college in Cork, going to be doctors,' Tom told me, 'and they have to study the skeletons of people to find out where all the bones are. That's why they have that skull and bones on their jerseys.' Even though I got in 'before a man' – and a very nice man, I thought, even if he was trying to kick Garryowen all over the field (only doing what he was supposed to do) – and even though Garryowen won, I don't think I really enjoyed that game, and my sleep that night was probably disturbed by the tap-tapping of Long John Silver's peg-leg and a voice bawling:

Fifteen men on the dead man's chest,
Yo-ho-ho, and a bottle of rum!
Drink and the devil had done for the rest –
Yo-ho-ho, and a bottle of rum!

13

COFFIN NAILS AND PICTURE CARDS

Anyone looking at the films made in the 1930s and even up to the 1960s will notice that all the characters seem to light a cigarette at every opportunity; even the lovely heroine and her lover will light up as soon as they sit down at a table in a restaurant. Smoking, in those days before the great cancer scare, was so common in all classes of society that a non-smoker was as rare as a non-drinker today. In the cinema it was not only in the film that cigarettes were being smoked; the vast majority of the audience smoked all through the film, so that there was always a fog of smoke between audience and screen. In buses and trains and cafes, almost everywhere except in the church and in one or two Dublin theatres, cigarette smoke was being exhaled and inhaled on every breath.

Children began to smoke surreptitiously when far away from their house and street – I smoked my first and last cigarette, sharing it with two pals, on the way home from a school hurling match – and some imitated poor adults who picked up butts from the street and got a few puffs from them, even by holding the very meagre butt on a pin! Hygiene, is it? We never heard the word, although the concept was enshrined in the proverb, 'cleanliness is next to godliness'. Even doctors were not aware of the cancer link which has caused such a change in public awareness of the dangers inherent in the use of tobacco. It was obvious to everyone that heavy smoking was deleterious to health, especially to the respiratory system. The cheapest and most common brand of cigarettes, having the lovely pastoral name of Wild Woodbine, were generally referred to, even by their users, as coffin nails. And the raucous coughing that so annoyed many a preacher in our numerous Limerick churches during the winter was not caused solely by the Atlantic mists coming up the Shannon. Little did we realise, as we looked forward eagerly to being next in turn to get the picture card when Dad bought a new packet of Woodbines, that every cigarette he smoked was chipping some time from his life. His winter cough, of course, was aggravated by the rigours of his occupation: being out on the coal-cart in all kinds of weather, inhaling coal-dust every time he emptied a sack, occasionally playing the sax in the smoke-filled dancehalls of those days.

Although our home was mercifully always free of violence, vulgarity, bad language and material deprivation, it would not be natural to expect that it should be entirely free of disagreement or the occasional bickering and squabble between the children. As for the parents, the only occasions when we ever heard any such disagreement are associated in my memory with smoking – perhaps this has been a subconscious factor in my own lifelong aversion to the habit. As the number of chicks in the nest increased and the financial strain of feeding and clothing them became heavier, my mother, who was a non-smoker like most women at that time, began to become more resentful of the fact that good money was 'going up in smoke'. She appreciated, no one better, the small alleviation of her husband's daily hardship provided by the fags, but it must have been a growing aggravation of her own daily hardship to consider how the money Da spent on cigarettes could have added to the meagre resources of her household purse.

We, on the other hand, would probably have been very disappointed if my father had given up smoking; we thought smoking was something every man did, and to be able to smoke in your own home rather than surreptitiously with your street pals was a sign of growing into manhood, along with getting into long trousers and leaving school at the statutory age of fourteen and getting your first job. Like all our pals on the street and in school, we considered ourselves fortunate that every new packet of cigarettes produced a new card for the current series. Duplicate cards would be swapped for ones we didn't have and superfluous cards became the currency for our street card-games of pontoon.

The cigarette card was also an important item in what can be called our extra-curricular education. Educational programmes on television and video can undoubtedly provide children today with information far beyond the scope of any book but these programmes have to compete in the child's memory with all the other stuff to which children are exposed in the modern media. Our media entertainment consisted of the black-and-white films we saw on an occasional visit to the cinema, if we could raise the necessary twopence (the equivalent of two weeks' pocket-money in the average family). And so those series of picture cards published by the tobacco companies were more intensely and repeatedly concentrated on than any book or television programme can be by a child today. Each series of fifty cigarette cards was devoted to a special topic, such as Wild Flowers, the Sea Shore, Famous Racehorses, Aeroplanes, and of course, Footballers, Sportsmen, Boxing, even Famous Greyhounds! At the back of each picture card there was a closely-printed and very informative account, and in the album which could be used to stick in the fifty cards, the printed text was reproduced beside the space for the picture.

Apart from the reading practice provided by each card – this in an age when books were not in such plentiful supply as they are nowadays (the paperback revolution did not begin until 1935 with the first ten Penguins) – the imagination was stimulated, curiosity aroused and material for discussion and argument provided. I remember being fascinated especially by the series on wild flowers and watching out for them when we went on picnics or rambling in the nearby Clare hills in the hope of 'skinning' an orchard.

We spent so much time in the open air, along the banks of the Shannon, playing in the Island Field, wandering 'out the country', that we had an innate awareness of flora and fauna, even if it did not amount to an obsessive love of nature – songbirds in cages were a common feature in houses, and some men made a business of trapping them with lime and selling them. We had a canary in our own house for some time, along with a dog and a cat, until the morning when we found it dead in its cage – the cat had managed to evade being put out in the shed for the night, and my father deduced that the canary had died of fright as our black pussy tried to leap up to the cage. My mother had a great love of wild flowers and she would never come home from our family picnics without something to put in a vase, even if it were only a bunch of what she called 'fairy grass' or a few sprigs of heather. From the Island Field or our forays into the Clare countryside we brought her anything that qualified as a flower, but we were disappointed when she ruled out the bright yellow 'wild daffodils', as we called them, because they were full of little creepy-crawlies.

The coffin-nail nickname of the Wild Woodbine brand of cigarettes proved true in my father's case when the racking winter cough resulting from a lifetime of addiction to that pernicious weed – 'hellish, devilish and damned tobacco, the ruin and overthrow of body and soul' as Robert Burton, author of *The Anatomy of Melancholy* (1621) called it – cut short his life when he was only sixty. But even before I arrived in the world as the sixth child, adding to his burden as breadwinner, he had deprived himself of the small luxury of a cigarette often enough to be able to make two investments which were to prove of fundamental cultural and educational value in our lives. Being himself more interested in music than in literature, he first bought a gramophone and some records, to which he added when he could afford to. Many of our winter evenings were spent playing records, often with the renewed caution not to wind the spring too much. We all had our favourite records, and mine was the old English ballad, 'The Farmer's Boy', which made us all very sad with the first half and glad with the second, and which I am still ready to sing at the drop of a hat or the filling of a pint:

> The sun had set behind the hills across the dreary
> > moor
> When weary and lame a boy there came up to a
> > farmer's door;
> 'Can you tell me,' said he, 'wherever there be
> One who would me employ –
> For to plough and to sow, to reap and to mow,
> And to be a farmer's boy . . . '

There were a few special records which were kept apart from the general stock and which we were not allowed to play except with special permission and on rare occasions. One was the recording made by the Sarsfield Fife and Drum Band, a selection of Irish airs entitled 'Old Erin', for the Parlophone Company in 1932, with my father playing the piccolo and my Uncle Danny conducting (he had also arranged the selection). The other special records were a few saxophone recitals by an American virtuoso named Rudy, who was my father's model. He played all Rudy's tunes himself in our kitchen, for his own delectation and ours, but of course he never got to play them for a larger audience in the city or county dancehalls.

The other purchase my father made instead of indulging in further supplies of Woodbines was a children's encyclo-paedia, *Newne's Pictorial Knowledge*, in six volumes, lavishly illustrated as the title indicates. These he bought from a door-to-door salesman with a down payment of a pound and subsequent payments of sixpence a week (for comparative purposes, it should be noted that the price of the daily newspaper at that time was one penny). Just as his own few select records were preserved in special thick covers, so these 'Knowledge Books', as we called them, my father covered in thick brown paper and kept in a special corner of the kitchen press. He urged us to use them as often as we wished but with care. They became for us a source of information on many topics and a further stimulation of curiosity concerning the history and content of the world we lived in. As with the records, we had predilections in the encyclopaedic field of knowledge, my own being the history of Greece and Rome. I knew about Romulus and Remus, the murder of Julius Caesar, Socrates and the glory that was Athens, before I made my First Communion, and I can still see in my mind's eye the illustration of the heroic stand of Leonidas and his three hundred Spartans at the Pass of Thermopylæ, the artist having centred his picture on one of the helmeted Spartan warriors with his head tilted back and an arrow stuck bang in the middle of his neck. We did not notice it very much as we pored over the pages and pictures again and again, but later on I realised that the history of England, written in the standard imperialistic vein, took up a lot of space in the history volume, whereas that little island called Ireland got no mention on any page.

14

'TOLLE LEGE, TOLLE LEGE'*

*'Take up and read, take up and read'
St Augustine of Hippo (354–430)

When I see in the bookshops today the amazing range of books by Irish and other authors for children of all ages, it is one of the few occasions on which I realise that in this area, as well as in material matters, children today are much better off than we were as we grew up in Limerick during the decade of the 1930s. We had, of course, a rich culture of storytelling, rhymes, songs and poetry, even if the loss of our native language had deprived our people of the traditional culture of their own race; but even in the language imposed on us, there was a dearth of good reading material, and of what was available very little had any connection with our own nation and society; most was imported from England.

In our own house, as I have indicated, gramophone records were more numerous than books. Whatever little leisure time my father had, he preferred to spend at his own art, either practising the saxophone and the flute, or copying and transposing music. But he would have been an avid reader if circumstances had allowed him to relax at the fireside reading a book and he encouraged us by extolling the pleasures and benefits of reading good books. His self-sacrificing and laborious purchase of the encyclopaedia, *Newne's Pictorial Knowledge*, for our benefit was an indication of his own intellectual values. Of the few other books he had been able to buy before the increasing family required all the financial resources from his two occupations, I remember especially Stevenson's *Treasure Island* (already mentioned), Canon Sheehan's *The Graves at Kilmorna* and *Glenanaar*, George Eliot's *The Mill on the Floss*, and some of the works of Dickens. My favourite was *A Christmas Carol*, even though the ghosts of Christmas, and that door-knocker being transformed into the face of Scrooge's dead partner ('Marley was dead . . . as dead as a door-nail') caused me many a nightmare.

Another and unusual book in our stock was a huge old American Bible which had been in my father's house in Watergate but he did not know what returning emigrant had brought it back from the New World to the Ould Sod even before he was born. We were more interested in the many realistic illustrations than in reading the exploits of King David or the tribulations of that poor afflicted man, Job, whose name was frequently on my mother's lips as it was on many a mother's. What I suffered from the ghost of Dickens's Marley was nothing to the terror I endured after seeing some of those biblical illustrations, like the one showing the last few people clinging to the upper branches of trees in the Deluge (living so near the Shannon, and seeing high tides coming up almost to the trees along the Island Bank, we could well imagine what another such universal flood might be like). An even more disturbing picture was the one that showed the ground opening under some chancers who had opposed Moses and set up idols, for which they and their relations, friends and followers were being swallowed live into hell! When the good nun preparing us for First Holy Communion began to tell us horror stories about hell – 'There was this boy who pretended he was going to Mass on Sunday but instead he went out in a boat and what do you think happened him? The boat turned upside down and he fell into the river. And where do you think that boy is now? I'll tell you where he is . . . ' – I could nearly feel the wooden floor of the classroom opening under me. No wonder some of my more nervous classmates wet the floor and even worse from time to time!

I doubt if the Bible was to be found in many Catholic houses in Limerick in my childhood (in how many would an inquiring angel find it today?). But there was another kind of religious reading material which was widespread. Apart from the newspapers, the principal reading material of Irish origin to be found in ordinary houses consisted of the pamphlets of the Catholic Truth Society of Ireland, which could be bought for a few pence from the small bookstand in most churches, and religious magazines like the popular *Irish Messenger of the Sacred Heart*, its companion magazine for women, the *Madonna*, and others such as the *Redemptorist Record* and the *Far East* of the Columban Missionaries to China. A regular feature in this last, 'My Diry', by the misspelling schoolboy Pudsy Ryan, was popular with young and old in those days of innocent amusement. These little publications, like many other aspects of the Catholic ambience of life in Ireland in those decades, are now sneered at by irreligious cynics; but even the poet Patrick Kavanagh bears testimony to the fact that they were a valuable source of reading material, not only in the towns, but also in rural homes where little else was available to adults or children. The CTSI pamphlets, in addition to their role in the religious and spiritual lives of their readers, were also an incidental source of adult education – some dealt with social questions, with figures in Church history and with topics like evolution, and these provided material for fireside discussion in those years before the television chat shows and soap operas changed Irish home life. Another popular item was the unsophisticated but wholesome *Ireland's Own* magazine, and two annuals that were eagerly looked forward to in our house were *Carbery's Annual*, written and published by the sports journalist P. D. Mehigan, which recorded the year's events in GAA games, and the *Wolfe Tone Annual* of Brian O'Higgins (1882–1949), devoted to Irish history. O'Higgins was also the designer and publisher of the only Irish-made Christmas cards that were an alternative to the Dickensian holly-and-robin imports from England.

In the cities and larger towns, the public library provided a regular supply of books for people who had the leisure and inclination to make use of them; but from what I have described of the living conditions in the working-class areas of Limerick, it will be obvious that there was little time or privacy available to the poorer people for the reading of novels or other long books. In the cities and towns where there were schools of the Irish Christian Brothers (founded in 1802 by Edmund Rice, a wealthy widower in Waterford who, at the time when Napoleon was trying to conquer Europe, took literally Christ's advice to the idealistic young man: 'Go, sell what you have, give to the poor, and follow me'; he was beatified in 1996), two further important items of reading material were available to the pupils and their parents.

The first of these was the monthly magazine, *Our Boys*, the solitary native antidote to the long-established *Boys Own* and the many other weekly English comics. These 'comics' were different from the American picture comics, a bundle of which came to us now and again from our Uncle Joe in New York (along with very welcome secondhand clothes – these ceased with the increase of his own family cares). The English publications, directed solely at boys, were really magazines of serious stories, closely printed, with only a single illustration at the head of each story. Although there were different magazines, with titles like the *Rover*, *Hotspur*, *Adventure*, *Champion*, they were all of a kind. I often wondered in later years, when I had become a professional writer myself, who were the poor hacks who churned out the stories for those publications week after week. Whoever they were, they knew how to write a story in that genre of heroic adventure and suspense. But again, as with the history content of the children's encyclopaedia in which my father had invested his hard-earned sixpences, these magazines were totally British and imperialistic in their topics and attitudes. Nevertheless, they were avidly read by boys in every city and town in Ireland – at threepence, they were far too expensive (three weeks' pocket-money!) for us ever to buy new, but there were a few huckster shops where they could be bought secondhand for a penny or a ha'penny, depending on their condition – and that noble idealist, Pádraig Pearse, would have thought his sacrifice of career and life for the Irish nation all in vain if the Lord God had let him see the youth of Ireland eagerly reading the exploits of Rockfist Rogan of the RAF and other such fictional heroes who gallantly maintained the civilising rule of Britannia over her ungrateful colonial subjects in India and Africa and defended her shores and skies against the Boche or the Hun.

The Christian Brothers' magazine, *Our Boys*, was only a monthly production, and its effect in counterbalancing the weekly flood of English comics was symbolic rather than significant but at least it made us aware, even subconsciously, of the fact that we had our own culture and traditions. At a time when some of the upper classes, Protestant and Catholic, were sending their children to English public schools, disdaining the established native Protestant colleges and the copycat institutions provided by religious orders for well-to-do Catholics, *Our Boys* even had a serial story about an Irish college, where the escapades of a genuine *garsún* named Murphy were at least more intelligible to us than the affairs of Billy Bunter or Smith Minor of the Lower Fourth. Another regular feature in *Our Boys* was the monthly story by Victor O'D. Power, a folksy tale narrated by an old travelling woman called Kitty the Hare, who repaid the hospitality of whatever farmhouse she happened to reach as night came down by telling the family one of her stories, beginning always with some such opening as: 'Oh wisha, isn't it a terrible night altogether, God save us all! It reminds me of a night a long time ago – let ye gather in here now to the fire, and I'll be telling ye – .' This feature was a favourite with the adults as much as with the children, and in many houses Kitty the Hare's story was actually read aloud at the fireside. Two facts that curtailed what might otherwise have been a universally beneficial circulation of *Our Boys*: firstly, because it was produced by the Christian Brothers, it was automatically debarred from entry into many schools owned by other religious orders as well as into the snob colleges, both Catholic and Protestant; secondly, even in the schools of the Christian Brothers themselves, sad to say, there were not a few pupils whose parents simply could not afford the few pence it cost.

Much more important in the educational area was the graded series of English Readers compiled by the Christian Brothers for the pupils in their primary schools, one for each class. These hardcover and copiously illustrated books were, in effect, a comprehensive anthology of literature in prose and poetry, and like the stories of Kitty the Hare, they were actually read with relish by the parents as well as by the pupils. Readers of all ages learned from them such fine recitation pieces as 'Caoch O'Leary', 'The Wreck of the Hesperus' and 'The Ballad of Inchcape Rock' (in which 'Sir Ralph the Rover tore his hair and cursed himself in his despair'). In school they were used for much more than straightforward reading lessons; they became the material for transcription, dictation, recitation, spelling tests and imitation composition.

Much as I loved reading, and consequently relished getting my hands on those school readers, there were two drawbacks connected with them as far as I was concerned. Like our clothes and shoes, schoolbooks were passed on from one member of a family to the next in line. In a family like ours, where I was number four son, the likelihood of my ever having the pleasure of handling a new schoolbook was minimal. (It did happen in the convent school and I can still smell and feel that lovely glossy new book!) Consequently, the average pupil had books that were held together, as we said uncouthly, 'with spits and chewing-gum'. The other disadvantage of those excellent school readers was that, because there was so little else to read, an avid reader, as I was, would always have read the book of the boy next above him in the family even before he got into the class using that book. And so, the daily reading lesson became a period of tedium conducive to that condition of daydreaming so dangerous in a classroom where the teacher's voice might suddenly rouse you with the command: 'Flynn! Go on!' And when you had no notion of where the previous reader had been halted, the consequences could be dire.

15

'ON BOKES FOR TO REDE I ME DELYTE'*

*The Legend of Good Women, Prologue
Geoffrey Chaucer (1350–1400)

It was our teacher John Liddy who urged us, when we were in Fifth Class in the primary school, to join the Carnegie Library. At that time, the library was situated in Pery Square, which to our way of thinking in the Island Parish, was foreign territory. We ventured 'up the town' only when shopping with our mothers or when going to the Friday night weekly meeting of the boys' section of the Holy Family Confraternity in the Redemptorist Church, so that the idea of walking all the way up to Pery Square just to get a book to read would appeal only to any afflicted child like me who was already an insatiable bibliophile.

On my first visit to the library, I got to see the packed shelves of books from the distance of the reception desk but I didn't even get to touch a cover. All I got was a very sniffy reception from the woman at the desk who first looked me up and down as if I was 'the thing the cat brought in', then handed me an application card which had to be signed by my teacher. 'And you'll have to promise to keep the books clean, do you hear?' With that parting encouragement, I went home, regretting that I had ever accepted my teacher's contrary encouragement. When I made my second literary pilgrimage all the way up to Pery Square, my card, duly signed by Mr Liddy, was sniffed at, turned over, and examined for possible King's Island bibliophobic germs; finally, after renewed admonitions about keeping the books clean, I was admitted into the Ali Baba cave of literary treasures.

Just to look at and then handle those books in their coloured dust-jackets gave me a sensuous thrill that I still experience when I handle a brand-new book. Never having been in a bookshop, I just wandered up and down, fascinated, picking out a book, replacing it, picking out another. I was so confused by the realisation that I could actually take home any one of those lovely books, free of charge, that I was in more of a dilemma than King Solomon wondering which one of his seven hundred wives or three hundred concubines he would order to his bed on any particular night.

I don't remember what I chose as my first free gift from the beneficence of the Scottish philanthropist, Andrew Carnegie. What I do remember is that the woman at the desk examined it as if it were the Book of Kells, and pointed out to me that there was a mark on the title page and a slight tear in the bottom edge of the back of the dust-cover, blemishes which she noted in pencil on the inside of the book itself. While I realised that she was being fair in thus ensuring that when I returned the book I would not be accused of causing those defects, it was obvious also that any further mark, blob, tear or other disfigurement on this precious work of literary art would be incontrovertibly attributable to the said Christopher O'Flynn of 2 Old Church Street, off Castle Street, in the Island Parish of St Mary's, Limerick, who might forthwith and without right of appeal be barred forever from the Carnegie Library, children's section (and his name probably noted in a blacklist in case he should ever dare to apply for membership of the adult section).

If I felt disgruntled and discouraged by my first encounter with officialdom in the Carnegie Library, worse was to come. On my second visit, I was replacing on a shelf a book I had been considering when I suddenly felt a heavy hand laid on my shoulder. I looked up into the face of a natty-looking man who was considering me with what in the books would be called 'a stern countenance'.

'What's your name?' says the stern countenance.

I told him.

'Where do you live?'

I had handed in a completed application card a week before, on which my name and address were written in block letters, and this card was just over there in the files where the sniffy dragon was watching from behind her reception desk. Nevertheless, I answered politely as brought up to do by decent and honest parents.

'I live in Old Church Street.'

The grim countenance was made grimmer by a frown.

'Where's that?' The tone implied that it could be a false address, such as the *Limerick Leader* told us every week the defendant had given to the sergeant. However, even at that early age of ten years I was always willing to dispel ignorance. I began helpfully: 'Do you know King John's Castle?'

He got really snotty then, God knows why.

'Of course I know King John's Castle! You don't live in the castle, do you?'

A real 'thorny-wire', I thought. But thorny-wires, like the genuine article (thorny wire: barbed wire), have to be handled with care. I could have told him that, being descended from a high king of Ireland named Flann, I had every right to be living in the castle, but that Cromwell and the Penal Laws etc. etc. But I decided to keep to the geographical facts.

'If you go straight on from Nicholas Street instead of going down by the castle to Thomond Bridge, the street you – '

He didn't have the manners to let me finish. A real bostoon, Granny would say.

'All right, all right! So, you're from the Island, are you?'

Any fool could have figured that out from the information already given; but only someone a bit more alert than a fool would have detected the social snobbery in the intonation. Naturally, then, I did not offer to give him a bar or two of 'There is an Isle'.

'Yessir, I'm from the Island – from the Parish,' I added, with my winning smile. And in my secret soul I added: Put that in your pipe and smoke it!

'And where do you go to school?'

'Quay Lane.'

'Where?'

'The Gerald Griffin Memorial School.' And put that in your pipe and smoke it!

'Where's that?'

'Do you know St Mary's Cathedral?' Always willing to help.

'Of course I know the – '

The hand that had been on my shoulder moved to my ear.

'What did you say your name was?' getting real ratty now, the little boolum.

I considered asking him if he was deaf, but instead I patiently repeated the personal Christian name, Christopher, and the ancient clan name, O'Flynn.

'Well now, young Flynn, be sure you take good care of these books, do you hear?'

I heard, in spite of his fingers wagging one of my ears.

It occurred to me to ask him did he administer this ear-wagging and admonition to all newcomers to the library, including the nice boys and girls who went to school to the Jesuits in the Crescent or to the nuns up in Laurel Hill where they learned to talk like the Protestants and say *gawdun* for *garden*. But, all the way from her little house below in Crosby Row, the Granny Connolly shook her old grey head and reminded me that *a shut mouth catches no flies*.

'If I hear any complaints about you, you won't be long in the library.'

In the safety of the secret soul, I spat: And the same to you – with knobs on!

I knew this 'piece of importance' must be someone higher up in the library than the dragon at the desk; later I learned that he was actually the Big Chief Bottlewasher himself, the boss, the librarian, one Robert Herbert by name, and – again from that generous weekly source of news and information, our own *Limerick Leader* – that he was one of the leading lights in various societies devoted to local history and archaeology, to whose journals he contributed articles from time to time.

If I had told my mother about either the desk-dragon's warning to keep the books clean or the welcome afforded me by the librarian himself, she would have gone up to Pery Square the next day and given them both 'Rocks o' Bawn' and the 'Rakes o' Mallow', a treatment often meted out to villains and blaguards in her stories. If the Granny Connolly had heard about the way her grandson was treated, she would have visited the Carnegie Library with a can of paraffin under her black shawl, and unless the librarian made a quick exit, his days of writing articles for archaeological journals would be at an end.

Both the librarian and the desk-dragon might have learned something about the level of civilisation in our house and in the Island Parish generally if they had been in our kitchen on the day I brought home my first book from the library. Having admired it, my mother told me to cover it with newspaper so that the lovely coloured dust-jacket would not be in danger of being torn or stained; and I did likewise with any other book I brought home, adapting the same sheet of newspaper to each new book – newspaper was a valuable and versatile commodity in those times. Having been read – and a good read it was when radio was still uncommon and television had not arrived, and when newspapers were still really *news*papers, sheets of closely-printed news with very few pictures, unlike today's lavishly illustrated bundles of stale news, strident space-devouring advertisements, gossip and scandal and self-opinionated spouting – the newspaper was put to many other uses: in the home, it was used as kindling and as lavatory paper, in small shops as wrapping paper. It even figured in our play when we made paper hats (to go with a wooden sword) or paper aeroplanes. I have mentioned in an earlier chapter how my mother used to wrap newspaper around our feet inside the stockings in winter. And a sheet of newspaper was put to unique use one day by a nun in the local convent school, and a young girl in our street, a classmate of one of my sisters, became an item in our folklore when the nun, judging the girl's skirt to be immodestly short, pinned a sheet of newspaper around the hem and packed her home to her mother in conventual disgrace.

To the earnest and erudite teacher who had advised his pupils to join the Carnegie library, I gave the positive account I thought he expected to hear. The only person to whom I bared my troubled soul was my elder sister, Mary, who had a wise head and was like a second mother to me. She was already out in the world, working as a machinist in a tailoring firm in Patrick Street and adding a few shillings to the household funds. She appreciated my resolve to have no more to do with the library but she counselled me to carry on and not to let people like them upset me. The library was for everybody, she said, and we were as good as anyone else. So, I carried on for over a year, until I finished in the primary school. I saw the librarian in the distance once or twice after that but he didn't bother me any more.

What I read in the library was more of the stuff we were reading in the comics from England, except that it was in book form. Apart from the books by Standish O'Grady based on the Cú Chulainn saga, the only book of native origin I can remember reading was *A Swordsman of the Brigade* by Michael O'Hanrahan (1877–1916), whose literary career was cut short by a British firing squad – early on the morning of 4 May 1916, he stood in the yard of Kilmainham Jail, side by side with Limerick's Ned Daly and the poet, Joseph Mary Plunkett, when three more names were added to the list of those Irishmen executed by order of a British court martial for having dared to use in the cause of Ireland's freedom the same martial methods by which England had conquered our country and held on to it for seven hundred years.

There were three kinds of book in the flood of publications from English publishers. Firstly, to add to the antics of Billy Bunter and others like him in the weekly comics, we got the series about a scallywag named William and his pals. I remember being puzzled by some of the dialogue in those books, and when I asked my sister Lily to enlighten me, she couldn't, but she glanced through the book and told me that it was terrible rubbish on which I should not be wasting my time and brains. Secondly, there were adventure books about Africa and India, and a similar series based on the First World War – *With Haig on the Somme*, *With Allenby in Palestine*, and so on. And finally, there were numerous books about English public schools where the chaps played rugger and cricket, and knackers (called 'cads') were regularly punished by all the decent chaps by being sent to Coventry. I thought Coventry must be some place like Glin in County Limerick where the Christian Brothers had an industrial school, a penal institution to which anyone could be consigned by the courts if he began to practise petty crime like stealing sweets or fruit or anything else from shops, or even if we 'mooched' from school once too often (and to which, unfortunately, poor orphans were also sent, as they were to similar institutions all over Ireland in those times). How I found out that the cads were not really sent to Coventry makes another story.

16

ENTENTE CORDIALE

On a fine Spring day during the Easter school holidays when
I was ten years old, having cajoled my father, as we
occasionally did, into letting me come with him on the coal-
car (we called it a car, not a cart, and my Uncle Danny had
once been secretary of the Carmen's Society, which included
many kinds of carriers), I first went with him to the stables
in Watergate where he tackled up our horse, Peggy. Dad
sorted out a supply of sound sacks (he used to repair torn
sacks with a big packing-needle, just like Mam darning the
socks by the fire). We then went to the docks, to Sutton's
coal-yard, where I stood watching as my father held each
sack open on a low wooden platform that had two handles
at each side. This was filled from the mountain of coal behind
them by two men with shovels, whose faces were much
blacker than my father's ever was when he came home at
night. All three carried on a chat while the bags were being
filled – these two men were old friends of my father; one of
them had played in the Sarsfield Band with him. When a
sack was full, the two men put down their shovels, bent to
the handles of the wooden platform, and lifted, while my
father turned, took the full sack on his back, and carried it
to the nearby car. Twenty sacks to the ton of coal, a
hundredweight per sack. Then my father guided the horse

over to the weighbridge just outside the office. He went up on the car and the man in the office signalled to him through the window; he had to throw a few lumps of coal out of some of the bags until the man gave him the all clear, and then he went into the office to pay – not like some of his customers, he had to pay on the nail for what he got. Then we drove off, and although I was very happy and feeling cock-o'-the-walk viewing all the ships and the men working from my perch on the car, I could see that poor Peggy wasn't feeling as lively as when we were driving down to the docks with the car empty.

I think my father only let us go with him on the car now and again so that we could see what the work was like, even on a fine day. He never chawed the rag with us about school but he advised us to have respect for our teachers and learn as much as we could. We all knew that he should have been playing the flute in some big orchestra instead of spending his days going around selling bags of coal but he never said a word about it himself, and we never heard him blaming his father for landing him and Uncle Danny into such a hard way to earn their living. But sometimes I heard my mother giving out about it when Da wasn't at home.

So, anyway, off we went this fine spring morning, along by the docks and across Sarsfield Bridge and out the Ennis Road, my father sitting at one side smoking his cigarette, and myself at the other side as happy as Larry, whoever he was. Today was a good day for my father, because he had an order for half-a-ton of coal for a big house out someplace off the Ennis Road. We'd be getting rid of half the load at one go, instead of the usual, a bag here, two bags there, and poor Da having sometimes to carry the bag up a few flights of stairs in some tenement, and maybe not be paid for it on the nail but 'I'll have it for you on Friday when he gets paid.' Some old women used even be haggling with him about the price, telling him that some other woman was getting the bag of coal sixpence cheaper from her coalman.

We knew how that was done but Da couldn't say it to the customers. From what I said about the way the ton of coal was weighed in the coal-yard, it can be understood that each sack of coal was not weighed separately; so, although the twenty sacks together made up a ton of coal, no single sack had exactly the one hundredweight people thought it had and a dishonest coal-beller could make twenty-one sacks out of the twenty by taking some coal out of each sack. Then he could sell a bag here and there at a cheaper rate, and cause trouble for honest men like my father.

One of his fireside stories was about that trickery. A couple of carmen he knew were sent out by one of the big coal merchants with a ton of coal for some rich old miser who they knew wouldn't give them a tip. First, they made an extra sack for themselves by taking some coal out of all the twenty sacks; but not satisfied with that, they dumped one sack out of the twenty with the one they made – that meant a bag each for themselves to sell or take home. They thought the old fellow wouldn't know, but they got a big surprise when they started carrying in the sacks, because there was the old gezebo standing at the back window of the house peeping out – and watching them as they carried each full sack into the coal-shed and came out with the empty sack, which meant he was counting. But the Limerick blaguards were too cute for him. One of them was a small, butty sort of a fellow and after they had the nineteen sacks brought in, he got into a sack out at the car, and the other fellow carried in this twentieth sack to the shed, then came out and gave the docket to the old geezer to sign. As soon as the satisfied miser was gone from the window, the small coalman came out of the shed and off the two blaguards drove.

On our way out the Ennis Road, my father told me that the man who owned the house we were going to was an Englishman who was a big boss in some firm in Limerick and his wife was a musician. She played the cello and my father had played with her in some orchestra for a few amateur shows, so that was how he had the big order. He often told us that the cello was a lovely instrument and one of the pieces he transposed for me to play on the flute was a cello piece, 'The Broken Melody' by Auguste van Biene. When we got to the house, a maid came out first, but then the woman herself came out and she was all dolled-up like one of the beauties you'd see in the cinema. She had a real lawdy-daw English accent, but she seemed very nice, not like a snob; she asked Da was I his son, and then she asked me would I like to come into the garden and play with her own son while my father was putting in the coal.

The garden was beautiful, lovely bushes and daffodils around the edges and a lawn in the middle that seemed as big as the whole road in our street. There was a young fellow about my own age, around ten, all on his own, kicking a football. His mother introduced us, his name was James, and although I felt terrible at first, kicking football with this English boy while poor Da was lifting half a ton of coal, sack by sack, into a big shed over at the side, after a while I got into action and we were having a great time. When the coal was all in, I thought that was the end; but then the maid came out with a tray and put it on a fancy iron table that had four chairs around it. She told us the lady and my father were going to have a cup of tea in the house, and we could have our lemonade and biscuits there in the garden. Da came over and asked me was I all right and I said why wouldn't I be?

That was the first English boy I ever spoke to, and the first Protestant too. And he was one of the nicest fellows I ever met, although at first I found it hard to follow what he was saying, and I suppose he had the same problem with my Limerick accent. We tucked into the lemonade and biscuits – fancy ones and chocolate ones that I wouldn't see even at Christmas – and after a while we were having a great chat, all about school and games and books. He liked the William books, but he said that even he couldn't understand some of the things William and his pals said. When he told me that he went to a big boarding school in England, and would be going back there next week, I told him about the school stories in the books in the library that were all about Smith Minor and the Lower Fourth and the bounders and cads who were no good at cricket and rugger. I asked him why the cads were all sent to a place called Coventry. He had a good laugh at that but then he explained to me that it was only an expression; the cads were not really sent anywhere, just nobody spoke to them or played with them or had anything at all to do with them. 'Ah, I see! That's just like our boycott,' I told him. And then, of course, I had to explain what that was, and I told him the story about Captain Boycott in County Mayo, which we had been told in school by Mr Liddy. We had another laugh when I asked him what was the game called truant that some fellows in the books used to play now and again, like 'Harris was very fond of playing truant . . . ' I told him that our word for dodging school was 'mooching' and he could hardly get his tongue around that!

He told me he never even saw a hurley or a crook, and he never played cat or serves. I thought at first that a rich boy like James must have a great time but the more I listened to him, the more I began to be puzzled. He was never in a fight and he never threw a stone at anybody in his life, while we were always fighting and 'flebbing' stones at one another or at any crowd from another quarter if we had a row with them. The worst thing was when I told him about fishing for thorny-backs in the big trench that ran all along behind the Island Bank, how we made a rod from a thin branch and a line from thread, and put a small worm on the thread (some fellows used a pin, but we didn't agree with that; a hook was all right for eels and fish, but the little thorny-backs could be caught just by letting them swallow the worm until it was in their throat and then pull) and how we used to watch them peeping out from the reeds – a cock with a red throat like a robin, a hen with a white throat – and put them in a jam-jar to bring home. He looked very sad about that, and he said he'd rather fish for thorny-backs on the Island Bank with us than play 'rugger' and 'paper-chase' in his fancy school.

Next he wanted to know why the Irish and the English were always fighting down through the centuries, and why the Welsh and the Scotch people were satisfied to be all the one with England but the Irish would not join in. I told him why but I had to go easy on calling the English any bad names. He was very interested in all that and he said none of the chaps in his school knew anything about Ireland or about our history; they thought we were savages, he said, like the Blacks in Africa and the Indians and the Chinese, and that we all had donkeys and pigs in our houses. When we had the lemonade and biscuits polished off, he brought me into a garden house and showed me all the stuff he had, a real rugby ball and the things for cricket, a lovely bicycle and things for playing croquet on the lawn. But in the shed he told me something that nearly ruined the whole excursion for me; he said that he hated the school he was in and he wished he didn't have to go back next week. He told me that the big boys in the school, fellows up to eighteen years or so, did nasty things with the young boys but he couldn't tell me what they did because they all had to give their word to tell nobody outside of the school. If it was found out that he had told somebody even in Ireland, he could be sent to Coventry himself.

I knew anyway that the nasty things were not just getting a kick in the behind or a clip in the ear or a belt in the gob like we gave one another. He was very sad that he had no brother or sister to play with and when I told him how many were in our family he said, 'Oh, golly, I wish I was living in your house!' I couldn't follow that thinking at all, because I was wishing I was living in his house! Then he made me promise to come out in the summer and play with him again. And when his mother called us he whispered to me, 'Ask your Dad if I can come with you on the cart, will you?' I said I would. Da looked as if he had enjoyed his cup of tea as much as we enjoyed the lemonade and biscuits. I said thanks very much to the lady and when we were getting on the car outside I told Da what James wanted, to go around the town with us on the coal-car. He said it was out of the question, couldn't even consider it, the mother would have a fit, and so on. I never played with that English boy again, because they all went back to live in England in the summer, which meant that while I lost my new friend, my father lost one of his best customers. But I knew from that day that all the English people were not like Cromwell and Queen Elizabeth and the Black-and-Tans, and I knew also that even if Protestants were different from us, whether a person was nice or not didn't depend on their religion but on how they behaved with other people.

17

'MUSIC HATH CHARMS . . .'

I remember everything connected with that day I spent going around Limerick with my father better than the day of my First Holy Communion. Maybe it's because, in a big family like ours, and with us all in the one room just like the stone-age people long ago in their cave – I only hope they were half as happy as we were – it was impossible for any one child in the family to have a long conversation with the father or mother, and on this lovely day in spring I had my Da all to myself. But also, I felt that my father was happier himself that day than on some days when he'd come home wet and weary in the winter or be worrying about people who hadn't paid him for the coal. I remember on one occasion, after we had moved to the new house in Thomond-gate, he was in bed with flu and he sent me to three houses with a note asking for payment for coal he had delivered: one house in Thomondgate itself, one in the Parish where we used to live and one in the Irishtown. Charity forbids me to name the people concerned but they were not poor. Charity does not forbid me to record that I came back with a score of one out of three.

Today my father had been paid on the nail for half-a-ton of coal. But he was happy for two other reasons, as he told me while we went around other streets delivering a bag of coal here and there. He was delighted when I told him about the great chat I had with the English boy, and how I knew more about English history out of our Knowledge Books than James did from his fancy college in England. But he talked to me too about music and he was glad that I had seen an example of what he was always telling us in the family, that music is the only thing that brings all classes of people together on an equal footing. Nobody asks you, he used to say, who you are or what you are, whether you're a Catholic or a Protestant or a Jew, where you live or where did you go to school; all they consider is this, can you play that instrument well, can you read music.

'Just like rugby, isn't it, Da?' I said, because we often heard him saying that in Limerick everybody was equal on the rugby field. The snobs from up the town or the Ennis Road were only the same as all our own lads from the Parish or any other quarter in the city.

'It's a bit like in rugby, but better again,' he said. 'As soon as the rugby match is over, the snobs go back to being snobs again and looking down on the working class; but if you're a good musician, every other musician respects you and treats you as an equal.'

In describing the idealistic scheme concocted by my sailor grandfather for the welfare of his family, I mentioned that the remaining two sons, being my father and his brother Daniel, were rendered unfit for successful participation in any commercial enterprise by having been infected with the virus, music. On the other hand, perhaps music was their salvation. Like most of their kind, the four O'Flynn boys felt that school was a prison from which they should escape as soon as circumstances permitted. Their father being a sailor who was away from home for long periods at a time, they had only their mother to convince that school was a waste of time, and she was probably glad to see them earning a few shillings. As their home in Watergate was in the area of the city markets, they were already earning a few pence on Saturdays by holding the horses while the farmers and their wives were selling their produce in the market. My father became so friendly with one farmer and his wife that as he grew older they asked himself and his brother Danny to come out and help on the farm somewhere in County Limerick. This had a sequel worth recording.

When the Free State troops attacked the Republican stronghold of Limerick during the civil war, many of the citizens left the city, finding refuge in Mungret College and other such nearby institutions. My parents, living almost within the shadow of King John's Castle, then held by the Republicans, took off with their two young children on my father's coal-car and went to stay with his country friends until the fighting had ended with the ill-armed Republicans being shelled out of the city. When relating this event in their lives, my mother, characteristically, gave it a twist in the tail by lamenting the fact that she was 'stuck out there with my two children, miles from anywhere and with nobody to talk to while your Da was out in the fields working with the farmer'. Meanwhile, back at the castle, empty now of British or Free State or Republican warriors, the local people were looting the well-stocked stores left by the British garrison when they pulled out before the civil war. 'No knowin' what was got out of it,' she said enviously. 'They got china and pots and God knows what else; one woman got bags of stuff for her hens and another woman got a lovely range.' While my poor patient father merely smiled and raised his eyes to heaven, we looked at our big iron range there beside us and wondered how that woman managed to carry a range out of the Castle Barracks to her own house.

It was the eldest son, Danny, who first became interested in music. There was a band of some kind in almost every parish in Ireland even at the time of Parnell, and apart from the political tragedy that he brought on the country because of Kitty O'Shea, he also did irreparable damage to the cause of music in Ireland because many a band was disrupted and many a fine instrument broken during the faction fights between the opposing sides. There is a photograph extant from the early years of the century showing a military band leading a parade across Mathew Bridge on the Abbey River (for non-natives I mention again that this is not really a river in its own right, but a loop of the Shannon which forms the Island). They are obviously returning from a Sunday church parade to St Mary's Cathedral, which can be seen in the background. This photograph is evidence of the fact that the British military bands brought music to every garrison town not only in Ireland but all over the British Empire; hence, among the debris of that empire to be found in former subject countries like India and Egypt, the native soldiers can be seen playing the brass instruments or the Scottish bagpipes their grandfathers learned to play in the British Army.

The bands in Limerick had the same provenance, being formed by ex-soldiers and their pupils in every parish. The army also had a summer militia, in which youths were given a few weeks' military training in camp. Our Uncle Danny and his pals in Watergate went off one summer to some such camp but fortunately what he saw there had the opposite effect to what the recruiting officers intended; otherwise he might have ended up like his younger brother, Tom, as yet another casualty among the millions of the First World War. But either in the summer camp or from some member of a local band, he learned to play the flute and became totally addicted. He had never been a good student at school – witness his 'playing truant' even in the Liverpool docks during their brief sojourn in that city – but now he began to study musical theory on his own, searching for books and music in the huckster shops. He was only about twenty years old when he was appointed conductor of the local band, the Sarsfield Fife and Drum Band, whose bandroom was located in the Irishtown, at the very spot where the forces of Dutch

King Billy were halted by the Irish troops under Sarsfield himself and pushed back towards the breach in the walls of Limerick on that historic day in October 1690. Soon young Danny O'Flynn was arranging music for the band and teaching men twice as old as himself to read music.

My father often confessed that he had no interest in music or bands until he was conscripted by his older brother who realised that the smallest instrument, the piccolo, can outplay, or outshrill, the rest of the instruments put together. Even more so in a flute band, where the single piccolo is capable of sounding like a blackbird or a lark above a harmonious cooing of doves and pigeons – which is why my father started all of us off on the piccolo. Apart from the flute being more cumbersome for small fingers, he maintained that once a pure tone was achieved on the piccolo, the flute would present no problems. We had some records of Sousa's marches for brass bands, one of them, 'The Stars and Stripes Forever', designed specifically to display those qualities of the piccolo.

And so the young conductor of the Sarsfield Band decided to entrust this instrument to his young brother, Richard, who was reluctant at first to join the band at all, but who later, Uncle Danny asserted – to our great satisfaction – became totally addicted to music and became one of the best piccolo players in Ireland! As proof of this, he instanced Dad's performance with the band of a famous virtuoso piece for the piccolo, 'The Deep Blue Sea'. And when the Sarsfield Band won first prize at the Tailteann Games in 1924, the adjudicator, Colonel Fritz Brase (the German musician imported by the Free State government to organise the military bands for the new Irish army) singled out the piccolo cadenza, which, he said, had been 'very neatly rendered'. We knew from the piccolo-player himself that the same Colonel Brase had been even more impressed with the young conductor of the Sarsfield Fife and Drum Band from Limerick. He urged Daniel O'Flynn to accept a commission in the Free State Army and the position of conductor of one of the new army bands, but the Limerickman loved his own band and his own city too well even to consider the offer. He continued with his motley group of dockers, tradesmen, coal-bellers, mill-workers, pork-butchers and factory-hands. Unfortunately, the musical benefit accruing to Limerick from his decision was countered by the continued deterioration in the livelihood to which their father's well-intentioned scheme had committed the conductor and the piccolo-player. Between their commitment to band competitions and other engagements such as regattas and carnivals, and my father's new sideline as a danceband saxophonist, they were both often unable to rise at dawn and tackle a horse to begin the daily grind of a coal-beller. They sometimes hired casual drivers with consequent financial loss and at other times lost customers who had given up hope of getting a delivery and took coal from some other man.

As children, we had divided loyalties, living as we did in the Island Parish where the great rivals of the Sarsfield Band, St Mary's Fife and Drum, had – and still have – a splendid bandroom which was also in use as a dancehall and for shows and concerts. To confuse us even more, in one of the apartments in the cottered old Bishop's Palace beside our house, there lived an old gentleman named Patrick Salmon, who happened to be the retired conductor of St Mary's Band. My father and our Uncle Danny spoke very highly of this man as an arranger and composer of music, and we were intrigued to learn that the meeting at which St Mary's Band was founded in 1885 was held in that same old Bishop's Palace. The rivalry between the Sarsfield and St Mary's was local and friendly; they celebrated mutually any victory over outside bands. In fact, both bands occasionally invited the conductor of the other band to act as guest conductor, and if any of the finer musicians in either band happened to be unavailable when a competition was imminent, a competent replacement was always available from the other band.

Anyone who has heard Bing Crosby singing that rollicking tune 'MacNamara's Band' will be interested to learn that the MacNamara of the title, together with some of his brothers, came from the Island Parish in Limerick; they had been members of St Mary's Band before emigrating to New York and carrying on their musical activities there. And when St Mary's new hall was built in the early 1920s, much of it by voluntary labour of the members and their friends, the New York MacNamaras and other exiles from the Island Parish contributed generously to the cost.

Although my father never realised his dream of having a danceband of his own, he did pass on his love of music to his family, helped, of course, by my mother's love of singing and her genuine appreciation of any musical effort in the house. And from the premier position of music in the cultural life of our family, there came one of my father's dicta for our guidance in life: 'Never pass by a street musician,' he'd say, 'because you never know – you might be there yourself some day!' To which piece of stoic philosophy my mother used to retort: 'God forbid! Wouldn't you at least have them playing in a band or an orchestra and not out on the street!' But she herself gave us the same counsel, although not with the same foreboding, about the poor people – they were never called beggars – who called to our door. No matter how low her household funds were, she would search and find a penny, or even a halfpenny, in her 'last resort' safe in the hollow statue of the Child of Prague on the mantelpiece. There was one visitor to our street who qualified under both headings, poor man and musician (of a kind!). He was a tall, thin, hungry-looking man, badly dressed and hatless, who used to stand in the roadway outside our door, cup one ear in his hand and begin to bawl out his ballads. If his performance took place late in the evening, he sometimes slept on the stairs in the hallway of the Bishop's Palace. My mother used to give him a cup of tea and a bit of bread, but my father was professionally interested in this poor man's style. He pointed out to us that the cupping of the ear was a practice of the street singers who, performing at fairs or other noisy venues, could hardly hear themselves above the din only for the cupped ear which acted as an echo-chamber. We used to try it out, and were delighted to find that it worked! I remembered that lesson when in the primary school we came across the poem about the blind fiddler, Raftery, in which he says:

> *Féach anois mé is m'aghaidh le balla,*
> *Ag seinm ceoil do phócaí folamha.*
> ('Look at me now with my face to the wall,
> Playing music for empty pockets.')

My father was delighted with the verse and he even went to the corner of our kitchen-living-room to demonstrate how the poor country fiddler would have made his own echo-chamber by actually turning into a corner of the country kitchen, with his back to the dancers. Many years later I wrote a play about Raftery in which I took the opportunity of letting audiences know that Brendan Behan's English version of those poignant words of the poor blind poet, a version much quoted by monolingual yahoos but with which I will not degrade these pages, is inaccurate, banal and vulgar.

That old photograph to which I referred earlier, of a military band crossing Mathew Bridge, shows adults walking along on both sides of the band, while a group of youngsters scurries along in front of the band. In our own day, it was the custom of the local bands to parade through the city on Sundays and on other special occasions. St Mary's Band always paraded to the parish church on the Feast of the Assumption, and gave a recital in the church grounds after Mass; for the annual retreat of the Men's Confraternity at the Redemptorist Church, the Confraternity being divided into three sections of the city, a band from the relevant area would parade to the church on the opening night and play hymns in the yard while the men were going in, repeating the performance and the parade after the devotions. We often almost choked on our Sunday dinner when we heard either St Mary's or the Sarsfield coming along Nicholas Street towards the castle. In spite of my mother's admonitions, we gulped down what was left and rushed out to join with the other kids in front of the band. We went out across Thomond Bridge. From the Treaty Stone we proceeded along Clancy Strand to Sarsfield Bridge where we turned back into the city, up William Street and back to the Irishtown with the Sarsfield or to Mary Street with St Mary's. By which time we would have been ready to eat another dinner; and such a long wait before the six o'clock Angelus bell signalled that Ma would be boiling the kettle for our tea! Even after my father and our Uncle Danny had retired from the Sarsfield Band, the band on its Sunday parade always halted at the corner of our street near the castle and played a tune there in honour of my father. He would come out to show his appreciation, while we galloped up to take our place at the head of the band.

And talking of marching with the band, there is a story in the folklore of our Island Parish about a night in 1932 – the year of the Eucharistic Congress, and also the year when De Valera and Fianna Fáil came to power – when St Mary's Band were marching up to support Dev at an election rally at the O'Connell Monument. They were marching along to the tap of the 'tipper' side-drum, and being joined as usual by adults and youngsters, when suddenly a few men pushed in and began to march along with the bandsmen – and no mistaking the tall, bespectacled man around whom the others were watchfully protective, none other than Dev, 'the Boy from Bruree' himself! The bandmaster immediately called on them to strike up. 'What march?' he was asked. 'Second to None!' he shouted. At which Dev turned round and cried out, with his Bruree grin, 'And that's what Fianna Fáil will be from now on, lads, second to none!'

The Sarsfield Band has long been defunct, but until

recently the façade of their small bandroom still stood in John Street in the Irishtown, with the dates and venues of their competition victories displayed in white stucco on a green background. This would have been worth preserving as part of Limerick's cultural history but it was considered by the city planners to be just another old wall to be reduced to rubble so that another office block or more ticky-tack urban apartments could rise up 'where Sarsfield drove the Saxon from the walls of Garryowen'. That storied old façade was the occasion of one of the most moving tributes ever paid to the contribution my Uncle Danny, my father, and their comrades in the Sarsfield Band, had made to cultural life in the city of Limerick. In 1963 St Mary's Band won the Senior Championship of Ireland in Wexford. On the following Sunday all the bands of the city joined with them in a victory parade from the bandroom in Mary Street through the city, and when the parade arrived in the Irishtown, the bands halted outside the fading façade of the Sarsfield Bandroom and St Mary's played a memorial tribute to their old rivals, the Sarsfield Fife and Drum Band.

As a child, I often sat in that bandroom with one or two of my brothers when the band were rehearsing but my fondest memory of the band is of a summer's evening when I was very small, probably about four years old, and the band was playing, not in the small bandroom, but seated on chairs outside, in the middle of John Street! And seated on chairs on the pavements were all the women from the neighbouring houses and from the side-streets, knitting or sewing while they enjoyed the operatic and other selections being rehearsed for the next band competition. People nowadays would be astonished to hear them rendering, from their repertoire for national competitions and local concerts, arrangements of airs from the operas of Verdi, Mozart, Donizetti, Rossini and others, as well as the popular trio of Irish operas, Balfe's *The Bohemian Girl* (1843), Wallace's *Maritana* (1845) and Benedict's *The Lily of Killarney* (1862).

Years later, I thought of that childhood scene on a summer's evening in John Street when I read that, prior to the erection of the O'Connell statue in 1857, the colonel of the regiment in the nearby New Barracks (now Sarsfield Barracks) used to put on summer evening recitals by the garrison band in the roadway at the Crescent, this for the delectation of the 'quality' in the big houses on both sides. (The Jesuits arrived there a decade after John Hogan's bronze O'Connell took possession of the site.) The ladies used to sit on their balconies sipping tea and enjoying the music – until Big Dan scuppered the recitals and caused the ladies to withdraw in horror behind closed shutters when his monument became the venue for election rallies. Doubtless those ladies would be surprised at the suggestion that the women of the Irishtown who used to bring out their chairs and their knitting to enjoy the recitals of the Sarsfield Band were just as musically cultured as themselves.

On a wall of the room in which I am writing these words there hangs a photograph of the Sarsfield Fife and Drum Band taken after their victory in the Tailteann Games of 1924, with their names and the dates of all their other victories inscribed. (Of course, other members would have come and gone over the years.) My father sits on the right of the front row, piccolo in hand; on the left of that row sits the conductor, my Uncle Danny. Together with their colleagues, they seem to be suggesting that the least I might do is to record their names in this chronicle. I do so now, on behalf of all the citizens of Limerick, in gratitude for their contribution to the cultural life of the city in their time. It should also be recorded that one man in the photo, M. Raleigh, made a further and unique contribution to the musical life of Limerick in the 1930s. 'Mikey' Raleigh was a veteran of the First World War, in which he lost a leg. He lived near us, down the Island Road, and when he retired from the Sarsfield Band he formed a boys' band, teaching the young lads in a shed behind his house. He and his band became a popular sight in the city for some years, as the lads marched along playing while poor Mr Raleigh limped along trying to keep up with them. Here then is the list of the members of the Sarsfield Band:

Back Row: J. Williams, P. Moloney, C. Nash (Drum Major), F. Heffernan, D. Neagle, M. Raleigh
Third Row: T. King, J. Field, C. Robinson, J. Scanlan, F. Moran, J. Keyes, J. Fitzgerald
Second Row: J. Twyford (Sec.), R. Smyth (Treas.), J. Cronin, P. O'Brien, T. O'Flaherty, P. McMahon, J. Johnson, J. McDonnell, P. Madden, P. Kelly, M. Doherty (Pres.)
Front Row: D. O'Flynn (Conductor), J. Collopy, P. Markham, T. Cross, J. Carey, P. Smyth, R. O'Flynn
Seated in front: Master J. Williams, Master J. Smyth

And now, as the old travelling-woman, Kitty the Hare, used to say to the readers of *Our Boys*, let ye all gather in to the fire in our old house near King John's Castle and listen to the story my Da is telling us:

That reminds me of the one about the great violinist, Fritz Kreisler. He was giving a concert one time in New York, and on the day of the concert he was trying to rest for a few hours in his hotel but while he was lying on the bed he was disturbed by what he thought was a cat screeching somewhere. After a while, he went to the window to throw something at the cat and he realised that it wasn't a cat at all but some fellow scraping on a violin on the street below outside the hotel. He went back to lie down again but he couldn't rest with the terrible sounds he was hearing. Anyway when he was going off to Carnegie Hall to give his performance, there was the poor old busker still at it. Kreisler took one look at him, then he rushed over and shouted, 'My dear man, you're not even holding the bow properly!' And he grabbed the bow and put the fellow's fingers on it. Well, off he went and gave the performance, a great success as usual. But when he came back to the hotel later on that night, there was the poor old busker scraping away still – but now he had a big placard on his chest saying: 'Pupil of Kreisler'.

18

'WHERE THE SHANNON RIVER MEETS THE SEA'

It does not meet the sea at Limerick, but farther west at Foynes, although the tidal effect is very evident up to the city. But we always include that lovely air in our repertoire of Limerick songs:

> Though my feet are planted in a far-off land
> There is somewhere they would rather be;
> Sure 'tis firmly planted in the dark brown sand
> Where the Shannon River meets the sea.

When my first ventures in the world outside our front door took me past the Bishop's Palace to the corner of the street, I would have seen Thomond Bridge at the bottom of the short sloping street beside King John's Castle. I would already have been brought in the pram down to the Island Bank, where the children and mothers from our streets spent much of their time in the summer. This bank was built to protect the Island Field from the river and it had a few small tunnels which allowed water into the deep trench at the Island Field side, a trench to which I have referred as our first fishing ground where we caught thorny-backs. The Island Bank began a short distance upriver from Thomond Bridge, and continued round by a section of the looping Abbey River to Athlunkard Bridge. The Corporation had established a primitive swimming baths – merely a fenced-off section of the river bank with dressing-rooms and two diving-boards – at the beginning of the Island Bank. Since admission to this privileged section cost one penny, it was never used by us natives of the Island but by the 'swanks' from up the town. 'A fool and his money are soon parted' (the Granny Connolly). Why should we lash out a whole week's pocket-money just to go in there and swim in the same river! We had our own swimming spots along the bank, three in number: firstly, a spot where small steps had been built into the bank to make access to the river easy; these we called the 'Fairy Steps' and it was here that mothers with babies sat on the grassy bank while their young children paddled in a little sandy area at the foot of the steps. Farther on along the bank there were two wider sandy coves, known respectively as 'Girls Sandy' and 'Boys Sandy', no explanation or comment necessary.

The social distinction promoted by the Corporation in the erection of that wire-mesh fence between the primitive baths and Mother Nature's two sandy coves was also apparent in the apparel worn by the respective swimmers; the swanks were always correctly rigged out in nice gear, while the poorer colleens at the Girls Sandy were often unashamedly attired in an old pair of bloomers; as for the boys, the flimsy swimming togs, often torn and repaired, that we wore were little better than the fig-leaves woven to cover the parts of Adam and Eve that had suddenly become dangerous when exposed. I recall that at one weekly meeting of the Boys' Confraternity in the Redemptorist Church, the Reverend Director, with some obvious embarrassment, cautioned us against swimming 'without a bathing costume' (in our pelt, we interpreted, as we discussed the decent man's advice on our way home) wherever there were girls in the vicinity. Fair enough, we judged. Anyway, at that stage in our manly development, we didn't want 'gerrels' hanging around when we played games or went for a swim.

Another item indicating social class was the inflatable rubber ring used by the swanks when learning to swim; again, Mother Nature provided for us, who we assumed were nearer and dearer to her, by causing bullrushes and reeds to grow profusely in the swampy trench of the Island Field and at some places along the river bank; the bigger boys and girls collected these and put an armful under the learner's chest – you felt as if you could float across the river! – and as the natural ability developed, fewer rushes were used.

Apart from swimming, we could use the river sand to make castles just as well as the children of the better-off were doing at the seaside in Kilkee or Lahinch. Our own visits to the seaside were confined to the rare one-day cheap excursions advertised by the Great Southern Railway as 'Sea-Breeze Excursion to Kilkee and Lahinch' or 'to Cork and Youghal', and even these became prohibitive as the number of children in a family increased. Which is why there was great excitement in the Parish as well as in other parts when the St Vincent de Paul Society organised an excursion to Youghal for the poor children of the city one Sunday in the early 1930s. I went on that outing with my three older brothers but all I remember of our day at the seaside is that some man spilt boiling hot tea on my leg as we sat in lines on the strand waiting for our grub, and he got me a big cream bun to stuff my gob and stop my screeching and to compensate for the blisters I could see rising like lumps of white jelly. Later, when the good V de P volunteers decided to give the mob of kids an orange each, they found they hadn't half enough to go round, and no one on hand to oblige with a miraculous share-out as Our Lord did with the couple of loaves and a few fish. The V de P men invented a new beach game: throw an orange up in the air and let the poor kids have a bit of fun tussling for it. With my brother Dick as my protector, I as the toddler sat well back from this loose maul in the sand, while our two older brothers, Tom and Joe, displayed their natural rugby skills by diving in valiantly time after time until the four deserving noble descendants of King Flann Sinna had an orange each.

The Island Bank also had a few small trees along its curving length and from these we took saplings to make bows and arrows. However, this unwitting sin against our Mother Nature had to be committed surreptitiously; not only did our own mothers disapprove but there was an official caretaker of the baths and the Island Bank appointed by the Corporation – the sinecure office had been given, at a salary of one pound per week (good money then) to the aged and almost blind Michael Hogan, the Bard of Thomond, some years before his death in 1899 – and he could 'bring the law on you' for any such vandalism. But what were we poor Indians to do, seeing that there was no other source for our bows and arrows? Like Geronimo and Sitting Bull and all the other great warriors we saw in the pictures, who rightly resented being told by the white man that they could not move or hunt freely in their ancestral lands, we considered that we had more right to the Island Bank and to everything on or near it, including the trench at one side and the river at the other, than any crowd of councillors sitting above in the Town Hall making rules and regulations to leave our young lives 'cabin'd, cribb'd, confined'.

As we grew older, the river offered fishing and boating as free and perpetual pleasures – for those who did not have to join their fathers and uncles in either of the two ancient working groups known in our parish as the 'Sandmen' and the 'Abbey fishermen'. The former dredged sand from far up the river and brought it to a section of the Abbey River near Baal's Bridge where it could be more easily unloaded; hence this quayside became known as the Sandmall. There it was bought by building contractors, who prized it above the sand from the pits up in the Clare hills and elsewhere. The Abbey fishermen were so called because most of the families who had been traditionally engaged in that occupation lived in that area of the Island Parish, adjacent to the Sandmall, known as 'the Abbey' from the ruins of the old Franciscan Abbey. These were the families whose livelihood vanished when the Shannon Hydroelectric Station opened in 1929. The building of this scheme involved the construction of a canal a few miles upriver from Limerick which diverted most of the water from the river's natural course. When the fishermen decided to follow the salmon into the lower section of the canal, where the water exited from the turbines, they were barred by the new state body, the Electricity Supply Board (ESB) established two years earlier. The subsequent 'Battle of the Tail Race' took its place along with tales of Sarsfield and Seán na Scuab and all the rest of them in the folklore of Limerick. The fishermen lost out in the end, with token compensation, and the tradition of the fishing families came to an end.

Although one might imagine that their working association with the river might make them wish to stay as far away as possible from it during their meagre leisure hours, both the Sandmen and the Abbey fishermen were among the foremost members of our local rowing club, Athlunkard, situated idyllically on the Abbey River. With the compulsory daily training imposed on them by their respective occupations, they were formidable opponents of the up-town amateur rowers of the other clubs, Limerick, Shannon, and St Michael's. It was said in our Parish that you could stand at the top of Athlunkard Street and give a good shout, and from the members of only a few families coming out of the houses in that street you could form a senior rowing eight, and a senior fifteen for rugby, who could take on any competition in Ireland. Add to those heroes the men from the Abbey and the Sandmall, and it is obvious why our Parish was so prominent in both sports. There was another Parish rowing club, the Curragower, of which my mother's brother, our Uncle Maurice, was a member, but they were unfortunate in having their clubhouse situated beside the Curragower Falls which gave them their name. I have indicated elsewhere that this is a grandiose name for a series of rapids caused at low tide in the river by a shelf of rock just downriver from King John's Castle. Picturesque as it seems, it is also dangerously tempting to young daredevils, as we found out when we essayed crossing the river there on a few occasions and had to retreat at a point where the swirling water would have washed us away.

It was always a big occasion when the annual Abbey River Regatta gave the men and youths of the Island Parish the chance to display their boating skills in their own boats of several types. There were also competitions like 'catching the duck' and 'the greasy pole' – in which we and our first cousins, the Brommels from Crosby Row, once cheered mightily in support of our Uncle Maurice Connolly as he made a brave effort out along the pole only to slip and fall into the river when almost within reach of the little flag at the end.

We always halted in our play or our swimming at the Island Bank when we saw a gig (as we called the rowing-boat) coming along the Shannon on a full tide. And just as our street rugby games mimicked the 'Tackle him low!' call, we cried, 'Pull – Shannon! Pull – Shannon!' as we formed our own 'crew' on the grassy bank with our arms linked around the waist of the one in front of us. And lest it be thought high treason or apostasy on the part of Parish children to call *Shannon* rather than their own *Athlunkard* in their imaginary rowing, that was the name that fitted our rhythm best; it was also, of course, the name of our rugby team, so it came 'trippingly on the tongue' to us. If there is any sight in all sport more beautiful and poetic than seeing a well-coxed and skilled senior eight moving along the Shannon on a full tide in the sunshine of a summer's day, it must be some game the angels play in heaven.

The movement of the swans on our river was, of course, something else altogether, a poem in motion that even the best Athlunkard crew could not match. When we could spare a bit of bread from our own supply – on summer days, our mothers often brought our dinner down to the Island Bank, a can of milk and another can of new potatoes, and plenty of bread and butter – we fed the swans, calling out to them, 'Here, Billy-Billy-Billy!' Even before we went to school, we knew the story of the Children of Lir, and even the wildest among us, or the most skilful wielders of our homemade fork-slings, would never throw or sling a stone at a swan. A few years ago, I stood nostalgically at Thomond Bridge and counted sixty-four swans on the river – that beat the 'nine-and-fifty' the poet Yeats counted 'upon the brimming water among the stones' at Lady Gregory's Coole Park in County Galway.

Besides being a source of relaxation and of livelihood, a river also has its dangers. In ancient times, every river had its own resident god, and drownings were regarded as a human sacrifice demanded by that deity as a tribute from the people who used the river for their benefit. Hardly a year passed by but the god of the Shannon exacted that ritual tribute, and stories of drownings in the past were added to with new tragedies year by year. There were also, of course, incidents of heroism, ending sometimes happily with rescue, sometimes with the loss of two lives. The stepped slips constructed at various points along the river wall for the convenience of the fishermen were the river-god's temptation to children. The steps below the castle at Thomond Bridge were to become the scene of a cataclysmic event in my own life, as will be seen in due course.

We were swimming at the Boys Sandy one summer's day when a young fellow of about fifteen decided to try to swim across the river, a thing against which we were sternly cautioned by our elders; he disappeared in the middle of the river as suddenly as if some river-monster had gulped him down. Some of the Abbey fishermen came very soon after and they found the body quickly. That was the first drowned person we saw but not the last. Before I graduated from the children's paddling cove at the Fairy Steps to the Boys Sandy, I saw a daring rescue carried out by the mothers who had been sitting on the bank above us, knitting and chatting. They were roused by the cries of the children below at the river – a small girl had paddled out too far and was floating away as gently as poor Ophelia on the slow tide. The women rushed and slid down the bank, formed a human chain, and the woman farthest out, up to her neck in water – I can still see her – grabbed the child, who, as the women said, 'hadn't a brack on her', only that her clothes were a bit damp, just like their own!

A grimmer aspect of the river-god is the seductive whispering of his waters as they entice the troubled soul to commit the ultimate act of despair. It must seem an easy solution to a mind overburdened with torturing worry, that gentle slide into the dark waters and the few moments of whatever agony has to be endured before the body becomes that limp and lifeless thing that horrified us as children on the bank of the river near our sunlit Sandy. In those times when sleeping or sedative pills were unknown – pills and powders for headache or constipation were about all that common folk had available to them – the gas-oven and the river or lake were the most common means of suicide, and in our own city as elsewhere there were occasional tragedies in one or the other form.

In order to save the family from the social and religious shame associated with suicide, an Irish coroner and inquest jury in the early half of this century usually brought in a standard verdict on what was obviously a case of suicide by drowning: 'The cause of death was drowning, but there was no evidence to show how the deceased came to be in the water.' And so, until the 1960s brought the beginning of a more honest and open society, even some of the bishops of Ireland piously proclaimed that we had the lowest suicide rate in Europe.

From going to the docks with my father, as well as from our own wanderings in that riverside region, we got to know many of the local ships as well as ones that were regular callers with coal, timber or grain. I used sometimes to accompany a pal of mine whose mother would send him to the docks with a box-car to buy a hundredweight of coal in one of the big coal-yards (it must have been cheaper that way than to buy from a coal-beller) and we took one handle each in pushing the load home. We always dawdled on the docks, watching the men slaving at loading or unloading the cargoes and wondering what it would be like to go to sea. One ship that was often mentioned in our family, I'm not sure why, was a local vessel called the *Lanahrone*, after a popular swimming and picnic spot on the river in Corbally (the name is a corruption of the Irish, *Oileán na Rón* – Seal Island). As we lay some nights, telling our stories or (softly!) singing our songs, whenever we heard a ship's siren from the river we said, 'That's the *Lanahrone* going out!' And in imagination we went with her down the dark Shannon under the stars, heading for 'those faraway places with strange-sounding names'. In reality, if it was the little *Lanahrone*, we knew she never went to any place more exotic than Liverpool or some such British port to pick up another cargo of those black stones that were the daily burden of our father's breadwinning. When the Second World War broke out in 1939, the small Limerick ships, in spite of having the Irish tricolour prominently painted on the deck and hull, were attacked by German submarines and planes, and several Limerickmen, including a neighbour of ours in the new houses in Thomondgate, were among the casualties when the *Irish Pine* was bombed and sunk off the south coast.

19

WONDROUS WORDS

In the comedy, *Le Bourgeois Gentilhomme*, by Molière (1622–73), the 'beggar on horseback', Monsieur Jourdain, hires various professionals to give him a crash course in the social graces and the arts, including literature. When he learns from his professor of philosophy that there are two kinds of speech, prose and poetry, and that the usual kind we use is called prose, he exclaims in astonishment: 'Good heavens! For more than forty years I have been speaking in prose without realising it!' In thinking back to our Limerick dialect of Hiberno-English, in which single Irish words still lingered along with many expressions which were a direct translation from the language our ancestors had spoken for thousands of years, I sometimes feel that we were doing the opposite for much of the time, speaking in poetry, or at least in poetic prose.

My mother was never *very tired* – she was *wallfallen* (that looks more like Anglo-Saxon than modern English). Her forebodings were expressed as, 'That's the rock he'll perish on' or 'That's where he'll meet his Waterloo.' And when the straw broke the camel's back, as others say, we heard, 'That put the kibosh on it!' That single word, 'kibosh' (stress on the last syllable, kye-*bosh*) is a history lesson in itself, as we learned later in school; it comes from the Irish, *caidhp bháis* (death cap), the name given to the impromptu scalping-tool used by the redcoats after the rebellion of 1798 when they lined a leather helmet with boiling pitch and clapped it on the heads of their Irish prisoners, known as Croppies (as in the ballad, 'The Croppy Boy') because of their close-cut hair-style. When the pitch cooled, the cap was wrenched off, taking the prisoner's scalp, and often his life, with it.

When we boasted that we had got 'millions of black-berries' up in the Clare Hills we did not know that we were using hyperbole; another example of which, again unwit-tingly, we enjoyed when we told the story about the little boy who said to an old priest in Confession, 'Father, I have an awful sin to tell – I *murdered* me sister.'

'What?'

'I *murdered* me sister.'

The old priest peered through the grill and saw the nipper who was confessing to sororicide. 'How many times, my child?' he says gently.

'Lots of times, Father – but I had to, because she pulls my hair and she wouldn't let go if I didn't *murder* her.'

When my mother said of an ambitious woman, 'She's putting her arms around the world now,' or described a child thus: 'Shur he's only a fistful!' we were not aware that we were hearing poetic prose. If she warned one who was inclined to step out of line, 'You'll have to draw in your horns now and put your shoulder to the wheel,' we took the message and were not aware that a carping pedant might sniff about mixed metaphors. The pedant might at least be impressed by the literary connotations of our folk way of saying that someone was guilty of what the Catechism called 'backbiting, calumny and detraction', which in my mother's speech became: 'Oh, she read and spelt him, she left nothing unsaid about him!' And she had a sardonic blessing for anyone who might show signs of being niggardly: 'Wisha, God spare you your spit!'

Supposing a professor of literature overheard the following

exchange between two men in our local Halpin's pub: 'Did he swally it?' 'Hook, line and sinker,' he would condescendingly interpret it as a conversation in plain prose in which two uneducated labourers were talking about a fine fish caught by one of them, whereas any child in our parish could have told the deprived academic that the men were talking about a mutual acquaintance who was extremely gullible.

Taking even a single word like *feather*, we would hear it used in various contexts, but always with that alchemical transformation which makes poetry out of prose. Praising one of us if we won something at school, my mother would say (among other things!), 'Well, God bless you, *a stór*, that's a feather in your cap!' Referring to the victim of a contretemps of one kind or another, she'd add, 'It didn't knock a feather out of him.' And the antics of politicians in general were summed up thus: 'All they're doing is feathering their own nest.' Of an astute child or adult it was said, 'There's no flies on that fella!' but when someone said, 'That child would hang you!' it meant that in his innocence he was inclined to blurt out in company things his parents had said in private.

Many of the words and expressions we heard from Granny Connolly and my mother came directly from Irish, as when one of them would say, 'Will you rise out of me!' (*Éirigh asam!* – 'Don't be bothering me') or 'Don't be drawin' the *tóir* of that crowd on us!' (I wonder how many members of the Conservative Party in Britain know that this Irish word, *tóir*, meaning 'pursuit', is the origin of their alternative title, Tory?) Some Irish words, like 'colleen', 'boreen', 'smithereens', 'banshee' (from *bean sí* – 'fairy woman') have found a place in the English dictionary. The most recent edition of *Chambers* admits that 'bother' comes from the Irish *bodhar* ('deaf'). There were many more such in our dialect that are probably unheard in Limerick today: words like *smathán* for a hearty kiss, 'drass' (*dreas*) for a turn at something (on the street we might say, 'Give us a drass, will you?' using the plural for the singular, a common transference), 'smathered' ('The poor fella was smathered in blood and mud!') and 'crawshawlin' (*cnáimhseáil* – 'complaining'). The expression 'making a feck' for humorously mocking persons or things – the person doing so was a 'feckmaker' – came from the Irish noun *feic*, meaning a sight or spectacle. Pejorative words, of course, are likely to survive longer than laudatory ones; we heard people described as 'bostoon', 'sloonawnee', 'loo-dramawn', and my Granny's strange word for a tall, thin person, a 'skooraloo' (Irish, *scodalach*). But we also heard a nice, homely person described as 'an oul' *grá-mo-chroí*' and a man who was tipsy was '*maith go leor*'.

This latter Irish euphemism was matched by many terms in English: a drunkard was *foolish*, a girl who gave birth to a baby while unmarried was *unfortunate*, and someone described as being 'a bit touched' would be labelled today as mentally unstable. When this affliction was more pronounced, the person was 'noora-strayna', a term which is obviously a folk corruption of the medical *neurasthenia*, but which has been compounded with another euphemistic expression referring to hereditary mental instability, when the Granny or my mother might describe a certain family thus: 'Ah 'sha, God help them, there's a strain in them for generations.' Another medical derivative was *a tisick*, used of a sickly child (Shakespeare uses it to mean a cough; the medical noun and adjective, 'phthisis' and 'phthisic', mean tuberculosis or similar wasting conditions). We liked the Granny's curt dismissal of a bumptious but unintelligent person: 'That fella is only a thick-a!' which implied that whatever little brains he had were in his backside. But I remember being very puzzled when I overheard from a fireside session of our domestic Cumann na mBan (our Aunt Dolly had come visiting with Granny from Crosby Row) a reference to some girl who had worked with my mother in Cleeve's caramel factory on Charlotte's Quay. 'Ah, poor

Josey!' my mother said, 'she was a great soldier-hunter.'

'She was,' said my Aunt Dolly, 'and the poor girl died an awful death after, over in the City Home.' I thought this to mean that the said Josie was some heroine – like Betsy Grey of Ballinahinch in 1798 or the women of Limerick in 1690 – who had fought the Black-and-Tans and the English Tommies in 1920 but had been so badly wounded that she died in agony in the City Home and Hospital (which was also the old poorhouse and a home for 'foundlings' as abandoned babies were still called). When I asked my mother another day to tell me more about the girl who fought the soldiers, she had to be reminded of the fireside chat, and then she said, 'Ah no, *a stór*, it wasn't fightin' the English soldiers she was, but the opposite.' Which left me even more puzzled than ever; but I knew that further questions were liable to be met with one of her rhymes: 'Ask me no questions and I'll tell you no lies, for inquisitive people are never made wise.'

A very strange word, *consplawkus*, was the favourite encomiastic expression of the Granny Connolly. When she was told that any of us had won a prize in school or elsewhere, she would praise us with that exclamation: 'Consplawkus to you, me boy, you're a chip off the ould block!' It was obviously a word of praise but neither we nor the good woman herself knew that it was Irish. I was to learn from my teacher in the primary school, Mr Liddy, that what the Granny Connolly was saying was *gan spleáchas* (literally 'without dependence'). When she heard any of us chanting our Irish lessons or reciting a poem in Irish she became even more enthusiastic – too much so, we thought, because, in that small room, we were often easily within range of her vigorous fist, which shot out and thumped you as she cried, 'Well, glory be to God, isn't it lovely to hear the bit of Irish!' And then, the tone becoming more severe, 'Learn yere Irish! 'Tis our own anyway! *Sinn Féin amháin!*'

A word in common use on the street and in the school

yard was our term for a bully, a species of which there are always some specimens in every street and school. We called the type a 'boolum', but not until we learned the original Irish term, *buaileam sciath*, did we know that our word was linking us with the ancient sagas of our Irish race, with those braggart champion warriors who came out in front of their army to *beat the shield* with the sword as a challenge to single combat for any warrior in the opposing force, and with that bloody ford in *Táin Bó Cuailgne* where Ferdia was forced by Queen Maeve to fight his old boyhood friend, Cú Chulainn.

The fact that I was a natural *ciotóg* (left-handed) but forced, according to the pedagogic doctrine at the time, to write with the right hand, caused my mother sometimes to remark, 'Look at him with his lefty cly.' If this was from the Irish word *clé*, which means 'left', it was an example of bilingual tautology. A bad violinist was called a *scrawby-looby*, someone who got a bad beating in a fight was *mollafoostered*, and the word *mashiated*, a forceful compound of mash and emaciated, could be applied to a person, an item, or food that was not in good condition. Since disputes were so often settled on the spot with the fists, we had many colourful expressions connected with fighting, so that a description of such a bout might include some of the following: a belt in the gob, a dig in the eye, a clitter in the ear, a box in the jaw (cf. boxer, boxing), a puck in the kisser. Threats might offer to put your eye in a sling, to give you a cauliflower ear, to put you into the middle of next week, and the common kick in the arse was even more rudely expressed as a fong in the hole. Money seems to give rise to slang terms everywhere; we had the common 'bob' and 'quid' for a shilling and a pound respectively, but also a 'make' (halfpenny), a 'wing' or a 'clod' (a penny) and a 'tanner' (sixpenny bit). The threepenny bit and the florin (two shilling piece) had no slang names, and the half-crown had been Americanised as a 'half-dollar'. The decimalisation of our currency has meant the loss of some of the coins themselves, while relieving children of the task of learning the twelve times multiplication table in order to tackle those complicated financial problems in arithmetic.

Two strange expressions deserve a note to themselves. The first, 'Oh, doll-dye-di', was an alliterative but slightly sarcastic comment on some action or on the integrity of someone's intentions. I have no idea of its provenance or etymology. The second was plain prose and was used to express doubt, but it is peculiar to Limerick, and its provenance is well known. From a book among the many on my 'Limerick' shelf, *Portrait of Limerick* (Robert Hale, London, 1982) by the historian and folklorist, Dr Mainchín Seoighe, a book that is a comprehensive and informative guide to both city and county, I quote:

A mile south of Ballyneety an impressive stone entrance on the right gives access to the ruins of Ballinagarde House, formerly the residence of the Croker family. The house was built in 1774. The saying, 'I doubt it, says Croker', has long been proverbial in County Limerick. Once, when the foxhounds met at Ballinagarde, old John Croker, who was seriously ill, was found seated in the hall, hunting-horn in hand. He wanted to see and hear the hounds and asked to be brought to the window. Having looked through the window for some minutes, he sighed. 'O sweet Ballinagarde, must I leave you?' said he. His son, Robert, a clergyman, heard him and said: 'You are going to a better place, father.'

'I doubt it,' said Croker.

And from an old ballad about Croker, Dr Seoighe gives us the incident as versified by the balladmaker:

He tried to persuade him to make him resigned
On heavenly mansions to fasten his mind:

'There's a land that is fairer than this you'll
        regard' –
'I doubt it,' says Croker of Ballinagarde.

Before leaving what has been of necessity only a cursory study of vocabulary and expression in the Island Parish of my childhood, I wonder if the reader has noticed that my mother's term of endearment was invariably the Irish one, *a stór*? (the word literally means 'treasure'). This was the only one we ever heard her use – she had none in English – and she used it not only for her own and any other children but even for adults; so that the rent-man, the gas-man, the Indian peddler who called with his big case full of silk scarves and other exotic items, even a garda síochána if he ever called, the tinker and the street-singer and any poor man or woman (never beggar, as I have noted already) would all and sundry be addressed with that affectionate term, *a stór*. And on the sad day a few years ago when we carried her coffin from St Munchin's Church out to the waiting hearse and we were waiting for the funeral to move off, among the people who came up and shook my hand in sympathy there was one man who said, 'When we'd be standing over there at the corner of the bridge, we loved to see her coming, because what she always said to us was, "God save ye!", never anything else, and we'd answer her, "God save you kindly, Mrs Flynn," and d'you know what, we always felt the better of it!' Back in the long-term exile of the Pale, I remembered that and also that my mother wished the same to 'every dog and divil that came the road' as she would say. I remembered too that when any of us left the house, whether to go to school, to work, to Mass, to a match, or to some faraway town or country itself, she never, ever said 'Goodbye.' Always, as she shook the holy water on us from the little doorside font, her farewell was the standard blessing: 'God speed you!'

20

RATLESS RHYMES

Several English writers in Elizabethan times, including Ben Jonson, Shakespeare and Sir Philip Sidney, advert to the strange fact that in Ireland rhymes were used to kill rats! In his *Defence of Poesie* (1580) Sidney says: 'I will not wish for you to be rhymed to death, as is said to be done in Ireland.' Any rats venturing up from the river to our streets would be quickly taken care of by the many excellent ratters among our dogs. I learned the real meaning of the phrase, 'he fought like a cornered rat' one day as we came home from the Island Bank and saw a rat in just such a corner of the river wall, unable to escape from our mongrel terrier, Spot. I never saw a rat even in the backyard of our old house but in winter the mice could be heard behind the skirting board, in which they gnawed holes in order to forage on our kitchen floor and around the range at night. Any child who has never observed, as we did so often, the household cat watching at such a mousehole, eventually catching, and then tormenting the mouse by flicking it in the air, letting it run, pouncing on it again, before finally killing it, is deprived of that early lesson. So, although we did not need to rhyme the rats to death, we appreciated the lesson in the rhyme we heard my mother singing at our own fireside, a rhyme that also taught us to beware of what Granny called *plámás* ('flattery').

Two little mice sat down to spin,
Pussy passed by and she peeped in:
'What are you doing, my two little men?'
'We're making coats for gentlemen.'
'May I come in and bite off the thread?'
'Oh no, Miss Pussy, you'd bite off our head.'
Says Pussy: 'You look so wonderful wise,
I like your whiskers and nice black eyes.
Your house is the nicest house I've seen
I think there is room for you and me.'
The mice were so pleased that they opened the
      door,
And Pussy soon laid them all –
Dead – on – the – floor!

Like my mother's songs, which ranged from hymns through operatic airs, Moore's Melodies, traditional ballads and Victorian tear-jerkers – over the Monday morning tub of washing she could render a miscellaneous selection with items like 'Sweet Heart of Jesus', 'In Happy Moments', 'I'll be your Sweetheart', 'The Fairy Boy', 'Hail Queen of Heaven', 'When Other Lips', 'Mrs McGrath', and many more – I must have heard this tragic tale of the mice and many other such rhymes even while I was in my mother's womb.

A rhyme we hated to hear was one my mother remembered from her own schooldays. It was in the form of a dramatic dialogue between the child reluctant to go to school and the wise mother who can see through all excuses:

Mother, I am tired today, and at home pray let me
      stay;
The air is warm and close and thick, and really I
      feel almost sick.

The mother's firm reply has been buried forever in my subconscious, but we often heard its content in our own mother's forthright reaction to any of our attempts 'to play the old soldier' as she called it. Even though we had no television or radio, we were often reluctant to leave our games or reading at bedtime. Then we heard, 'Early to bed, early to rise, makes a man healthy, wealthy and wise.' And we laughed when we heard father and mother swapping their versions of 'Patience is a virtue, have it if you can, never in a woman, always in a man.' (I forget the other version!)

Many rhymes were connected with food. Whenever my mother brought home a bag of fresh doughnuts with her shopping, invariably we would have the song-story of the little boy who went in to buy a doughnut with a damaged penny:

Oh she looked at the penny and she looked at me
And she said, 'Young man, shur you can't fool me!'
There's a hole in the penny, and it's gone right
            through.'
And sez I, 'There's a hole in the doughnut too!'

And when fish was frying, we would hear: '"Oh God bless us and save us!" sez ould Missus Davis, "I never knew herrin's was fish!"' The making of pancakes gave rise to the sad tale of poor Jack, which we sang while the first splash of creamy batter was going on the pan:

Last Monday, next Sunday
When Jack went away,
His mother made pancakes
Though she didn't know the way.
She twisted them, she turned them,
She made them so black,
She put too much pepper in 'em
And she poisoned poor Jack!

The standard nursery rhymes of English folklore were common in our anglicised Ireland too, but we had a sufficient stock of local and topical rhymes to balance their cultural effect. Before I went to school, I had picked up at our own fireside an anthology of nonsense rhymes and sayings like this (I indicate the Limerick pronunciation): 'Me uncle hit me ankle and gev me heel a sore toe.' A more elaborate example of the genre was: 'Ere last night about three weeks ago an empty car full of bricks went over a dead cat and nearly killed him; the cat is now in hospital sitting at the corner of a round table breaking stones with a glass hammer.' And if you have enough of your childhood innocence left to enjoy that, you'll probably have heard this one:

> I went to the pictures tomorrow,
> I got a front seat at the back,
> I fell from the floor to the balcony,
> And I broke the front bone in me back!

The jokes page in *Our Boys* was also the source for some of our rhymes; from it we culled parodies like this one on Longfellow's plangent 'A Psalm of Life':

> Tell me not in mournful numbers that I have an
>   unthatched roof,
> 'Tis the hairy head that lacks sense: baldness is of
>   thought a proof.

And it may have been from the same source that we got this alliterative tongue-twister:

> 'Let us flee!' said the fly.
> 'Let us fly!' said the flea.
> So they flew to the flaw in the flue.

One of my mother's caustic comments – this one if we had been helping her to search for something she had mislaid, only for herself to find it – 'You wouldn't see a hole in a ladder!' was linked in my mind with one of our nonsense rhymes:

'I see,' said the blind man,
'A hole in the wall.'
'You're a liar,' said the dummy,
'You can't see at all.'

The influence of the cinema on society was shown in one of the rhymes the girls chanted while hopping a ball in one of their pavement games:

Charlie Chaplin went to France
To teach the ladies how to dance.
Heel and toe, over they go,
This is the way he taught them so.

Another song-rhyme indicates that even in our Island Parish we were aware of the personalities and events in world politics:

Please get off the grass, and let the ladies pass,
Here comes Gandhi riding on his ass;
Never mind the weather, never mind the rain,
So long as we're together – up she goes again!

There was a separate repertoire of rhymes and songs using the airs of the well known marches and jigs and reels we were hearing so regularly from all the bands in the city. One example must suffice; it is one my mother often sang as she dandled the baby on her knee:

Oh, good morning, Kate! Good morning, Nell!
And where are you going? says Nellie.
I'm goin' down the town for a piece of mate
An' I'll buy it from Mary Kelly.

Of all the mate that's in the pig
The centre is me fancy
Dee-dyedle-um, deedle-um . . .

A rhyme that was probably known all over Limerick was inspired by the clock on Cannock's department store, the chimes of which could be heard at a great distance in those traffic-free days. Perhaps because of the river, we could hear it as we lay in bed on summer nights telling our stories. Whenever we heard it striking the hour, no matter whether in bed, on the street or down by the river at the Island Bank, we immediately began to chant along with its chimes:

Here is a man, what do he want?
He wants ca-li-co; how many yards?
One, two, three . . .

Like the Irish poets of former centuries whose successor he considered himself to be, the impecunious Bard of Thomond, or the Poet Hogan as our Granny always called him, was in the habit of tossing off the occasional or topical quatrain, most of them satirical. Some of these, along with his masterpiece, 'Drunken Thady and the Bishop's Lady', formed part of the poetry we heard at the fireside before we ever went to school. The one we enjoyed most concerned the statue on Sarsfield Bridge, a statue we had never seen. The statue in question was that of Viscount Fitzgibbon, who was killed in the famous but foolish charge of the Light Brigade at Balaclava (1854) during the Crimean War. He was the son of the notorious John Fitzgibbon, the first Lord Clare, one of the chief opponents of Catholic Emancipation – he declared that giving Catholics in Ireland the same voting rights as Protestants was 'folly and madness' – and one of the principal architects of the Act of Union in 1800 which meant the end of the Irish Parliament in Dublin.

After the death of Daniel O'Connell in 1847 the

Corporation of Limerick decided to erect a monument in his memory, and they allocated the site at the Crescent for the purpose; but while they were collecting funds, the mayor and his cronies in the aristocracy declared that they were going to put up a statue there in memory of the Crimean hero. The Corporation, supported by the irate citizens, refused to hand over the site at the Crescent, and the Fitzgibbon statue was erected on Wellesley (now Sarsfield) Bridge, leading from the Ennis Road into the heart of Limerick's business centre. It stood there, flanked by two Crimean cannon, in spite of several efforts by persons unknown to dislodge it into the Shannon, until one dark night in 1929 when the fairies came in from Ballynanty and shook fairy powder around the hero's wellington boots, with the result that the statue was blown away into the dark waters below and never seen again. And it is related in Irish legend that it was another tribe of those ancient Celtic fairies that came into Dublin from the Wicklow Hills one night in 1966 and celebrated the Golden Jubilee of the Easter Week Rising by blasting Nelson off his tall column outside the GPO in Dublin, a task that had been found legally impossible by all Irish governments and all Dublin Corporations since 1922.

When the great day for the unveiling of the statue of Viscount Fitzgibbon was drawing near, the Mayor of Limerick happened to meet with the strolling Bard of Thomond and asked him to prepare, for a suitable fee, some lines of verse appropriate for inclusion in his speech. To his surprise, the Bard told him that he had suitable lines composed already, and he recited them *con brio* for his worship, as follows:

> Here he stands in the open air
> The bastard son of the great Lord Clare;
> They call him Fitzgibbon, but his name is Moore,
> For his father was a cuckold and his mother was a
>   hoor.

It was obvious to us children that the grown-ups got a great kick out of that particular effort by the Bard, but of course the real point was lost on us until life and the street provided us with a glossary; we knew the word *hoor* as a descriptive term applicable in varying contexts, but a man having a *cuckoo* (as we thought) for a father was something we had never heard of before, and – 'ask no questions, etc.'

A 1916 memorial stands on Sarsfield Bridge where the Crimean hero in bronze lost his footing and fell into the Shannon, but many people in Limerick are not aware that the fine granite base on which he stood was acquired in 1954, the Marian Year, by a committee set up in our Island Parish – a committee that included several of my old schoolmates in the Parish, and also the man who, according to my mother, did more for the Church in St Mary's Parish than any priest, the sacristan, William Bartlett – with the objective of erecting a shrine in honour of Our Lady on a site in St Mary's Park. Near the entrance to the estate, an area that had been a swampy, rat-infested dump was cleared and prepared by voluntary labour and, with materials supplied free by firms in the city, the granite base was put in place. The fury of the ghost of the Bishop's Lady would be nothing to the fury of Lord Clare if he had been allowed back from 'his own place' as Peter said about Judas, to be present on the Feast of the Assumption in 1954 and see the then Parish Priest, Monsignor Lee, unveiling a beautiful marble statue of Our Lady – the statue also was a gift (not a penny was spent on the entire project) – with an inscription in Irish on that granite base. The city bands were in attendance to entertain the multitude and to render their own tribute to the Mother of God who was appointed heavenly protector of our Parish Island Field and all who dwell therein when the Corporation built the houses there in the mid-1930s and renamed it St Mary's Park.

Because of our domestic situation, sharing a house-and-a-half – and a common stairs – with another family, the

Sheehans, whose mother's name was Mary Anne, we were strictly forbidden to recite the following delightful rhyme anywhere outside the four walls of our own kitchen-living-room:

Mary Anne the dancer never said her prayers,
Catch her by the two legs and haul her down the
    stairs.
The stairs made a crack, the divil broke her back,
And all the little ducks said: 'Quack, quack, quack!'

We needed no prohibitive caution from father or mother to avoid reciting the next one if our beloved Uncle Danny happened to be visiting:

Dan, Dan, the dirty man,
Washed his face with the frying pan,
Combed his hair with the leg of the chair,
Dan, Dan, the dirty man.

Before ever my mother took me by my pudgy three-and-a-half-year-old hand and led me to meet the renowned Sister Felicitas, head nun at the local Convent of Mercy, my brothers had taught me what they said were Irish and Latin rhymes. I listened often, of course, while the older siblings chanted genuine Irish poems and prose as part of their school 'ekers', so I was a willing student when they coached me in this rigmarole: 'Tá sé swally-a-handcart, two dob-dobs and a chaney-alley, a ha'p'ny nick-nee-nock and a bottle of Yorkshire Relish.' The 'Latin' rhyme they taught me was not even related to the worst of 'bog' Latin. In cold print – I never saw it written – it may be easier to decipher than it was for me to unravel when they chanted it at me by the fireside after they had laboured at their genuine homework; so, I'll try to make it look the part: 'Indeltarris, inoknoniss, inmudeelsiss, inklaynoniss, gotay tyevee, mayray tay.'

Rendered into correct English, allowing for some grammatical licence, it goes like this: 'In dell tar is, in oak none is, in mud eels is, in clay none is; goat ate ivy, mare ate hay.'

Some years before I was born, the activities of a medical practitioner who was also a proselytiser gave rise to another rhyme, to the air of 'John Brown's Body':

Oul' Doctor Long he has a shoe-shop in hell.
He sells pinnywinkles at the top of Pinnywell.
If I had a pinny, I would buy a pinny rope,
And hang Doctor Long for meddling with the
       Pope!

When we moved from fireside to street, we acquired additions to our stock of rhymes, but we also learned the distinction between decency and vulgarity, between modesty and obscenity. Certain words and phrases that were commonly heard on the street, even the euphemism 'feck' for the most common vulgarism – we called that 'the soldiers' word', and my mother commented: 'My father, who fought in the Boer War, would go mad if he heard anybody calling it that! He said himself and his pals never used language like that!' – were taboo once you stepped across the threshold where the *lares et penates* of the households of ancient Rome had been replaced by the Holy Family and the saints, with statues and holy pictures in every room of the house.

I digress to record that the only non-religious picture in our house was a copy of *The General Absolution of the Munsters at Rue de Bois*. We used to gaze at that picture while my father was telling us about his young brother who died in the war, wondering which of the soldiers was our Uncle Tom, and we could all recite what was printed under the picture, the words of the chaplain, Father Gleeson, seen on horseback blessing the ranks of soldiers, because my father explained to us their significance in the context of the sacrifice the Irish soldiers had made in the Great War for the cause of Irish Home Rule. Telling the Munsters on the eve of a big push that many of them might die in the coming battle, the priest said: 'That your dust may rebuild her a nation and that your souls may shine as stars in her sky.' Incidentally, that same picture was the cause of severe shock to me when, on a day some time in the late 1960s, I walked into O'Donoghue's pub in Merrion Row in Dublin, along with a friend of mine, a red-haired and loquacious banjo-player named Luke Kelly who was to achieve musical fame with the Dubliners; while the barman was filling our pints I happened to raise my eyes to view the backdrop of bottles and other items on the cluttered shelves behind him – and there, high up on the wall, was the picture of Father Gleeson and the Munsters at Rue de Bois, but in a copy much more soiled and fly-marked than the one that had been as venerated in our home as any of the holy pictures.

I was still only a child when I became aware of the fact that there is some evil thing in human nature that can distort ordinary words and actions into something repulsive or vulgar or even obscene. I was going with my eldest brother, Tom, who would have been about eleven at the time, across Thomond Bridge to Mass in St Munchin's Church, as we sometimes did, not out of disloyalty to our own St Mary's, but for convenience. I began to chant a rhyme I had picked up from some source. I know the rhyme still, and there is no word in it that is blatantly obscene or vulgar, but I know now why my big brother shut me up quickly but gently, and warned me never to sing that thing again, especially at home, because it was dirty – that was the word he used, and he was right. As we grew older, the street and the school yard inevitably added to our store rhymes that varied from the mildly naughty to the blatantly vulgar and even to the plain dirty or obscene. These things, like their equivalent in dirty jokes, imprint themselves ineradicably on the *tabula rasa* of the young mind, even of a child who finds learning anything in school to be difficult. Like some of the banal Tin Pan

Alley songs we heard so often, like much of what we are bombarded with in print and on the television today, I wish I could blot them out of my mind. That will only happen when, like Croker of Ballinagarde, I have to move on to what will, I hope, be 'a better place'. I have resolved not to sully these pages with any such vulgarity or obscenity – God knows there is more than enough of both to be found even in the graffiti that children write on walls today, let alone in what adult minds concoct in the guise of entertainment or literature.

Fianna Fáil led by Eamon de Valera came to power in 1932, the year of the Eucharistic Congress in Dublin. Another general election took place the following year, when Dev was returned again. And no doubt the Pope in Rome would have been surprised to learn that in Old Church Street near King John's Castle in Limerick the papal flag was being carried along with the tricolour on both sides of the street during election campaigns by opposing bands of children. Meanwhile, up at the meetings in the Crescent, presided over by the statue of the Liberator, our adult counterparts, the Blueshirts and the IRA, were beating hell out of one another in the name of democracy and freedom of speech. My mother used three political labels for the neighbours and inhabitants of adjacent streets: some were Cosgrave's Blueshirts (Fine Gael), some were Republicans (Dev's Fianna Fáil) and one or two families she was unsure about, because 'They used to be terrible Red-White-and-Blues.' From one side of our street, the Republican faction chanted a new addition to our repertoire, to the air of the American Civil War song, 'Tramp, Tramp, Tramp':

Vote, vote, vote for De Valera.
Kick Billy Cosgrave out the door.
When we ketch him out tonight,
We will show him how to fight,
And we'll crown De Valera King of Ireland!

To which the young Blueshirts across the road replied with equal gusto, to the air of the ballad of 1798, 'Kelly the Boy from Killane':

What's the news, what's the news?
De Valera sold his shoes
For to buy ammunition for his men.
He was atin' pinny buns
Whin he heard the Free State guns
And the sly little divil ran away!

Obviously a ditty composed by the propaganda machine of the new Free State government during our own regrettable civil war in 1922–23. But we jibed the opposition that their song was actually complimentary to De Valera, a man who was willing to sell his own shoes to buy a few bullets for the betrayed cause of the Irish Republic, while the Free State army was generously supplied with guns and ammunition and artillery by their new friend, John Bull.

Our political horizons were widened by world affairs, and the Italian invasion of Abyssinia (Ethiopia) in 1935 gave us a new ditty – it probably came via the wireless, now becoming less of a rarity, although we did not acquire a set until many years later – and this expressed our support for the poor barefooted black men we saw in the newspaper photos, trying to hold back the Italians – who were using bombs and even poison gas – with a few rifles:

Will you come to Abyssinia, will you come?
Bring your own ammunition and your gun.
Mussolini will be there, and we'll blow him up in
       the air.
Will you come to Abyssinia, will you come?

The outbreak of the Spanish Civil War in the following year was not a likely source of any rhymes or songs but it led to confusion in our young minds because of the fact that while the papers reported the terrible things the Communists were doing to churches and priests and nuns in Spain – one photo that seared itself into the memory showed a line of riflemen aiming at a statue of the Sacred Heart – it was our own old enemies, the Blueshirts, who were being called on by their volatile leader, General O'Duffy, to go out to Spain and fight on the side of General Franco and the Catholics (much to the relief of De Valera) while some of the IRA were organising another company to fight for the Republicans, whom we understood to be the Communists.

With the coming of the Second World War, some politician quoted Viscount Grey's 1914 remark: 'The lamps are going out all over Europe.' Except for a few tragic incidents like the bombs on Dublin and Belfast, Ireland was spared the real horrors of war, but the rationing of food and fuel, and the scarcity of many commodities, meant that we all had to 'draw in our horns' – a metaphor taken from the snail, as Oscar Wilde would have put it. So, I finish with the rhyme we chanted whenever we came across a snail on rain-soaked walls or paths:

> Shah-la-muddy, shah-la-muddy,
> Stick out your *haw*-rens!
> All your children are roarin' an' *baw*-lin'!

We waited for the horns to appear, thinking that the snail had heard and obeyed our command. At the touch of a finger on the shell, we could make him draw in his horns again. It was only in school that we learned that our 'shahlamuddy' was a corruption of *seilmide*, the Irish word for a snail.

21

'SHADES OF THE PRISON-HOUSE'

> . . . trailing clouds of glory do we come
> From God, who is our home:
> Heaven lies about us in our infancy!
> Shades of the prison-house begin to close
> Upon the growing boy . . .

> *Wordsworth, 'Intimations of Immortality from Recollections*
> *of Early Childhood'*

Just when my education was proceeding so well – at home, in the street, all around the castle and Thomond Bridge, down the Island Bank, out in the fields and hills of Clare – my mother decided that it should be interrupted. She sent me to school. There was another occupant in the pram, my brother Maurice, and as I was now three and a half years old, and probably annoying the poor woman with my guff and gab, she took me by the hand one fine summer's day in 1931 and led me up the street to Halpin's pub at the corner of the New Walk, then on down to the Convent of Mercy gate and along by the wall of the girls' school to the open gateway of the long passage leading down to the boys' infant school. If I had known my Dante then, I would have seen over that gateway the 'darkly coloured words' he saw inscribed above the wide open gateway to Hell, concluding with that soul-searing line:

Lasciate ogni speranza, voi ch'entrate!
('Abandon all hope, you who enter here!')

When I was confronted by the principal of the boys' infant school, Sister Felicitas (none of the pupils could say that name, so she was known as Felickstas), I felt like a midget looking up at that huge black and white giantess. In the medieval style of religious habit they wore up to Vatican Two, only the nun's face could be seen (no wonder a little boy was said to have told his mother one day that he found out nuns have legs!). The face I was looking up into had very red cheeks and blue eyes, and all that black and white stuff spreading out and down from it made me feel that she was a terrible witch going to whisk me off to her hut in the woods and eat me without salt. This formidable nun was well acquainted with our family; my brother Dick was still in the infant school, and Joe had just gone up to the 'Monks', as the Christian Brothers were still called then, to join our eldest boy, Tom. The two girls, Mary and Lily, were in the higher classes of the girls' school. So, the chat between mother and nun went on up there above my troubled infant head; something like this:

'Ah, Mrs O'Flynn, how are you? And you're bringing us another of your fine boys! And what's this little fellow's name?'

'This is Christy, Sister. He's a bit young, God bless him; he's only three and a half but he'll have his brother, Dick, to keep an eye on him, and he'll be out of harm's way here with you, if you can take him.'

'Take him, is it! Mrs O'Flynn, if you had a hundred children I'd be glad to get them!'

'Oh, God forbid, Sister! Haven't I another one

crawlin' around under my feet at home! I had to leave one of the girls minding him until I get back.'

And so she left me. And that was the day my childhood ended.

There were other new pupils abandoned by their mothers all around me, some of them sniffing, one or two bawling, 'Ma! Ma! Where are you? I want to go home!' But all the sniffing and the bawling stopped when Sister Felicitas produced a box of sweets and gave us all one each. They were toffees, wrapped in paper that had the words *Milseáin Uí Ghadhra* printed on them. I knew those words and what they meant, Geary's Sweets, because the factory where they were made was in Newgate Place, between the Court House and my Granny's house in Crosby Row. The factory used to be the old Newgate Prison and Geary's also made biscuits, not like Jacobs, but big ones, one kind that were square and plain, the other round with currants. Granny told us that the Geary's were great Republicans and 'Ireeshans', as we called people who spoke Irish, and that's why they had the name in Irish on the sweets.

Children who are stuffed with all kinds of sweets and chocolate and crisps in these affluent times could not possibly understand what a single sweet meant to us. It was even a sign of true friendship to bite off a piece of your solitary toffee and give it to your pal. We sat in the long tiered benches, all eyes, sucking away, while below us at the table Sister Felicitas was having a confab with our new teacher, Miss Mack.

The first fact I learned in the infant school, purely by observation, was that Miss Mack was not a hunchback. Along with the 'Latin' and 'Irish' rhymes my brothers had taught me, they had prepared me to begin my academic career by teaching me a rhyme about this teacher, Miss Mack. (I don't know which of the 'Macs' she belonged to: in Limerick, MacNamaras, MacCarthys, MacDonnells and all the rest of them became one big clan of Macks.) So, before ever I saw her, I had learned that 'Miss Mack, broke her back, tumbling over a haystack.'

Apart from my wonder at her athletic feat in tumbling over a haystack – it was one of our own enjoyments out in the country to try to climb up and over a haystack, much to the natural fury of any of the owners who saw these savages from the city invading their fields and wrecking their work – I had concluded that Miss Mack must now be a hunchback, or at least hobbling around like the old witch in Hansel and Gretel with the aid of a stick. But this small, dark-haired, thin-lipped woman I was considering while I sucked my toffee was as straight as a rod and the only stick I could see was lying on the table. I knew from my helpful brothers what it was – a pointer, officially for pointing out things on the blackboard and on the coloured chart on the wall but used also for slapping on the hand or giving a wallop across the legs and shoulders.

When Sister Felicitas left, Miss Mack introduced us to one of the great mysteries of school life in the Ireland of that time (at least in the schools for the common mob). We were all to be given a new name – our name in Irish. I was well prepared for this, of course, from the family hedge-school. But I felt as if this was a third christening, added to the two my mother used to tell me about. So, Miss Mack inscribed us all on her roll-book – she had no problem with us true Celts, the Os and the Macs (like herself), but she did some humming and hawing and sucking her pen with the names of the descendants of the Vikings and the Normans and the Cromwellians and all those other gangs who came to trouble us down through the centuries.

Anyone who went to school in those years will remember that the educational equipment in the infants' classroom consisted of a blackboard on a stand, a coloured chart for Irish which had lots of pictures, a box of *marla* (plasticine, which had originally been in separate coloured sticks but was now in grey-brown lumps) and *cipíní* (little sticks of various colours for making shapes and houses etc.), a slate for each child with a rag to clean it, and the pointer in the teacher's hand.

Many people of my generation will have another memory from those days, that of the 'Black Baby' who swallowed coins. I am annoyed when I read pejorative references to that gadget, as if our religious teachers were in some way racist by having it there at all. This is an imposition of later attitudes on previous ones, and is an error in logic and in the interpretation of social customs. Just as we used the word 'tinker' merely to express what the man's way of living was, so with the words 'nigger' or 'black' there were none of the racist connotations these words carry today; in fact, when we sang the Stephen Foster songs about black slaves on the plantations, we felt great sympathy for them, and we enjoyed the humour in the funny songs like 'Campdown Races' just as we thought the blacks themselves would do. And everyone had as high a regard for Paul Robeson as for any singer in the world.

Unfortunately, from my mother's perpetually strained resources, I was never able to put a ha'penny or a penny on the little doll's begging tongue, and I envied the children who occasionally did so. And when Sister Felicitas gave us a special talk on the missions one day, and told us that if we brought in half-a-crown (two shillings and sixpence!) a poor little abandoned baby in Africa would be christened with our very own name, I knew enough arithmetic to figure out (twelve pence make one shilling, etc.) that she was actually talking about *thirty* weeks of our standard pocket money! I don't think I ever even saw a half-crown until I made my First Holy Communion and went on the collection tour to neighbours and relatives. So, one of the incontrovertible facts in my life story is that no little African child was named after a certain little *garsún* growing up in Limerick in the early 1930s.

My most lasting impression of my first day has nothing to do with the classroom. When we were brought out to the yard we were shown over in one corner a half-roofed structure and informed that the lavatories were in there. My pre-school instructors had warned me about that place. The unroofed part was the wall against which we were to piss, and back from that, under the half-roof, there was a step up to a long wooden seat which had round holes cut in it. One of our street rhymes recounted the gruesome fate of a little boy named Icky Ocky, who was one day engaged in adding his fertilising contribution to the soil under an apple tree when 'a rat came up and bit his botty – one, two, three!' This, we were warned by the older boys in the street, could happen to you if you sat on one of those round holes in the school lavatory. Consequently some timid infants, and not just in the 'Babies' class, were so afraid of risking being bitten by rats that they tried to defy the call of Nature until they got home; inevitably, Nature called too strongly now and again, and a child was sent home to his mother in dirty disgrace, accompanied by a neighbour.

I was selected for this unwelcome job once, and it was no joke walking up the street with a poor mee-awe (*mí-ádh*, 'misfortune') who was bawling his eyes out and sobbing, 'Me mudder'll murder me!' I told him not to be crying and his mother would fix him up and so on and so on, but when we got to his house, it turned out that he knew his own mother better than I did, because she took one look at him and then she caught him and gave him a couple of clitters on the back of his head and shouted at him that he was 'after disgracin' me in front of the nuns and the whole parish!' Then she turned on me – on me! – that had brought the gezebo all the way up along the public street. 'And what are you standing gawkin' at, young Flynn? Did it ever happen to yourself, did it? And you can tell the nun from me that the least she might do is clean the poor child and not send him home with the shit down along his legs for everybody to be makin' a feck of him!' I thought I was going to get a clitter in the gob myself; so, I just turned and ran all the

172

way back to the safety of the school. And I only had enough breath left to tell Sister Felicitas a lie. 'His mother said thanks very much, Sister.'

Another and more disgusting consequence of the alleged rat menace was that even the brave ones who dared to sit on the round hole were in such a hurry to get off that much of what should have gone down the hole was deposited on the wooden surround. Whoever had the job of cleaning that place every day after school should have got double pay. Considering also that modern toilet paper and the ritual washing of hands were unknown, I am surprised that we did not all die of typhoid or diphtheria – some did, of course, in the fever hospital out in the City Home aforementioned.

That walled-off structure in the corner of our school yard was the cause of trouble for me towards the end of my sojourn in the infant school. I was nearly six and a half years old, and preparing for my First Holy Communion – I know, because this was one of the facts that compounded my wickedness in the eyes of Sister Felicitas. One of my pals was a neighbour who was the most physically skilful of all our crowd; while most of us could stand on our hands with our feet against the wall, we envied this fellow who could actually walk around the street or the school yard on his hands! He could climb a tree or a wall where none of us could follow, although in games he was useless and was always picked nearly last for one of the teams. This acrobatic gezebo was the cause of our calamity. One day there were four of us together about to perform against the wall in the Rats' Hole, when the competitive instinct in my pal put a bright idea in his otherwise fairly dull brain. 'Hey!' says he, 'we'll see who can piss the highest up the wall!' Our pre-school education on the street having prepared us to accept and enjoy any challenge, we all agreed.

It was no contest. Apparently, not only his hands and legs, but all other parts of this potential cat-burglar were more powerful than the average equipment of the young citizens of Limerick. Not only did his effort go higher on the wall than ours, it went out over the top of the wall. An unkind Fate had arranged, with the precise timing that only unkind Fate can control, that at that very moment two lady teachers were strolling along the yard, officially supervising the playtime, and passing by the wall on the other side. The one nearer to the wall was named Miss Bogue, a tall, severe sort of a woman. When she felt moisture spattering down on her out of a clear blue sky, she knew it wasn't the stuff the clouds turn into away up there. When she realised what it was, she was in on us before we had time to button up and dash out to mingle with the mob in the yard. We were hauled before Sister Felicitas who lectured us severely, referring specifically, as I have said, to the fact that we were just then being prepared by herself for our First Holy Communion in St Mary's in a few weeks' time, and assuring us that she would tell our parents who would have more to say to us. Then she gave us the cane, four each. I wouldn't be at all surprised, however, if the Recording Angel heard Felicitas telling that yarn to her cronies in the convent that same evening, with tears of merriment in those bright blue eyes of hers. I think she was that sort of a decent woman, because as time went on I realised that she hadn't said a word about it to my mother. Apart from the common punishment and lecture, there was a further worry in the matter for me. The teacher who suffered the effects of my pal's superlative effort, Miss Bogue, like Miss Mack, was also enshrined in one of our rhymes as follows:

Miss Bogue, the rotten rogue
Wants a man to give her a *póg*.

She was never my teacher but she was in charge of us sometimes when we were eating our lunch in one of the classrooms in winter and she unwittingly 'grigged' us, because, while we munched at our few bits of bread and butter, she would sit at her desk reading the paper and slowly peeling a banana, from which she bit a little as the skin went lower. Most of us had never eaten a banana, and little did the good woman know that we would have been glad to see her drop dead on the spot so that we could have a 'rawk' for what was left of it at her sudden demise. We would even have gnawed the skin if she gave it to us, just as we often did with the pith of orange peel. Now it so happened that Miss Bogue was an occasional customer of my father and she sometimes gave me a note for him, requesting a few bags of coal to be delivered to her house. I was in dread that she might decide to punish me further by cancelling her order and I knew how much every bag meant to Dad. But fair dues to the woman, she never mentioned the thing again – maybe she was too embarrassed; she probably had to go home that day and wash her hair and her clothes – and only a short while after the incident she gave me another order for my father.

As I did with the Sarsfield Band, I think it only just that I should at least record in this chronicle the names of the nuns and lay teachers who taught me and thousands like me. Sister Felicitas was the head, as we said, and the other nuns I knew were Sister Claver, a small pale-faced person, Sister Mercy, the opposite, a tall nun with a long nose and chin (her name always puzzled us, because she was Sister Mercy and a Sister of Mercy) and Sister Conleth, a small, quiet, bespectacled nun whom I was afterwards to encounter when I joined my brother Dick to serve on the altar in the convent. Sister Conleth was the sacristan, and we liked her very much. She was as nice and courteous to us acolytes as to the priest or the bishop. The lay teachers, in addition to Miss Mack and Miss Bogue, were Miss Kavanagh, a dark-haired woman, and Miss O'Sullivan, a red-haired cross woman who walloped my little brother Maurice one day at the stage when I was his protector. I can still see him coming towards me in the yard at playtime, with tears in his eyes, and his sobbing story about being slapped. Miss O'Sullivan was walking up and down the yard at that very minute and she would have been dropped in her tracks if I had been armed with a rifle or a revolver like the cowboys in the 'pictures'.

We were in the senior infant class when I learned another extracurricular lesson about school and education and all the rest of it: being stupid and slow to learn is a bad thing but sometimes being clever and quick to learn can get you into trouble too. A few times a year the girls who were training to be teachers above in the Mary Immaculate College near the Redemptorist Church were sent out to practise teaching in the schools. They were always dressed in a long navy dress with black stockings and a big shiny medal of Our Lady hanging from their neck. When they came, there would be one in each class with the usual teacher, and they taught a few of the lessons. Sister Felicitas was our teacher this year and of course she wanted to have the students going back with a good report of how we answered in the lessons – especially as the training college was run by the Sisters of Mercy, and one of the nuns from the college would come with the students.

When Felicitas knew the students were due, she used to do a cute trick: she put all the eejits up in the front bench – the school desks in those days were long benches like the seats in a church ('furrums' we called them, in official English 'forms') – where they were right under the nose of the student, and put all the smart alecks sitting up on the last bench where the student was staring straight at them. When the student taught a lesson and started asking questions she usually forgot the 'Silent, O Moyles' under her nose and pointed at us at the back. Sister Felicitas herself used to stand behind us, just to make sure we didn't start talking or fooling. Usually we piped up all right, especially if it was English or sums, but Irish was the big problem, not because we were not well taught by Herself, as we had been by the previous teachers, but because we often did not know what the student teachers were saying. Many of them were from Kerry or Cork or other such faraway places – we didn't know why at the time. It was because of the preparatory colleges established by the government in the 1920s to give young people from the Gaeltacht free secondary education and then move them on to the teacher training college to become teachers, thus ensuring a national supply of primary school teachers who were both native speakers of Irish and professionally competent to teach other subjects through Irish. Whatever benefit accrued from that system for the revival of the Irish language, it was a serious injustice to students in the non-Gaeltacht areas (which included the cities and major towns) who could compete only for the remaining places in the training colleges.

On the day I have reason to remember clearly, the visiting nun from the college was sitting in a corner watching an unfortunate student trying to get answers out of us after she had taught us a lesson in Irish. The poor girl probably had what would be called a fine Kerry *blas*, but it came across to us native speakers of Limerick Hiberno-English as something like the Red Indians talked among themselves in the pictures before they turned to the cowboy or the US cavalry officer and said, 'No can let White Man do' or something similar. So, things were not going well at all, and to make matters worse the severe-looking nun in the corner was scribbling notes in a book, and we could hear Felickstas behind us sniffing and snorting, probably thinking what the nuns in the training college would be saying about herself and her stupid little feckers in St Mary's and she with the great reputation of being one of the best teachers in Limerick!

Anyway, after several unanswered questions, the student teacher opens her gob and lets out another one: 'Wagga-wagga-wagga-wagga-wagga?' says she - at least, that's how we heard it – with a strained smile on her poor face. Suddenly I got a fierce thump in the small of my (very small) back –

the hambone fist of Sister Felicitas – and she hisses in my ear: 'Christy Flynn! You should be able to answer that!' Mother o' God, even if I had the answer on the tip of my tongue, I wouldn't have been able to get it out. As it was, I bit my tongue and nearly fell down on the head of the fellow in the bench below me.

When that student went away with her dragon boss, we got an awful scorching from poor old Felicitas, how we had let her down, how she didn't know why even the best boys in the class were all gone stupid on her, how there was no point now putting any of us in for the *feis* this year because even the good Lord and his Blessed Mother could see we had forgotten everything she ever taught us and we'd be no match for the children from any ordinary school, let alone the Ireeshans from the Model School above in Ballinacurra. We just sat there and let her spout it all out. The Granny Connolly, as ever, was whispering to me from up the street in Crosby Row: 'Remember, *a stór*, a shut mouth catches no flies.' I'm sure Felicitas herself knew right well what the problem was, and she probably had a good chaw about it with the nuns in her own convent and above in the college but there was no point in she talking to the likes of us about it.

The *feis* for which Sister Felicitas threatened not to enter us dunderheads was the Thomond *Feis*, an annual festival of Irish cultural events organised by the Gaelic League. This included competitions for all the schools in everything to do with the Irish language – storytelling, recitation, dialogues, plays – and also in Irish dancing. There was even a senior inter-county hurling tournament connected with it. My father brought us out to a Thomond *Feis* match one day just to let us see the great Mick Mackey. We saw little of the match itself but we saw Mackey after it with a blood-stained bandage around his dark head. I have recorded that great day in a passage in the five-thousand-line poem I wrote to celebrate the centenary of the GAA in 1984.

Sister Felicitas, like many other teachers, both lay and religious, was an enthusiastic vicarious competitor in the annual *feis*, entering any of her pupils who had a natural gift of the gab and a competent grasp of the *Gaeilge* for everything and anything she thought we had a chance of winning. From our point of view, there were two great advantages to being 'put in for the *feis*'. The Sisters of Mercy had a few convents in Limerick; they were also in charge of the training college and the City Home and Hospital out near the Ennis Road; so, they had a grand big car for shifting nuns from one place to another, also maybe for when they went on their summer holidays to Lahinch or Spanish Point. Sister Felicitas didn't want her well-trained little competitors in the *feis* to arrive above at the Gaelic League Hall in Thomas Street weary in body from the long walk, and consequently maybe not so sharp in the oul' brainbox for the contest with the enemy from whatever quarter. So, with the blessing of the Reverend Mother (maybe even with the permission of the Pope himself!) we little nippers, having been washed and scrubbed and combed by the mothers, were packed into the holy nuns' car (or the nuns' holy car) behind the big driver in his hat and belted overcoat, and driven in style ('like Lord Gough himself,' my mother said) through the town. That was the first car I ever sat in – but not the first vehicle: I mentioned a trip in a lorry earlier. Our neighbours, the Ryans in Castle Street, bought lorries after their horses were destroyed in a fire and one Sunday in summer, when I was still a toddler, they took the whole street out to Cappanty Woods in Clare for a picnic. I was lifted into one of the lorries and sat with my sister Mary holding me. I remember nothing at all of the picnic, only being in that lorry and it trundling along the road.

The second advantage of the *feis* depended on a good performance – there were money prizes on offer: a pound for first place, ten bob for second, five bob for third. The year before I made my First Communion, Sister Felicitas put me in for recitation and storytelling (that was the first time I heard of *Séadna*, the Irish folk version of the Faust legend that was rendered into a dramatic poem by Goethe and into an opera by Gounod, and I can still recite the long opening passage from the famous book by An tAthair Peadar Ó Laoghaire, which was the piece Felicitas got into my skull for the contest: *'Bhí fear ann fadó agus is é ainm a bhí air ná Séadna. Gréasaí ab ea é. Bhí tigh beag deas cluthar aige ag bun cnoic, ar thaobh na fothana, srl.'*) But there was another competition called *An Chlann is Fearr*, in which three members of the same family were examined in Irish conversation; my brother Dick was in the top class in the school but the next one above him in the family, Joe, was gone to the primary school; so, what did the bould Felicitas do but send out a summons, via Dick and myself, to have Joe present himself with us at the convent a few evenings each week. Then she marched us over to the school with the other brainboxes and sat us in a room if it was wet, on the grassy patch behind the school if it was a sunny evening, and we were drilled in our Irish stories, poems, and conversation practice. Joe didn't mind a bit, because he loved that sort of stuff. He was the one that started me off writing, when he wrote poems and one of them won a prize in the *Irish Press* children's page edited by Captain Mac. It was called 'By Shannon Shore' and my father was never tired of reading it out for Uncle Danny or anyone else who came visiting. I decided to try my own hand at it, and sometimes I wish to God I never did; but that's another story for another book. If TB hadn't sent Joe to heaven when he was only nineteen years old, he would surely have become a writer as good as any in Ireland.

The big day came and off we went once more in the holy nuns' car. It had black curtains on the windows, but they were tied back when we were in it; everyone knew what they were for, so that the nuns wouldn't be distracted from their prayers and holy thoughts when they were driving through the city. For the same reason, whenever they had to go out – they always went in twos – they had a black veil over their face; and when we met them coming along the pavement we were trained to step out on the road and salute the nuns like we did the priest. In spite of all the veils and curtains, however, we heard it said in the fireside gossip that the nuns saw more and knew more about what was going on than any mother of a family; they were always questioning the children in school, and besides that, some of the mothers would go and talk to the nun about any trouble in the family before they'd go to the priest himself.

That *feis* was a glory day for us, because not only did I win with my story, *Séadna*, and my poem, but the three of us, Joe, Dick and myself, knocked spots off all the other trios, even – and this is what made us the real heroes in the eyes of Felicitas – even the Ireeshans from the Model School. That school was a special one set up long ago when the British government was still ruling Ireland but now it was owned by the Department of Education, and it was supposed to have a much higher standard of Irish than the ordinary schools of the nuns and the Brothers. All the people in Limerick who were 'outsiders' from the Gaeltacht, like guards or teachers from Kerry or Connemara, or who wanted their children to be really the tops in Irish, sent their children to the Model. Of course they considered people like us to be only trotting after them, trying to pick up a bit of what they called 'school Irish' that wasn't the real thing at all. No wonder then that Felicitas was crowing for weeks after as if we had won the Triple Crown for Ireland instead of just the three of us winning *An Chlann is Fearr*. But I was sick and tired of it all after a while, because for ages after, every time some nun or inspector or anyone else like that came along to the school, she hauled me out to recite a poem or tell the story about that eejit of a cobbler below in County Cork who sold his soul to the *Fear Dubh* for a purse of gold. The gold that interested the three musketeers of the O'Flynn clan was the prize money we brought home to my mother when Felicitas got it from the *feis* committee later on. We always got a great kick out of being able to bring home any money, because we knew how tough life was for Mam, trying to feed a gang like us and keep clothes on our backs as well as pay rent and gas and everything else, including the insurance every family paid every week in case somebody died and the coffin and the funeral had to be paid for. But she always gave us a 'backlift' out of any such prize money. So, as a result of our achievement in the Thomond *Feis* that year, the three of us, Joe, Dick and myself, were able to suck Cleeve's toffee – the dearest but the best – for weeks afterwards.

One of my solo efforts had repercussions that made me wish I had never heard of the Irish language or the *feis*. Sister Felicitas decided to enter me for a competition called *Teagasc Críostaí* and if you don't know what that is, dear reader, you know as much about it as I did when herself hauled me out of the class one day – we were in our final year in the infant school, and I had made my First Communion the previous summer – and informed me that she was entering me for a new competition this year (as well as the usual ones!). She then produced a small book in Irish, in which she had made several marks with her red pencil. This, she told me, was the Catechism in Irish, and the marks were on the questions prescribed for the *feis*, the answers to which she would teach me. We all had, of course, a similar small book in English which we called the Kadiksum, and we were already able to chant such basic facts as that 'God is the Creator and Sovereign Lord of Heaven and Earth and of all things.' We also had acquired, from our big brothers as usual, the unorthodox answers which Sister Felicitas and the other nuns never heard. So, with our natural instinct for survival, we were able to chant in the school yard or when adventuring in the Clare Hills, such heretical definitions as: 'Who made the wurreld? Me fader an' all de udder min!'

And we even adapted the Catechism's final ridiculous item, 'What means Amen? Amen means "so be it".' We said: 'Amen means so-be-it, a little dog with four feet, runnin' down O'Connell Street, cryin' out: Pigs' toes tuppence each!' Thus the Holy Spirit took care of us, showing us even from our tenderest years how to protect our minds and our souls from the pernickety theologians who can sometimes be an enemy within the Church of Christ.

After a few sessions with that loving but forceful pedagogue, Sister Felicitas, I was soon able to astonish the Granny Connolly by repeating at my mother's instigation questions and answers from the book. 'Wait'll you hear what this fella is able to say – he's learnin' his Catechism in Irish, if you don't mind!'

'Well, glory be to God above! Did we ever think we'd live to see the day!' And then I had to chant: *'Cé hé Dia? Is é Dia an tAthair uilechumhachtach, cruthaitheoir neimhe agus talún agus gach uile ní.'* Then, inevitably, came the proud Granny's thump on my chest or shoulder, and 'Consplawkus t'you, me boy, you're a chip off the oul' block! Learn your Irish, *a stór*, 'tis our own anyway – *Sinn Féin amháin!*'

Came the day, and the examiner for the *Teagasc Críostaí* competition in the *feis* was a big hairy old priest who seemed to be half-blind or else it was that I being so small the poor man couldn't see me at first on the other side of the table. Anyway, after peering around for a while and finally locating the leprechaun from the Parish, he did the usual introductory quiz: *'Cad is ainm duit? Cad is aois duit? Cá bhfuil tú id chónaí?'* – a cake-walk for any experienced competitor from the stable of the mighty Sister Felicitas in St Mary's. Then he got down to the theology *as Gaeilge*, and when he was finished he sat back in his chair staring at me for a while; then he let a blast of Irish out of him that nearly knocked me out the window. All I could pick out of it was that I was a *garsún ana-mhaith ar fad*, a cliché encomium we often heard from Felicitas herself or from the student teachers; but he added another mouthful in which I caught the words *sagart* and *lá éigin, le cúnamh Dé* which made me worry that the old man was getting his lines crossed and offering me a vocation to the priesthood instead of the prescribed prize, one pound sterling. Life can be more complicated for a child of seven than for a man of seventy.

About a fortnight later, I was hauled to the top of the class again and my theological mentor gave me an envelope containing a few pound notes, the spoils from the other competitions in which she had entered me, and also a small shiny prayer book, the latter, she said, being what the *feis* committee had sent her as being a more suitable prize in *Teagasc Críostaí* than the pound which was the usual first prize in the competitions for storytelling, recitation, conversation, etc. Inevitably, when the next inspector called in, she used me as a distraction to impress him with dollops of the stuff she had packed into my poor skull. But on the day I arrived home with my envelope and prayer book the reaction was very different. My mother was very glad of the 'godsend' in the white envelope, she praised me for the achievement on all fronts and gave me the usual 'backlift' for myself. Then she began to brood on that shiny white Irish prayer book, with its coloured pictures just like our First Communion prayer books, and its price clearly marked thus: 2/–. I could say the price in Irish, *dhá scilling*, and I knew the Irish for a prayer book was *leabhar paidreacha*, but as for the contents, I could only make out a word here and there. And I did not need my mother's frowning observations to know that the difference between the pound I had expected to get and the price of this Irish prayer book was eighteen shillings, which was a considerable sum in the budget of any family in our street, in any street, halfway through those hungry 1930s. But when my beloved Ma announced that she had decided to go down to Sister Felicitas in the morning and 'have it out with her', I wished my angel guardian would appear, put me under one of those big white wings, and carry me off to heaven, at least temporarily.

The next morning, I stood between the pair of them at the top of the class, and I saw Felicitas nodding her head in agreement as my mother, in her forthright fashion, made comments about the person or persons unknown who, in her opinion, had tried to pass off a miserable little two-bob prayer book 'that the poor child can't even read – and after all his hard work learning jawbreakers in Irish about God and all the rest of it!' in lieu of the usual pound prize. And the poor child stands there below the line of fire, with all the other kids gawking at us with their gobs open and their ears cocked trying to figure out why I was in trouble, or maybe they were just getting a kick out of seeing Felicitas on the receiving end of the fiery stuff my mother could spout when she got her dander up. In the end, she threw the book at Felicitas (well, plonked it down on the desk very firmly) and advised her to 'send it back where it came from'. Also, Felicitas was to inform 'that crowd of Ireeshans above in the Gaelic League' that never again would any child of my mother's compete for anything in their *feis* if they did not forthwith give the pound prize as promised – and not even the eighteen shillings' difference would we look at.

We didn't have to look at it or at anything at all for that matter. The weeks dragged on and no more was heard from 'that crowd of Ireeshans above in the Gaelic League'. But my mother and the Granny and Uncle Maurice and Uncle Danny and the whole clan got great mileage out of that incident of my Irish prayer book; in fact, in the long run, I began to consider that I came out of it much better off than if they had given me the usual pound prize, from which Ma would have given me a shilling, because, in sympathy for the poor little *garsún* who had done so much for God and Ireland, and then been done out of his prize, the Granny Connolly gave me a shilling out of her pension, and her noble example was followed by the uncles who gave me sixpence each. Better than the money even was the summing up by the Granny, giving all the young listeners a fine punning line for our further amusement: 'That crowd of Ireeshans,' she growled, 'with all their fine talk about getting the whole country to talk Irish! 'Tis soft the wool grows on them! There's better men and women died for Ireland that hadn't two words of Irish! Bad cess to them anyway, they'd give you a pain where you never had a window!' We would have enjoyed that peroration all the more at the time if we had known what the Granny was really wishing anyone when she wished them *bad cess*. It was only years later, in our further school studies, when we came across the word 'cesspool' and looked it up, that we enjoyed retrospectively that Elizabethan malediction of the dear departed.

Before Sister Felicitas packed us off up to the Monks in Quay Lane, there was the First Holy Communion to be got through. It is not with even the slightest hint of disrespect that I speak thus of what we were always being told would be the greatest day in our lives. (They told us also that our schooldays were the best years of our lives, which should be classed with my mother's fairytales.) The Holy Spirit knows that, humanly speaking, I enjoyed many a rugby match, or a day spent skinning an orchard and otherwise skylarking out in the Clare Hills, or marching with a band, any band, around the city, much more than the day of my First Communion. There was too much tension associated with all the preparation for our first Confession and the practising for the reception of Holy Communion, learning the hymns, being drilled in what to do with your tongue and your teeth. Did the priests and the bishops of our time forget entirely what Jesus Christ did when the mothers brought the children to him, and Peter and the other disciples were trying to hunt them away? He took them on his knee and blessed them; he didn't try to teach them the 'Our Father'; that was a prayer for his disciples, the future bishops of the Church, but in our time it was only one of the items we had to learn, along with that Catechism that did more harm to religion than even dialect did to the Irish language! And of course, the greatest anomaly of all in that area was that the bishops and the priests, whose mission in life was given them by Our Lord in the command: 'Go, and teach all nations,' never taught any child a prayer or a line of the theological Catechism; they conveniently imposed that as an extra (unpaid) task on the nuns and Brothers and lay teachers.

The first Confession was an ordeal for every child in those times. We had the notion driven into us that your soul was originally spotless but that it had gathered all sorts of stains; these were your sins, and you could only get your soul clean again by telling the sins to the priest. Most of us would be trying to make up some sort of a list – like that little nipper in the story who murdered his sister! – but I had two really big things for that first terrifying session in the dark box (again, dear Holy Spirit, why did you ever let the stupid officials of your Church invent that spiritual torture chamber?). The first was the terrible sin I thought myself and my three pals had committed the day we had the pissing competition in the Rats' Hole and caused poor Miss Bogue to go home and wash her hair. My second big sin was even worse, because it was blatant disobedience to my own poor mother.

One night, a few months before the First Communion day, my father was away somewhere in the country playing at a dance. When my mother told us it was time to go to bed, I announced that I was going to stay up until my father came home. Most mothers would give a brat like that a *paltóg* in the ear, and send him up the stairs with what my mother herself called 'a runnin' kick'. But my mother was wiser. She just said quietly, 'All right, but you can't wait here, because I'm going to bed, and I'm locking the door; so, you can wait out on the street.' With that, and before I had time to change my tune to one of wailing repentance, I was caught and thrown out the front door on to the dark street. I can still hear the banging shut of that door in Old

Church Street. But I must have had the makings of a first-class juvenile delinquent, because I didn't cry or kick the door; all I did was move up the street and over to Chris O'Brien's shop, which commanded the view down by King John's Castle to Thomond Bridge. I had the idea that the car with my Da and the other musicians must come in that way, because that was the way 'out the country' in our life.

I sat under the lighted window of the shop and kept my eyes on the bridge. I could hear the river as it passed under the bridge and went rushing along through the Curragower Falls below the castle. After a while, looking at the yellow light of the streetlamps, looking at the big dark castle, looking at the bridge, I began to think of – who else? If I had stayed there much longer I would actually have 'seen' the Bishop's Lady coming up over Thomond Bridge and making for me to carry me off and throw me in the Shannon like she did with poor old Drunken Thady. Fortunately, Chris O'Brien came out from her shop to put up the shutters, and she got as much of a shock when she saw me sitting there as I would have got seeing the Bishop's Lady. When I told her why I was there, she took me into the shop and presented me with a big square cream bun; then she brought me down to my house and banged on the knocker. I'm sure my mother was only waiting for that knock, whether from myself or anyone who had found me. She was out like a shot, but keeping her cross face fixed. My deliverer had me drilled in an act of contrition, and I was able to work up the tears genuinely enough because I was frozen and terrified by now. And, as mothers will, she took me in, sat me by the fire, made me a cup of cocoa and even a cup of tea for herself. And, of course, I shared my big square cream bun with her. And like that story in the Gospel, how the good big brother was fed up when he saw the way the father made such a fuss of the blaguard son, the next day I was in danger of getting a couple of clouts from some of my own brothers when they heard all about the cream bun and the cocoa.

When I told the priest in St Mary's lovely new church that I had two big things to confess, he told me not to be worried. When I managed to tell him about the pissing competition and Miss Bogue's hair, I could see him peeping out through the grill at me with a big grin on his puss; that upset me more than if he had told me I might go to hell. (I was wondering after did he happen to know Miss Bogue?) The second big sin he took a bit more seriously, but he said he knew I loved my mother and that I'd never give her such trouble again. And he only gave me three Hail Marys the same as I often got afterwards when I had nothing to tell the priest only that I was fighting with another fellow in the street or in the school yard, or that I was talking in the church or rushed through my morning or night prayers without thinking of what I was saying.

When I was back in the Island Parish on a visit recently, I went to St Mary's Convent and visited the nuns' cemetery beside that high old wall of the thirteenth-century Dominican Priory. I stood at the grave of Sister Felicitas, that valiant woman, and asked her to pray for me in heaven. Only God knows the good that single nun did for our Parish and for Ireland and for the human race, and there were many more nuns and brothers and priests like her, the uncanonised saints of Ireland in our time.

22

A PIECE OF A GOOSE AT CHRISTMAS

The County Cork priest, Peadar Ó Laoghaire (1839–1920)
whose novel, *Séadna* (1904), based on the Faustian folktale
he had heard from a neighbour's daughter in his childhood,
provided the Gaelic League with its first popular book, tells
a story in his autobiography that is amusing but also
incidentally more revealing of the landlord-tenant problem
in nineteenth-century Ireland than many an academic thesis.
I translate (the conversation part is in English in the
original):

> I remember a certain day when I was, I think, three
> years old . . . I saw a lot of strange people out in the
> yard and they whispering and talking. I gathered that
> some important person was coming and that they were
> waiting for him. Now and again I'd hear the word,
> the Master, and Mr Saunders. At last a big well-fed
> gentleman came in, and he sat on a chair in the middle
> of the house and all the strange people came in after
> him. My father was one of the men who came in. It
> was he put the chair in the middle of the house for
> the gentleman to sit on. There wasn't a word out of
> anybody. At that time, I myself wasn't shy or afraid of
> any kind of a person, high or low. Over I went and I

stood in front of the gentleman.

'Good morrow, Mr Saunders,' said I, welcoming him.

'Oh, good morrow, boy! Good morrow, boy!' said he and he caught me by the shoulder and drew me over until he had me between his two knees. 'Tell me, boy,' he said, 'did you eat any meat today?'

'Don't you know,' said I at once, 'that I ate a piece of a goose long ago when it was Christmas?'

I thought all present would drop dead that minute with the laughing. The gentleman himself laughed too, and he let me go . . .

A day came later when I understood perfectly what made them laugh. It was to raise the rent that the 'Master' had come that time. When he asked me about the meat he was only looking for an excuse. If I had said that I had eaten meat that morning or the day before or a week ago, he'd have the excuse he wanted. He could say, 'You people have meat to eat every week. That shows you all have my land too cheap. You'll have to pay me higher rent.' But when the child could only boast that he had eaten a piece of a goose long ago at Christmas, that took the ground from under any excuse for raising the rent. That's what set them all laughing. The gentleman himself laughed too, but I think his was 'the laugh of burnt Johnny'. He let me go quick enough anyway. He didn't want any more of the goose!

A hundred years later, in our homes in Limerick, if even the weekly eating of meat was to be the criterion, a modern Mr Saunders would certainly have his excuse for raising the rent but the Christmas goose was still the *pièce de résistance* in the culinary calendar, and its purchase at the market was a ceremony in itself. Our weekly expedition to the markets up at the end of Mungret Street, my father's native heath, was always an adventure. While my mother wandered around looking for the best value for her meagre money, and usually meeting friends and relations for a chat, we explored the noisy crowded market itself and the neighbouring shops, one of which was a workshop selling stools and *súgán* (straw-bottomed) chairs – and brand-new hurleys, at which we gazed in longing and frustration, thinking of the crude crooks we used on the street. We were fascinated by the poultry and the barrels and boxes of vegetables and apples. The temptation to pilfer an apple was very strong but my mother had us strictly warned – and we were helped by the fact that she herself supplied each of us with an apple, free of charge!

The packaged goods in the supermarkets today are a contradiction of the old adage which advises us never to buy a pig in a poke. In the shops and markets of our childhood, that adage was respected by both seller and buyer. When buying a pound of rashers even in the best grocery stores, such as Liptons, Nelsons, the Home and Colonial Stores, the customer saw the rashers being sliced off by a machine and weighed on the adjacent scales, and butter was taken from a huge block with wooden bats dipped in water, then weighed and wrapped. There was wrapped creamery butter on sale, in pounds and half-pounds, but it was more expensive than the farmers' butter; anyway, we preferred the salty taste and the buttercup colour of the stuff the farmers' wives had made themselves. Because it was homemade, it could vary in taste and quality, and I never saw my mother or Granny buy a pound or two of it without first scraping off a bit with a penny and tasting it. In the market, my mother procured us all a free apple by the same method: she would scrutinise the barrel or box of apples on offer by the countrywoman, pick up one, bite it, chew with her head in the air like a wine connoisseur and then hand the apple to one of the waiting hands below. If she liked the sample, she might buy a dozen; if not, she shook her head and moved on; but if she had more than one of us dragging along, she would sample elsewhere until each gob was stopped.

The goose was the material symbol of Christmas for our generation, just as the Star of Bethlehem and the crib were the spiritual images that impressed themselves on our souls and minds from the first time our mothers brought us to kneel and gaze in wonder. After Christmas Day, it was the custom to go on a tour of the cribs in the city churches, comparing them critically but also saying a prayer at each one. The primacy of the goose is evident from our traditional rhyme for Christmas, a rhyme that was probably another import from the land of Dickens across the water, but we chanted it happily:

Christmas is coming and the goose is getting fat;
Please put a penny in the old man's hat.
If you haven't a penny, a ha'penny will do,
If you haven't a ha'penny – God bless you!

The purchase of the Christmas goose was the greatest shopping event of the year. And when it was brought home it was hung in the shed, well-protected, until the night when it was to be plucked. The feathers were kept to make a pillow or a cushion and the wings became brushes for the range and the hearth. The goose itself 'died a sudden death' on Christmas Day (that was always our metaphor for any item that was consumed with gusto and *in toto*), but the giblets (often thrown away nowadays) and the carcase made great soup.

The making of the Christmas plum pudding was a ceremonious exercise in which it was the custom for each member of the family to give the mixture a stir. On the street, a new cry was added to the usual hawkers' lines: 'Holly-an'-ivy, tuppence a bunch!' And the people who pushed a box-car from door to door selling bundles of firewood were kept busier than ever. The simple chain decorations were bought in Woolworths, where the toys, especially the tin drums, piled in pyramids high up behind the counters, were almost a cause of severe neck-strain for us. Comparing the modern Christmas dinner with those of my childhood in that old house in the Island Parish, apart from the replacement of the succulent goose by the paler and more insipid turkey, the main item of difference is the amount and variety of wine today in contrast with its total absence from the Christmas table then. The only wine we knew of was the wine we poured into the chalice when we were serving on the altar. We saw advertisements for Buckfast Tonic Wine and knew that it was made by monks somewhere in England, but we thought it was some kind of medicine. In our own house, as in most houses then, there was never any intoxicating drink; however, my mother kept a few bottles of stout in a fireside press – no one was supposed to notice! – for the Granny, who, having polished off the first bottle, which put her into good form, caused us to wink surreptitiously and to mouth silently her inevitable proverb as she yielded to my mother's coaxing to have another: 'Ah shur, God bless you, Lily, I suppose I might as well – shur a bird never flew on one wing, as they say!' But if wine was unknown in our houses, a big stock of lemonade and other minerals was laid in for Christmas, and after a few days of glorious guzzling, we realised, as we did at Easter when it was the custom to eat as many boiled eggs as you wanted, the truth of Nerissa's observation to her mistress Portia in *The Merchant of Venice*: 'They are as sick that surfeit with too much as they that starve with nothing.' My mother's version of that would be less elegant but more colourful: 'Oh, I'm lorded! I couldn't eat another bit of this world's food, an' I'll be crawsick if I as much as look at a bottle of lemonade for the next week!'

If the goose was the centrepiece of our Christmas fare, the pig was the source of whatever other meat we had throughout the year. Limerick had the finest bacon stores in Ireland at that time and Limerick ham became renowned far afield. The ham and bacon from those stores rarely if ever appeared on the table of the poorer classes – except for the occasional rashers or sliced ham (this latter being real ham, not the packaged rubber of today). There were some concoctions like brawn and 'German sausage', used mostly for work lunches, but for the dinner, when there was meat at all, it was inevitably some part of the pig, and while the rich were dining on the backside or the belly of that much-maligned animal, we had what I still would claim to be the tastiest parts. There were shops that specialised in the sale of offal, and not only of pigmeat, but also of items from the sheep and the cow. In the window, a pig's head was often the centrepiece of a display of backbones, crubeens, eye-bones, spare ribs, skirts and kidneys, tongue – and I would need my mother back to list all the others.

Not, of course, that we had meat every day. The canon lawyers of the Church had decided that Catholics should abstain from meat on Fridays. My mother added Wednesday, in honour of St Joseph, the saint who was even more important than the Franciscan Anthony in her prayers. And economics usually added another day or two, or even three, some weeks. But who needs meat every day anyway? Not only some humans but even the mighty gorilla is a vegetarian. We were quite happy to dine on a big plate of colcannon, on a big lump of bread-pudding or on new potatoes and milk, and when meat came our way, it was not regarded as anything exceptional. I must confess, however, that I always begged my mother, when a pig's backbone was on the menu, to give me the tail – even my own children wouldn't believe me when I told them that it was tastier than any lamb chop or steak. And when there was money for them in the winter, we often had crubeens (*crúibíní*, pig's toes) and knuckles for tea, and we didn't even have to cook them because the Granny of the family who shared our house, the Sheehans, a grand old lady whom we all called Nana Ledane, lived in the nearby New Walk, beside the convent, and she sold pig's toes and knuckles ready for consumption. She had them boiling in huge black pots on the range, and they were much in demand all over the neighbourhood, a penny for a crubeen, a ha'penny for a knuckle (that's like the pig's ankle, the short part above the crubeen). Nana Ledane's was the Irish equivalent of the Italian fish-and-chip shops. She also sold salt, which she cut in bars, like a pound of butter, from a big block, and from the bar we grated salt into the open salt-cellar. Sometimes, Nana Ledane's black pots brewed discontent – she would make a present of a few knuckles to her granddaughters, the Sheehan girls, and they, with our two sisters, would sit on the steps at the (closed) side door of Halpin's pub across from her house, sharing the spoils and grigging us, their own brothers, with a great smacking of lips and licking of fingers, and absolutely refusing to throw us even the scrap that you'd give to a mongrel dog!

A special shop in the Parish sold the packet-and-tripe which was said to be the reason why the women of Limerick were able for those mercenary Dutch, English and German besiegers who wanted to take over our Shannonside town in 1690, and also why we produced such great rugby players down through the years. Whatever about that, it was a ritual on Saturdays to go to Treacy's with a can for the packet-and-tripe that formed the regular Sunday morning breakfast. An alternative to the packet-and-tripe was Matterson's (or any other) black and white pudding and sausages. Like the scrumptious coconut creams we got from our Uncle Maurice Connolly in Nelson's grocery shop in William Street (when shopping 'up the town', my mother always dropped in for a chat with her younger brother, the baby of their family) the pudding and sausages we consumed on Sunday morning after Mass – or on a winter's night for our tea if times were good – cannot even be imagined by the generation who think that what we buy nowadays in the supermarkets is the genuine article.

But there was a day when I was nearly (I say nearly) put

off all porcine products for life, including those delicious white puddings that came off the pan with lashings of gravy to dip your bread in. (We dipped bread also in the boiling hot cabbage-water that put life back in our freezing fingers and toes when we came rushing in at lunchtime in winter.) I was one of the many flag-sellers in the annual St Patrick's Week collection for the Gaelic League – we were recruited for this by one of the city's most prominent Ireeshans, Mr Toohey, or Mícheál Ó Tuathaigh. But this man was an Ireeshan with a difference, because he was one of our own, a teacher in the Christian Brothers' primary school in the Parish, and a man who was a cause of pride for us because of his activities on behalf of the Irish language. In the effort to find contributors somewhere away from the many other wielders of token flags and collection boxes, I ventured into O'Mara's bacon factory. I would have been ejected at once if anyone in authority had noticed me, but a small nine-year-old was so insignificant in that noisome and noisy shambles that I wandered all over the place and saw sights that God himself and certainly the makers of sausages and puddings never intended for the innocent eye of a child. I saw the pigs being slaughtered and disembowelled; the butchers had trouble enough with their victims without even bothering to shout at me to get to hell out! I wouldn't have heard them anyway above the screeching of the pigs. I could understand even better now why the two well-fed pigs in my Aunt Brigid's backyard, or the others in Mrs Murray's on our street, were so reluctant to go for a nice ride in the low cart from the bacon factory. I certainly was in no mood to recite 'This little piggy went to the market'.

When I saw the girls at the long tables making sausages and puddings, I was going to run away from the stink and the mess back out to the street and fresh air when one of them called me by name. She was a friend of my sister Lily and the poor girl wiped her hands on her factory coat, rooted somewhere inside it and produced a penny for my box. That

197

good example was followed by a few of the others at the table with her. So, saying my official *Go raibh maith agat* first, as per instructions from Mr Toohey, I added on a few more spontaneous Parish thanks and blessings that would have done credit to any tinker at our door selling his tin cans and pots. And on the following Sunday morning, fortified by Mass and Holy Communion, as well as by the memory of the pennies I got from those generous Limerick lady sausage-makers, I was able to put all unpleasant connotations out of my young mind and tuck in with the rest of the gang to a fine feed of white and black pudding for breakfast.

Among the regular visitors to our street there was a woman from Park, an area close to the city whose inhabitants were said to be descended from the Danes in the time of Brian Boru but who now were peaceful enough, and their principal occupation was growing vegetables. Annie the Cabbage-Woman, as we always called her, came with her donkey and cart selling vegetables. We had no milkman in those years but every street had its milk shop, where farmers brought the milk in churns, and it was dispensed into our jugs or cans by the pint or quart. We saw the beginnings of the bottled milk when the government brought in a scheme to give milk and a bun to the poor children in schools, like the dole and the free beef that came in to alleviate the economic crisis caused by the dispute with Britain over land annuities.

Like most mothers, mine baked very good bread of her own but this had to be supplemented with loaves from the local Tubridy's Bakery in Athlunkard Street. She also, when funds were sufficient, baked rhubarb and apple tarts; but her speciality was potato cakes and we wouldn't call the king our uncle, as she said, when we sat in to a feed of them, coming hot from the oven, with the salty country butter melting into them and a big pot of tea to wash them down. For some reason, the boiling of the kettle for tea often caused my mother to burst into a strange song, which she told us she used to hear when the First World War was on and the British were holding recruiting meetings in Limerick as they did in all the towns and cities. The Sinn Féin crowd used to interrupt the meetings, she said, with songs like this one, which she called 'Hochin' the Kaiser' (that 'ch' like the 'ch' in Irish *loch*), meaning 'Cheering for the Kaiser':

> What'll we do if the kettle boils over?
> What'll we do? We'll fill it again!
> What'll we do if we marry a soldier?
> What'll we do but we'll marry again!
> A month in jail for hochin' the Kaiser,
> When we get out we'll hoch him again! . . .

There was more to that once dangerous ditty but I can't remember the rest.

When as children we weren't otherwise engaged, like sitting on the pavement making guns out of broken slates – the slates had come off the old roofs in storms and we used a small stone to chip out the shape of a gun, the real skill being required when it came to fashioning a trigger: one tap too hard and it was gone! Michelangelo would have admired our patience and maybe given us a few tips – during which craftwork one fellow would relate dramatically to the rest the entire plot of some film he had recently seen, we were often on the go out in the countryside. On such expeditions we were always ready to supplement our domestic diet with anything a bountiful Nature or the unwitting farmers had to offer. The gathering of mushrooms in a green meadow early in the morning is an experience never to be forgotten by anyone who enjoyed it. My mother boiled them in milk to make ketchup or fried them in butter. There was also the ritual gathering of blackberries and hazelnuts in season. And, as the farmers and their wives knew only too well, we were always on the lookout for an orchard or even one or two apple trees.

In our own playground in the infant school we had an illustration of the story of the forbidden fruit. Adjoining the wall of the playground were the back gardens of two houses in nearby Peter's Cell, in which lived related families both named Gilligan – the boys from both families were schoolmates of ours. From one of those Gilligan back gardens, the branches of a pear tree rose above the wall, and no sooner did minute peareens begin to appear on those branches than the competition to get them began. In spite of dreadful seasonal warnings from Sister Felicitas and the other teachers, and even when one or other of them was supervising the yard, a stone was likely to be let fly at those unripe little pears. If the yard happened to be unsupervised for a few minutes, 'Give us a lift!' was the cry (a further item in the training of future line-out jumpers for Shannon!).

Anyone caught *in flagrante delicto*, of course, suffered retribution as swift as that imposed on those two loodra-mawns who didn't know how well off they were in the Garden of Eden. In spite of being thus exposed in the infant school to this modern version of the Fall, when we went rambling in the countryside an apple tree, provided it was not too near the farmer's house, was a magnetic attraction that needed no Father of Lies to coax us into sin. If my mother only knew how many sweeteens we forced off the branches when we 'skinned' an orchard, she would not have been able to sleep soundly at night for fear of the gardaí coming to haul us off to Glin. In reality, we played fair: we took only what would stave off the immediate hunger, raiding only briefly and always at a safe distance – a lesson we learned one day when I was up in a tree throwing down apples to an accomplice, and our sentry failed in his duty. Fortunately, the angry farmer fired a warning shot in the air as soon as he came out of his house, and rabbits would not have disappeared quicker than we did before he got anywhere near us. When nothing better was in season, we were not disdainful of the common turnip, which we broke into pieces with a stone. And we had another of Granny's proverbs (even the chivalrous and noble-minded Don Quixote eventually got tired of hearing the proverbs of his improvised squire Sancho Panza, but we relished Granny's, even if we sometimes mimicked her) to tell us: 'When all fruit fails, welcome haws.' We took this literally – ripe red haws are tasty but they only fill you if you're a robin or a chaffinch or a tom tit. We would have needed to consume them by the thousand and that would have taken a lot of chewing and spitting out stones. Before they ripened, the haws made ammunition for the pea-shooters we fashioned from the hollow stalks of plants in the ditches.

One place and one occasion when we saw real fruit in cornucopian plenty was when we were recruited – only certain trusted families – by the nuns to help with the picking of the raspberries, gooseberries and currants in their extensive gardens. These are now, alas, a vanished glory, vandalised initially by drink-and-drug intruders and more recently by the bureaucrats who allowed a ring road to be driven through them. The beautiful convent itself stands empty and awaiting the inevitable demolition.

If we were warned in the infant school to refrain from attacking Gilligans' pears, as we trooped along after the aged sister who was our supervisor in the convent gardens we were made to feel that the ground would open and swallow us directly into hell if we as much as popped a raspberry or a blackcurrant into our little Parish gobs. We were given a cup of milk and a hunk of bread and jam at our break, and a few apples each when the day's work was over, but the holy nuns themselves knew quite well that a boy or a girl would have to be another Aloysius Gonzaga or Bernadette Soubirous not to succumb to temptation in that particular Garden of Eden.

The bishops who made the laws about Friday abstinence did not have to dine on a mackerel or a pot of colcannon (I often wonder what the parish priest's housekeeper dished up for his Reverence on Fridays) but they were worse than those Pharisees who were condemned as hypocrites by Christ because they made burdens for others to carry but never raised a finger to help. No priest or bishop ever came around our streets asking the mothers how they were managing to feed their big families, on Friday or any other day

Two stories come to mind as illustrations of the ridiculous effects of that old Church ruling about abstaining from meat on Fridays. The first concerns my mother. Her brother, our Uncle Maurice Connolly, married a girl named Birdie Murphy who proved to be an enterprising business woman, opening a clothes shop in the Irishtown and another later on near the railway. On some occasion when she was going by train on a business trip to Dublin, Birdie kindly invited my mother to go with her. My mother heartily enjoyed this unexpected outing but it was afflicted at an early point by canonical rectitude − the pair of them were just about to tuck into a fine breakfast of rashers, eggs and sausages on the train when my mother suddenly remembered that it was a Friday (I'm sure Birdie momentarily regretted inviting her just then!) and so the fragrant rashers and sausages were left untouched and those two decent Christian women from Limerick had to concentrate on a fried egg with tea and toast to sustain them all the way to Dublin.

The other story comes from *Dialann Deoraí* ('Diary of an Exile') by the late Dónall Mac Amhlaigh, a fine and largely self-educated writer who died in exile in Northampton (his mother, he told me, was from our Island Parish). This account of his life as a hospital porter and navvy in England in the years after Hitler's war contains an episode that almost made me curse the canon lawyers when I first read it. Dónall was among the hundreds of 'McAlpine's Fusiliers' and others who were working on the construction of the Rugby tunnel. As the tunnel progressed, the contractors decided that it would be more economical to have the sandwiches they supplied for the lunch-break brought in to the workers, rather than have them making the trek out and back. One day, as they sat around in the tunnel opening their packets of sandwiches, one worker exclaimed, 'Great, lads! Ham today!' Whereupon Dónall, realising that it was a Friday, reluctantly took the slices of ham from his sandwiches and gave them to his nearest mates. Foolish, perhaps, in the eyes of the world, but a sacrifice and an example of loyalty to principle that merited noting down by the Recording Angel in that tunnel just as the diligent diarist himself used to record the day's events back in his digs at night. *Go ndéana Dia trócaire ar a anam dílis.*

In addition to the Friday regulation, our family had another and distinctive price to pay for the difference between the real Christianity of Jesus Christ and what some theologians and bishops make of it. Just as they had put an end to the crossroads dancing on summer evenings, the bishops of Ireland had decided some time, not only that adults should observe a strict fast – 'one main meal and two collations' as the Cathechism informed us – during the forty days of Lent but also that there should be no dances. Instead of telling them to feck off for themselves and preach the Gospel as the Divine Founder of the Church had ordered them, the people accepted this ruling, just as they accepted the Friday abstinence, as if it were part of the Ten Commandments or one of the Articles of Faith. So, my father and all the other musicians who earned part or all of their income by playing music in dancehalls were out of work for the whole of Lent – and no bishop or priest came and asked Richie O'Flynn or any of the rest of them how they were going to pay the rent and feed the family until Easter Sunday dawned and we could all feel happy again and dance with episcopal approval. My father and mother never made any complaint, in our hearing anyway, about this deprivation. As I look back on those years and wonder how in God's name they did manage to feed us, and even to provide us with a sixpenny Easter egg from Woolworth's, and a few dozen duck and hen eggs from the market to celebrate the Resurrection, I find it difficult not to curse retrospectively those who were responsible for that extra hardship in their lives. And I'm sure the sensible bishops I count among my friends today agree with me (not in the cursing, of course!).

A good story my mother told us about food was how she lost her first 'situation' as a live-in nursery maid in the house of a Catholic business family 'up the town'. She was only thirteen years old and she felt so lonely that one day, when she took the two children for their daily walk, she decided to visit her mother in Arthur's Quay. The dinner was just ready there and the rich kids were sat in and they 'got their ears back', as Ma said, to whatever was going. But next evening, when brought down from the nursery to dine with their parents, they turned up their little noses at the fancy grub and the little boy asked petulantly, 'Why don't we ever have nice food like we got in Lily's house yesterday?' The services of Lily Connolly were dispensed with on the spot and she arrived home in tears to her mother, who, no doubt, said, 'Well, bad cess to them and may the divil make a ladder of their backbone! Sit in there, *a stór*, the kettle is singin' an' we'll have a nice cup o' tay – an' thanks be to God an' his blessed Mother, we never died o' winter yet!'

My father had one of his own stories ready whenever we had black pudding for tea. Like all good raconteurs, he enjoyed his own repertoire so much that his audience would groan when he said, 'That reminds me of the one about . . . ' To our protests of, 'You told us that before, Da!' he would counter, 'Ah yes, but it's a good one, though!' and proceed to tell it again! And strangely enough, we relished it again. I did not realise at the time that I was learning there at our own fireside the difference between literature and mere narration, that the art is in the telling, not in the tale itself; which is why we can read *Pride and Prejudice* over and over again, but one reading ends our interest in the book that is merely a story. Dad's 'black-pudding' story was about the poor farmer who helped a leprechaun and got three wishes. When he got home he told his wife about it, but then he forgot and because he was so tired and hungry he said, 'Oh, I wish I had a nice black puddin' for me tay!' And it appeared on his plate; upon which his wife said, 'You eejit! I wish it would stick to your nose!' It did. And of course the only way they could get it off was – ?

23

'FOR WHOM THE BELL TOLLS'

The first dead person I ever saw 'laid out' on his own bed was Mr Lee, an old man who lived down Broad Lane opposite our house. There were no funeral parlours in those days, and a corpse, having been ritually washed by neighbouring women and then dressed in the customary habit (a shop in the Parish sold them, brown or black for adults, blue or white for children) still looked very dead, with its yellow face and a rosary beads twined in its white fingers. A strange custom connected with the ritual washing was that the piece of soap used was never used again in the house; it was thrown after the cortège as it moved away from the house. My sister Mar told me that the girls used to be on the watch for that bit of soap and they would snatch it up for use in their pavement games of 'house'.

The way they dicky up the corpse in the fancy funeral parlours today, with cosmetics and other tricks of the trade, and dressed in the best clothes, one would think they were trying to tell you what Our Lord said about the little daughter of Jairus, 'She is not dead but sleeping.' It reminds me of the story about the Limerickman who went to Kilkee for a fortnight's holidays and dropped dead after a week. When he was laid out in the modern style in the funeral parlour in Limerick, in his best suit and the face touched up, two of his old cronies stood looking down at him and one fellow says to the other: 'Bygor, Michael, d'you know what: he's lookin' the better of the week in Kilkee!'

The most important fact about human life, that we all have to die some day, was never hidden from us in our childhood. When anyone in the neighbourhood, or any relation anywhere, died, even the youngest children were brought along to see the corpse and kneel and pray for the soul of the deceased. When poor Mr Lee died my mother brought me, the toddler, along with the others down to the mourning house. And when I saw Mr Lee there on his bed, I was more surprised than fearful, because we had been used to seeing him ambling along, an old man with a white beard and a hard hat and a blackthorn stick, and here he was turned into a Franciscan! I knew that brown robe and the white girdle well from seeing the Franciscans around the town and also from visiting their church in Henry Street. I thought Mr Lee must be some kind of a saint, that God turned him into a Franciscan priest when he died because he had been so holy. My mother explained the mystery to me later on, that Mr Lee had been a member of the Franciscan Third Order for lay people, and they were allowed to wear the habit at their meetings and also to be buried in it.

The first funeral I attended was a very small one, only one carriage, for a very small child, and she was my first cousin, Peggy Bromell, one of my Aunt Dolly's children in Granny Connolly's house in Crosby Row. Her father, Alfie Bromell, had the little white coffin on his knees, and my mother and her sister, Aunt Dolly, and a few other children of the two families, were all packed into the carriage. That was a very sad day, even the children were crying their eyes out. But some funerals were not so sad, if the person was very old and everybody was saying they were just as well off gone to heaven. At funerals like that, we were always likely to get a bottle of lemonade and a few biscuits when the adults were drinking the (eternal) health of the 'ould stock' who had been buried. My mother told us that when she was a child in Arthur's Quay at the turn of the century, old-fashioned wakes were still held, with clay pipes and tobacco and snuff and 'lashin's' of food (often putting the poor family into even more debt, along with the cost of the funeral if they had not kept up the weekly insurance).

We lived in the times before penicillin and antibiotics and other wonderful drugs were discovered. Most people died at a younger age than would be the average today and the death rate in children was much higher, with scarlet fever and typhoid and diphtheria and pneumonia and measles all whipping off children even from the richest of families, although of course the poor suffered more casualties.

As we got bigger, some fellows would be on the lookout for a carriage bringing people back to our streets from a funeral, because when the carriage was going away again they would sit on the bar at the back and get a ride. If the driver noticed, they might get a slash of his long whip. We didn't like to try that, because we knew many of the funeral drivers; they were carmen who knew my father and Uncle Danny and they only drove for the funerals as a sideline, when they were idle from carrying coal or timber or anything else for firms in the city.

The treatment of sickness was a haphazard business. Diseases, apart from measles, meant going into the fever hospital in the City Home. A nurse came to the schools now and again and a doctor about once a year, and sometimes they gave notes to children to tell their mother to take them to the dispensary up in Gerald Griffin Street to get medicine. One nurse who came to the infant school tested our eyes with a chart of letters, and she gave some children a note to go and get glasses. She probably gave it to some fellows who had perfect eyesight but didn't know the alphabet; so my mother said anyway. I got a note but my mother threw it in the fire. 'For the love and honour o' God!' she said, 'that fella can thread a needle for me, and putting glasses on his nose will only make him blind before he gets married!' I was very glad she thought so, because if you got the glasses – they were the steel-rimmed charity glasses, the swanks wore horn-rimmed – all the other fellows called you 'four eyes' and if you fought them and the glasses got broken you were in trouble. I wasn't so lucky in the matter of the dentist, however, and when I got a note from the nurse my mother took me out of school on the day appointed and brought me up to the clinic at St John's Hospital, where Dentist Coogan, a terrible red-faced baldy man, roared at me when I bawled. 'What's wrong with you? I'm not hurting you! Be quiet, be quiet!' And who was the best judge to know was he hurting me or not? But there was a lovely lady of a nun there, one of the Blue Nuns of St John's Hospital, and she was very nice to myself and my mother. They had a little confab about the terrible Coogan and the nun was patting my head and telling me I was a very good boy. Unfortunately I had to go back there a few times more and it was all the worse because I knew what I was in for.

Everyone had to go to the dispensary up in Gerald Griffin Street for medicine if the nurse gave you a note but people could also go to see a doctor if there was anything wrong with them. Like the City Home and Hospital, the dispensary was a leftover from the Victorian idea of health care for the poor. There were rooms along one side of the big hall, with a doctor's name over each door, and forms out from the door at each side. There were two officials, Mr Coffey and Mr Keane, who had to sort out the people and decide which doctor to send you to. After getting a note from the official who asked what you wanted or what was wrong with you – I got tired of hearing my mother explaining every time about my asthmatic chest or the strange pains in my knees and the backs of my legs – you had to sit on one of the forms and wait, shuffling along just like when we went to Confession in the church. I often heard my mother saying that the officials were decent men who treated everybody with fairness and patience but that some of the doctors would never get into heaven because they treated the poor people like dirt. They didn't spend much time examining us, and my mother and the other women used to say that some of them would give you the same prescription for a broken leg, gallstones, consumption or if your ear was hanging off.

When my mother got a prescription from the doctor she had to go in to another section, hand it in and then sit down again with all the other people and wait, wait, wait, until suddenly a shutter in the wall was opened and everybody stopped talking, because there was a man's face in the opening and he was shouting names: 'Murphy! O'Brien! Flynn!' and if you weren't on the 'kee veev', as they said, and didn't hop to it, he might pass on and you'd have to wait till the very end to collect your medicine or pills or whatever. There were three kinds of medicine as far as we knew: red, yellow and white; and all sickness, complaints, injuries and diseases could be cured by the swallowing of some one of them or a combination of two or three. Then there was iodine, the stuff for cuts; it took away the pain of a cut from a stone or a hurley or anything else because it gave you a much worse pain, but they said it killed all the germs and you wouldn't get blood poisoning. We knew about blood poisoning in our family, because my mother's older sister, Mai Connolly, who worked with her in the caramel factory on Charlotte's Quay, died of it. They used to wrap the caramels by hand when my mother started working there at the age of thirteen. Later on machines were brought in (my mother told us that caused the first strike of women workers in Limerick) and it was when she was working on one of the wrapping machines that Mai cut her finger in it. She thought it wasn't bad, so she didn't bother about it. A day or two later the trouble started, her hand and her arm began swelling; she died in the City Home from blood poisoning.

The only thing we liked about going up to the dispensary with our mother was that sometimes when she was waiting for the medicine we went out on the street. There were two undertakers' shops in that street, Griffin's and Cross's. (Mr Cross used to play the big drum in the Sarsfield Band with my father and Uncle Danny, and so it was to him that all the funerals from the families of men in the band went, including our own when Joe and Lily died. The next Cross generation buried my father and mother.) For their games on the pavement in our Island Parish, the girls used to go into the sweet shops and ask the woman had she any empty boxes. They would use these in their own 'shop'; so, while we were waiting for my mother at the dispensary, we used to stand just at the door of Griffin's or Cross's, where you could see the men shaping the coffins, and say, very nicely: 'Mister, have you any empty boxes?' There was one man in Griffin's, an old fellow with a big moustache and an apron and a black hat, and we used to get a great rise out of him. He was a real thorny-wire; he'd come chasing up the street after us with the saw or the hammer waving above his head and shouting what he'd do to us if he caught us!

In all our houses people used cures of their own, like making poultices with bread in hot water to slap on anything that was festering. When we had a cold or a cough in the winter my father would cut up lemons, boil them and make real lemonade with lots of sugar. That would sweat the cold out of you, he said. All the small shops, like Chris O'Brien's in our street, sold powders for headaches and other complaints but there was one medicine we had to take and it must have been invented by the devil himself: senna tea. Some Victorian quack told the mothers of Britain and Ireland that it was essential to give their children a monthly purgative to keep their bowels in order, and he recommended boiling senna leaves and giving the child a cup of the water. It was guaranteed to clear out all the pipes in the little one and leave him or her running around as fresh as a spring lamb – until the pipes got blocked up again with all that rich food (!) and the purgative process must be repeated. One Saturday morning every month we were confronted with this mug of hell's brew by our devoted mother and in spite of all the tears you could squeeze out and swearing you had no 'pains' or anything, you were told, 'Not one bit of this world's food will pass your lips until you drink every drop of that!' It worked all right, it worked too well for the likes of us who were far from being Little Lord Fauntleroys or cossetted bundles of flab. In that Island Parish, as is clear by now, we spent all our free time in the open air running and walking, playing vigorously on the street or in fields, swimming in season, even spasmodically fighting, and although we were not overfed we had good nourishing natural food that kept the natural processes in proper order.

The people in our Parish had more faith in Sister Carmel's dispensary than in the Corporation one up in Gerald Griffin Street. She was one of the nuns in St Mary's but like the nuns over in the City Home, she wasn't a teacher but a nurse or maybe even a doctor. She had a small dispensary near the boys' infant school and she gave out medicines there. She was like an angel, so kind and patient, and the mothers got better advice from her than from the barking bullies of doctors in the other place. One item that she made herself was a pink ointment with a lovely smell that she gave out in little roundy boxes. That ointment was as good as the holy water, my mother said. It was put on everything from a sore to a blister, from a sprained ankle to a pain in the back, and all the people swore by it. I think it was felt that because Sister Carmel was a holy nun, God put a special blessing on that pink ointment. The nuns dispensed more than medicine from that little centre of mercy, and many poor families in the area were helped to survive by the milk and bread and other items that were discreetly put under shawls without any of the rigmarole of dockets or sitting on a seat waiting for your turn to be prodded and sniffed at by the doctors in the city dispensary.

When we got measles or chickenpox it meant a week in

bed at home and then a week getting back to form, so that meant two weeks off school. The first week you'd be sick and not fit for anything, but the second week was a gift – nothing to do but read a book or play cards (if you had anyone to play with). When we were in the primary school my brother Dick got the measles and I heard my mother saying that measles was a contagious disease and that the rest of us would surely get them now and it was just as well for her to get it over with. That night in bed I got my back well up against Dick's back and I said prayers to Saint Anthony and Saint Christopher and many more to give me the measles, please! The next morning my mother examined me – and the miracle had happened! There were a few little red spots starting up here and there on me. I thanked all the heavenly helpers who had arranged such a quick infection (as I thought) and I settled down to endure the few days of fever and then to enjoy the glorious days of recuperation free from school. (We didn't realise that the measles could polish us off as quickly as many other infections.) It was during that second week that our hard-earned holiday was ruined on us.

One day Dick and I were playing draughts on the table in the kitchen. My mother was out shopping but Mrs Sheehan was in her own kitchen keeping an eye on us. There was a knock at the hall door and when Mrs Sheehan opened the door who was standing there but Guard White. This man was the school attendance officer for the whole city; he went around on his bike every day to schools, checking with the principal about absentees. If a pupil was missing for more than a day or two and no explanation had been sent in by a parent, he would call to the house. And if he happened to see a child of schoolgoing age on the street as he cycled around during school hours he would get off the bike and interrogate the stroller. We were all afraid of our lives of Guard White, because he had the power of summoning the parents of anyone under the age of fourteen who was 'mooching' or otherwise not complying with the law of compulsory education.

After the first summons and a warning from the district justice, the next offence could result in the child being taken away from home and committed to Glin Industrial School down the river near Foynes, there to remain until he was sixteen, along with the orphans and juvenile criminals, learning a trade and being beaten 'black and blue' – so we heard from inmates when they came on their summer holidays all dressed up in boots, stockings and rough suits better than they ever were when they were at home. We found out when we grew older that Guard White was, in fact, one of the nicest of all the gardaí in Limerick city and that was why he had been given this job; but we were in such terror of him that even when my father gave us a day off school for the christening of the last arrival in our family, Patrick Joseph (destined to become a school principal in Limerick himself), and presented us with sixpence each to celebrate, we were afraid to go twenty yards up the street to buy sweets at Nonie Mack's shop until we had peeped out a few times and assured ourselves that Guard White was not coming along Nicholas Street on his bicycle!

Apparently, when he called that morning to Quay Lane school, Guard White had been given our names by the headmaster, Brother O'Callaghan, surely by mistake and because the poor brother was probably confused by all his other problems, which included the full-time teaching of his own sixth class. He knew our family well, having had the two older boys, Tom and Joe, in the school before Dick and myself, and he knew both our parents; also, he was a great teacher who was loved by the whole Parish. Whatever about all that, here was the Law at our front door, demanding information as to reasons of long absence from school of Richard and Christopher O'Flynn, brothers, of 2 Old Church Street off Castle Street. So, good Mrs Sheehan acted as foster-mother for us. She called us out and if the measles hadn't succeeded in killing us, the sight of Guard White nearly struck the two of us dead on the spot. It certainly struck us dumb, because we could hardly stammer out an answer when he started on the interrogation. Mrs Sheehan took over and explained the situation and we recovered enough breath to be able to gasp out that our mother had given a note to our neighbour across the road, Seán Daly, to give to Brother O'Callaghan. Guard White finally accepted that Mrs Sheehan and the young O'Flynns were telling the truth but he said that he would check again at the school.

And was that the end of the matter? Remember the incident of the Irish prayer book! When my mother arrived home with her shopping, the poor woman got a shock when she saw our faces. She thought we were having a relapse of the measles and she could see us being carted off in the ambulance to the Fever Hospital. Between Mrs Sheehan and ourselves, she got the story. And just like poor Sister Felicitas, Brother O'Callaghan had a very angry woman to deal with the next morning. And as had happened with the prayer book, although we were appalled at first when she said she was going to the school 'to have it out with him', we did well out of the contretemps in the end, because on her way back from the school she bought cream crackers, our favourite coconut creams and a few big oranges. We had a right party thanks to Guard White and Brother O'Callaghan getting their lines crossed and for the rest of the week we were cock-o'-the-walk and petted even more because of the additional suffering we had endured from *them*.

24

'KNOCK AT THE KNOCKER, RING AT THE BELL'

If in the religious dimension of our lives the feasts of Christmas and Easter were the high points, the pre-Christian culture of our Celtic (and maybe even more distant) ancestors lingered on in three other great festivals. On May Eve we had Bonefire Night (the *Walpurgisnacht* of Goethe's *Faust*), on November Eve we had Hallowe'en, and the day after Christmas, a day dedicated in the Church's calendar to St Stephen, the first martyr, was for us the Wran's (Wren's) Day.

In the early pages of this chronicle I recorded among my first impressions of the world outside our window the sight of that great fire blazing in the middle of the road, and I referred to Douglas Hyde's insistence, in *A Literary History of Ireland*, that 'bonefire' is the correct name, not 'bonfire' (as in common usage nowadays and in the title of one of Seán O'Casey's plays, *The Bishop's Bonfire*). Not only as a matter of general interest, but particularly in view of what happened in our street on the night of the bonefire, it is worth quoting at some length from Hyde's work.

Another druidic practice which is mentioned in [King] Cormac's glossary is more fully treated of by Keating

[Seathrún Céitinn, or Geoffrey Keating, the scholarly priest, poet and historian, 1580–1644] in his account of the great pagan convention at Uisneach, a hill in Meath, 'where the men of Ireland were wont to exchange their goods and their wares and other jewels. This convention was held in the month of May, and at it they were wont to make a sacrifice to the arch-god, whom they adored, whose name was Bél. It was likewise their usage to light two fires to Bél in every district in Ireland at this season, and to drive a pair of each herd of cattle that the district contained between these two fires, as a preservative, to guard them against all diseases of that year. It is from that fire thus made that the day on which the noble feast of the apostles Peter and James is held had been called Bealtaine (in Scotch Beltane), i.e. "Bél's fire".'

In a footnote to this passage, Hyde adds:

The Christian priests, apparently unable to abolish these cattle ceremonies, took the harm out of them by transferring them to St John's Eve, the 24th of June, where they are still observed in most districts of Ireland, and large fires built with bones in them, and occasionally cattle are driven though them or *people leap over them* [my italics, for later reference]. The cattle were probably driven through the fire as a kind of substitute for their sacrifice and the bones burnt in the fire are probably a substitute for the bones of the cattle that should have been offered up. Hence the fires are called *tine cnámh* (bone-fire) in Irish, and *bone-fire* (not bonfire) in English.

Bonefire Night and the witches of the *Walpurgisnacht* have been amalgamated with Hallowe'en in Dublin and many other places (St Walpurgis, who had nothing to do with the witches' festival except that her feastday coincided with it, has at least a legitimate claim to be included in Hallowe'en) but for us in Limerick in the early 1930s it was the public social ceremony marking the beginning of summer on May Eve (and most readers will remember from their school lessons that Bealtaine, which Keating tells us means 'the fire of the god, Bél', is the Irish name for the month of May). For a few weeks before May Eve, the boys of our enclave went from house to house collecting fuel of all kinds for the fire, or money in lieu thereof, singing at every door:

> The First of May is a very fine day
> Something for the Bone-fire!
> A piece of stick or a piece of coal,
> A ha'penny will not break your soul.
> Knock at the knocker, ring at the bell –
> And give us a pinny for singin' so well!

Every house, even the poorest, contributed something, literally 'a piece of stick or a piece of coal' or a ha'penny or a penny – perhaps there was an old superstition that it was unlucky not to do so. From the local shops, and from the fathers who worked in certain factories or other likely sources, timber boxes or other material was contributed. Any money collected by our door-to-door efforts was spent in our local shops on sweets, biscuits and lemonade for the big night but that meagre store was generously supplemented by the adults, whose own hearts were gladdened by an offering of stout and *uisce beatha* from our local Halpin's pub. Because our bonefire was built in the middle of the street, between the front door of our house and the wide opening of Broad Lane opposite, it was not constructed in the pyramidal fashion seen nowadays when Hallowe'en fires are situated on some open space of waste ground. Our bonefire was one of quality rather than quantity but of a goodly size and maintained as the night wore on.

On the night itself the people brought out chairs and stools and placed them in a wide circle round the unlit mound. An elderly woman would then be asked to light the fire. The local musicians, my father with the saxophone, Tom Glynn with the violin, and Granny Duffy with a melodeon, got into gear, and the food and drink, along with our purchased goodies, were distributed generously. Fine individual voices contributed solo songs and other songs were sung in unison by the whole gathering as the fire burned high and bright. On that night, we might well have been a tribe isolated from all the rest of humanity, and it is with some wonder, considering the extent of vandalism today, that I recall no incident of misdemeanour or dissension among young or old during all those long hours while the celebration (or ceremony?) went on. It was as if something in our genes, or some spirits of our ancestors returning to participate in the bonfire ritual, told us that this was not just a party but a religious ceremony. And it was when the supply of fuel finally began to peter out, and the fire to die down, that the remnants of that ancient religious ceremony manifested themselves.

When the older people had taken themselves and the small children off to bed, and the chairs and stools were being taken back into the houses, some of the bigger boys would go back down the street, to about the gate of the Protestant churchyard, and then run up to the fire and jump over the now lessening flames. And as the fire went even lower, some of the big girls would dare to imitate their brothers. This is why I have italicised the words *people leap over them* in Douglas Hyde's account of the bonfires. In later years, I read that this was actually a fertility rite which was practised in Celtic countries in pre-Christian times; at the time, of course, we thought it was just another dare and the smaller boys were envious of their big brothers who could do it. I often wonder if the priests and the bishop knew or cared about this practice; surely the spirit of poor old

Mainchín must have frowned on those neo-pagan fire-leapers almost on the very site of his first church!

There was still another custom to be observed, one not mentioned by Hyde. When the fire had become a low mound of glowing embers, my mother would say to one of us, 'Go in home and get the shovel.' This was the small fireside shovel for taking out ashes. Like every other mother on the street, my mother took a shovelful of the bonefire's embers and placed them in our own grate, with the comment, 'With the help of God now, we won't be without a fire for the coming year.' And the God in her prayer was not the old Celtic Bél, even if she was unwittingly performing a ritual that had been part of his worship.

Hallowe'en in our society was not a public festival, but a domestic one, celebrated by each family in the privacy of the home. We didn't even call it Hallowe'en – our name for it was 'Snap-Apple Night'. Nor were we aware that the name meant 'the Eve of All Saints' – in spite of our daily recitation of the Lord's Prayer, which included the phrase 'hallowed be thy name'.

On the Saturday before Snap-Apple Night my mother made a special trip to the market to buy a big supply of apples and nuts, and for each of us she bought what she and Granny and everyone else called an 'eye-fiddle', a Hallowe'en mask. It was only when we met our excellent teachers in the primary school in Quay Lane that we were able to delight the folks at home with the news that this was another piece of 'pure' Irish, *aghaidh fidil*, surviving in colloquial speech from former centuries; who knows but the term might go as far back as the fires of the god Bél? My father made the 'snap-apple' which gave the night its name. This consisted of two lengths of wood, one of them pointed at both ends, which were nailed together crosswise; on the two pointed ends he stuck half an apple, on the unpointed ends he put a stump of candle. The 'snap-apple' was then hung, by a cord attached to its centre, from a hook in the ceiling, my father gave it a spin and we, gathered in a ring, had to try to *snap* one of the apple pieces with our mouth, hands behind the back. I wonder if there was some origin in ancient pagan rituals for this also, as for the bonefire practices?

For the tea on that night there was the special barmbrack – a name that is another survivor from long ago: *báirín breac* means literally 'a small speckled loaf', i.e. a loaf with currants or something similar. Traditionally, the *báirín breac* should contain three tokens, a ring, a small piece of cloth, and a chip of wood. It was carefully sliced and the pieces kept together on the plate so that these items could not be seen, and then whoever got the slice with the ring would be the first of the family to marry, whoever got the piece of cloth would be the first to die (the cloth representing the burial shroud), and whoever got the chip of wood was destined to emigrate (the wood symbolising a ship). So the tokens were traditionally interpreted, but many mothers, including ours, would not tempt Fate by including the piece of cloth in their ominous recipe.

In addition to the centrepiece of the snap-apple, we played other games such as trying to scoop up small coins with the tongue from a basin of water and 'putting a tail on the donkey' in which something more or less like a donkey was drawn on a sheet of paper and pinned on the inside of the door; the donkey, however, like a Manx cat, had no tail, and the object of the exercise was for the player to add a tail at the appropriate anatomical point on the animal while blindfolded. The resulting additions were a cause of great hilarity even to the unsuccessful competitor who had put a tail on the donkey's ear or back left ankle or even a few inches above his head. And when we tired of the games, we sat around the fire and worked on the nuts and apples while resorting to our customary telling of stories, recitation of riddles and general raking over the old embers of traditional lore and legend.

We did not realise it at the time, but we were living in

the last age before radio and television changed, and changed utterly, the domestic life as it had been lived since the time of our prehistoric cave-dwelling ancestors. When the stone was rolled to the cave's opening, or when we closed the front door at night, each family was on its own, depending on its own members for entertainment and discussion, for looking back on the past and planning the future; nowadays, that google-box in the corner and that radio on the shelf bring all sorts of intruders through the walls to spout their views on life at the occupants, to cajole them into buying goods they don't really need, to silence their conversation and inhibit their discussion, and to stultify their own powers of entertainment with endless hours of the products, good, bad and indifferent, of the commercial entertainment factories.

I should record here that the first time I remember hearing the radio was on the day of the All-Ireland hurling final in September 1934, when Limerick drew with Dublin, and the second time was a few weeks later when Limerick won. On both occasions I was sitting on the pavement with other children outside the open window of our neighbours, the McCoys; the old men and most of our mothers were packed into the kitchen; our fathers, having by hook or by crook scraped the few bob together, were gone up to Dublin on the special cheap trains. At that time, the only non-domestic entertainment in our house was that small gramophone with its pile of heavy 78 rpm records and smaller 45s. John McCormack and Fritz Kreisler *et al*, far from having a deleterious effect on our domestic culture, were so beloved and familiar as to be almost familial. It would be nearly ten years more before the first radio-set came to put an end to domestic civilisation as we had known it on our hearth, and then its arrival was not the exciting event it would normally have been. My father bought a secondhand set somewhere, the only one he could afford, in order to try to brighten the final months of life for my sister Lily, who was then in the final stages of tuberculosis and facing death with a cheerful

222

resignation that was and still is a mystery to all who knew her. She even made jokes about the good nuns after their weekly charitable visit when they brought her a few eggs that made up, Lily said, for all the prayers they said with her! Like my brother, Joe, she asked only to be allowed to die at home rather than be taken into the new sanatorium at the City Home, which, in those early years of the TB scourge, was regarded as more like a deathhouse than a hospital.

In that pre-television age, even on Christmas Day there was no reason for staying up much beyond midnight, and so on the following morning, St Stephen's Day, people were up not much later than on an ordinary working day. And the first sound to be heard on the streets on that morning was the song of the Wran Boys.

As with all other such activities, I was pleading for permission to 'folly the wran' for a few years before I was allowed by my parents or accepted by the local lads, including my own older brothers. Over the years, I graduated in office until in the final year before we moved house I was the leader of the troops; but even by then the old custom was on its last legs, due to a combination of social developments and the fact that adult groups of Wran Boys in the city, who collected in the pubs where we would not even be allowed to sniff inside the door, used to get drunk and disorderly, sometimes even clashing with rival groups in the continuation of old feuds.

On St Stephen's Day we rose with the dawn and fortified ourselves with a good plate of porridge for the day's traipsing around from house to house and from street to street. Then we blackened our faces with soot from the chimney, dressed in our sisters' cast-off skirts or father's cut-down long trousers, with coloured scarves and old headgear of any kind, and armed ourselves with a few branches of holly from over the pictures in the kitchen. The gang gathered on the street, usually with one or two mouth-organ players in the group, and the leader decided on the route to be followed, beginning with our own street. An important consideration was not to encroach on the territory of any other group; this could lead to a clash like those which were causing the gardaí to be preoccupied with the adult groups.

The song that was standard all over Ireland, I suppose, was always our first effort:

The wran, the wran, the king of all birds,
Saint Stephen's Day was caught in the bush.
Up with the kittle and down with the pan
And give us our answer and let us be gane.

Our repertoire continued with the following verses (note the adaptation to local use in one of them) and after each verse – banging louder on the door that had not yet been opened – we sang the same refrain we used when collecting for the Bonefire:

Knock at the knocker, ring at the bell,
An' give us a pinny for singin' so well!

We followed the Wran three miles and more,
Three miles and more, three miles and more,
We followed the Wran three miles and more
On a cold and frosty mornin'.

The little Wran he was so funny,
He caught in a bush while we were runnin'.
Up with our sticks an' we gev him a blow
An' we hurled him down to Crosby Row.

Now 'tis all too plain to see,
Too plain to see, too plain to see,
Now 'tis all too plain to see
An' we'll hang him up in a holly tree.

We follied the Wran from block to block,
We chased him into a porter shop,
We dipped his head in a barrel o' beer –
An' we wish ye all a Happy New Year!

Our own mothers, of course, were the first to make a tinkle in our collection box, and as we went farther afield we sometimes had to back off from hostile groups; but all in all, by the time we returned to base, leg-weary and needing to assuage the soreness of throat, we had enjoyed our carrying out of the old custom and we had a fund sufficient to provide a party in the house of one or other of the Old Church Street Wran Boys. A single incident that stays in my mind from one of our Wran's Day expeditions occurred as we were passing by King John's Castle and wondering if it would be safe to venture across Thomond Bridge into the territory of the Soda Cakes. (We decided against it; to us, that was highly hostile Apache country on occasions like this – as will be seen from a later incident.) While we held our pow-wow at the castle side of the bridge, we saw a white-bearded old man in a heavy black overcoat and hat coming slowly from the Thomondgate side, leaning on a stick. Such passers-by were fair game just as much as the householders; so, we surrounded him and struck up with one of our songs. He seemed to be somewhat critical of our performance and when we finished he spoke to us in Irish, in an accent like some of those Kerry student teachers in the infant school. All we could say was, '*Níl fhios agam*,' and '*Ní thuigim thú, a dhuine uasail*,' the negatives which had been drilled into us for use when an inspector's question was totally unintelligible. The old man spoke slower, obviously choosing his words to suit our limitations in the ancestral tongue. We comprehended: he was asking us if we had any Irish song for the Wran. We had none. He shook his old head then and let another blast out of him, plainly a lamentation for what had happened to Ireland and the Irish (both people and language). And then he produced a little purse and gave us a *flóirín*, as he called it, a lovely shiny two-shilling piece with a fine Irish salmon leaping on it, the biggest single contribution we had got in the whole of that Wran's Day.

The memory of that silver *flóirín* brings to mind the coin my mother put in our hands on occasions like the first Monday of the year or when anyone was starting out in a new job. 'There's a bit of hansel for you, *a stór*,' she said. She told us it would bring us good luck; in our eyes, it made a welcome practical addition to her lovely salutation, 'God speed you now, *a stór*,' and the holy water she sprinkled on us from the little font beside the door.

25

PICNICS, POEMS AND PLAYS

It was our next-door neighbour, Mrs Nealon, a grand, homely, *grá-mo-chroí* woman, who was the organiser of the street picnics. She was a native of Sixmilebridge out near Cratloe Woods and I suppose she felt the call of the open fields much more than our mothers who had grown up in the city. After Mass and breakfast on a Sunday morning in summer, many of the mothers and children would set off, with the kettles and the baskets containing cups and provisions for the day divided among the bigger boys and girls.

We must have looked like a small tribe of migrating Indians as we straggled along by the castle, across Thomond Bridge, and headed for the Clare Hills, the mothers chatting among themselves, the children grouping naturally according to age and sex. The road led from the last houses in Thomondgate up over the railway bridge and on out past the Delmege estate (now a housing estate called Moyross). Our family were always a bit hushed passing by the big iron gates of Delmege's, because we knew from my father that the son of that family, Captain Delmege of the Munster Fusiliers, had been wounded and captured by the Germans on the same day, 10 November 1917, in that very same attack at Passchendaele in which our Uncle Tom had been killed.

Sometimes, as we headed on out the dusty country road, we were reminded again of the Great War by seeing one of the living casualties shuffling along the road towards us, looking like a tramp in old clothes and soiled tennis shoes. This man, whom we called Captain Roche-Kelly, belonged to one of the 'up-the-town' families in Limerick. He had been shellshocked in France and since then he lived in a hut up in Cappanty Woods (one of the venues for our picnic outings) and only ventured into the city, speaking to nobody, to collect provisions at a shop where the family had an account for him.

We walked for about three miles before turning off at Brennan's Cross (so called from the nearby house of the Brennan family, who had been active in the Anglo-Irish struggle) and going down a few hundred yards more to our favourite spot not far from the village of Meelick, known as the Blaych (Bleach), a grassy mound overlooking a small stream, beside which there was a disused limekiln. It was probably the place where in previous times sheets and other linen were left out to bleach, a custom that has given its name to the County Limerick village of Toornafulla (*Tuar na Fola*, meaning 'the bloody bleaching-green', an indication that on some day long ago something other than linen was spread out on that green field). The women settled on the grass while we got down to playing all around the place and paddling in the stream. Some of the bigger boys had dammed the stream sufficiently to make a small pond, and it was there that the toddlers began to learn that a human being is related to a fish by being held flat out in the water and given the first lessons in swimming. Brambles and dead wood were collected from the hedges for the stone-enclosed fires, and when the kettles were singing, each mother called, like the hen clucking her chickens to her. Everyone knows who has consumed it with an appetite sharpened by fresh air and vigorous exercise, that the mug of tea made like that and accompanied with well-buttered hunks of bread, is a more enjoyable meal than any fancy stuff in even the finest restaurants.

So the day passed, with more games and splashing in the stream, and a second repast later to finish off the provisions. And then we gathered up our bags and baskets. There were no plastics bottles or cups in those days, and the only litter we could have left was the paper the food had been wrapped in; but our mothers were both tidy and economical, and so the bleaching-green by the stream was always left as we had found it. There was a small bridge where the road crossed the stream, and on some Sundays a man with a melodeon came there and we sat around enjoying the music and the sight of our mothers joining in the dancing with the local people. (Those traditional merry-makings 'at the crossroads' were also found by the Irish bishops to be unChristian occasions of sin and were duly banned, like the dances in the halls during Lent.) We sang all the way as we walked home in the cool of the evening.

On Sundays in summer, when a street picnic had not been planned, my mother took us on a family picnic to Fairy Hill near Parteen – still an isolated village then – or to the Church Fields beside the river in Corbally – another green area that has since been covered with houses. My father never came with us; he would have been working late the night before, and would as usual have barely managed to struggle to the last Mass at twelve noon, a weekly occurrence that caused my mother to chide him jokingly about being late and giving bad example to the children: 'You'll be late for your own funeral,' she said, 'and you'll be late at the gate of heaven itself!' Dad countered this by claiming that, as a saxophonist, he would be warmly welcomed by St Peter no matter when he arrived, as a change from all those harp-twanging angels! No matter how late he had been at the coal drudgery the night before, if he had no dance engagement on Sunday night my father would go over to the stables in Watergate around Angelus time in the evening, tackle up the horse, and come out to take us home in style – after he too had enjoyed a mug of tea *al fresco*!

It was my brother Joe that brought out the poet in me, in emulation of his own poems and especially of his prize-winning piece in the *Irish Press*. I became addicted to the point where I had a copybook almost full of verses on all sorts of topics and themes. These have been lost to posterity and all I can remember is the opening stanza of one of them, perhaps it was my first, which was inspired by a butterfly and went like this:

> I see a butterfly upon a stalk,
> A wondrous thing with wings of golden hue,
> And as with dainty mincing tread it walks
> I can but say: 'How beautiful are you!'

I have studied many a butterfly since but never seen one walking, even with 'dainty mincing tread'. But I give 'the boy the Flynns' some credit, he at least had a grasp of metre and rhyme (no wonder, having been exposed to the recitation of poems since he was a baby). And *wondrous* and *golden hue* indicate that he must have been reading a lot already; nobody in the Island Parish uttered such weird language.

My poems became a cause of acute embarrassment for me one day when the charitable nuns were visiting, and one of them happened to be my old teacher, Sister Felicitas. When she asked my mother how I was getting on in the primary school, the poor woman let the cat out of the bag by mentioning that not only was I doing very well but that I was also writing 'lovely' poems. The nuns asked to see them, and I had to produce the box in which I kept all such items, including my illustrated *History of Ireland* and ditto *Life of Our Lord*, both works dating from my red-pimple period – when I was recovering from the measles fever, and probably still suffering from hallucinations, I asked my mother to supply me with a pencil (the ballpoint had not been invented), some crayons, and two copybooks, in which I executed the above works, now lost with those poems of my primary school period.

Having stood like an eejit in front of those two nuns, reading some of my poems about topics like that 'wondrous thing with wings of golden hue', and having watched the two of them charitably pretending to admire my coloured illustrations of the life of Christ and of selected scenes from the history of Ireland, I resolved that the material responsible for my agony would have to be destroyed. Posterity be damned! said I, or something similar and suited to my vocabulary, as I tore up those copies and consigned them to the flames a few days later when my mother was out and 'the coast was clear'.

My career as a juvenile playwright lasted a bit longer. It was one of the Nealon girls next door, Breda, who was instrumental in introducing me to the art of theatre when she organised, as the girls sometimes did in a variation from their usual street games, a 'concert', imitating the shows which were a common feature of life in every parish in those years. This performance, which would be put on in someone's backyard in summer, or in the house itself in winter, comprised songs, sketches, dancing and recitations. I was brought along to the concert in the Nealons' house by my sisters. Although I understood very little of the entertainment, I was happy that night for a different reason – I was sitting close beside another of the Nealon girls, a younger girl named Áine, who was the first love of my life at that tender age of about three. She was not, however, the first of the daughters of Eve to kiss me; that experience came from another blonde – I seem to have had a precocious predilection for blondes, although eventually I married a brunette – who was my first cousin, Mary Bromell.

One evening the Granny Connolly arrived at our house with the two eldest of the Bromell children from Crosby Row, little Mary and her older brother, my namesake, Christy (who died in his teens, like our Joe, but from blood poisoning, just like his mother's and our mother's sister, Mai, after her accident in the caramel factory). She was no sooner taking off her shawl than she ordered any of us who were in the kitchen to clear out and play with our Bromell cousins on our street ('And not be sittin' there with yere ears cocked listenin' to every word we're saying!'). When someone dared to pipe up that it was actually raining out there on Old Church Street, we were instructed to 'play in the hall so, can't ye?', the hall being the narrow tiled passageway between the front door and the stairs. (There must have been some very important matter to be discussed at our fireside that evening.) We sat on the wooden stairs, and poor little me began to cry; I suppose I felt that my mother loved that old Granny more than me. And it was then that my affectionate little blonde cousin, Mary, put her arms around me and told me not to cry and gave me a big *smathán*. And it's a wonder her usual 'two wings of a bird' didn't poison the Granny Connolly that night, what with all the terrible things her young grandchildren were saying about her out there on the stairs in the cold hall while she and my mother held their conference at the warm fireside. Eventually, there were as many children in the Bromell family as in our own, except that little Peggy died. All the other girls, like Mary, grew up blonde and beautiful, surely breaking many a heart far afield from Crosby Row.

Inevitably, my writing of poems and stories led to the writing of plays. These were largely influenced by the films we were seeing, swashbuckling as in *The Three Musketeers* and our namesake, Errol Flynn, in *Robin Hood*, or horror stories like *The Hound of the Baskervilles*. I had no trouble gathering a company from among the boys and girls of my own age and younger, and as our Uncle Danny had recruited my father to play the piccolo in the Sarsfield Band, I conscripted my younger brother, Maurice, as an actor who could be trusted to learn his lines, turn up for rehearsals, and follow the director's instructions faithfully and without querulous objection. (As every director knows, actors can be so troublesome – they *will* have their own ideas.) The director of my plays was the only person the author thought capable of that task: himself. I also designed and made the tickets (from cardboard) and the publicity leaflets (from the pages of an exercise copy). The big problem was that we had no theatre; our yard was a small one and was further reduced by having two sheds built in it. One of my company, a classmate and one of my best pals, Eric Woodrow, who lived down the road leading into the Island Field, had a much bigger yard behind his house and he negotiated its use with his mother. She kindly agreed to let us use her yard on Saturday afternoon but, Eric reported to me glumly, on condition that we put his two smaller brothers in the show! We got over that problem by giving them walk-on parts – they were barely able to walk anyway.

Being both author and director, it might be thought that I would not be inclined to act as well; but the whole point of the exercise, as far as I was concerned, was the opportunity to dress up and be Robin Hood or a musketeer or someone of that heroic ilk. And so I had to take on the leading role in all of my plays, slaying my unfortunate brother Maurice on several occasions after desperate bouts of fencing with wooden swords. From the commercial point of view, my plays were a great success. All the neighbours and relations bought tickets – a penny for adults, a ha'penny for children – but on the night (or I should say the Saturday afternoon) no adults were able to come and get value for their money, all being otherwise engaged at housework or shopping or at rugby matches.

And so our audience consisted entirely of a mob of kids

whose mothers had bought them tickets just to get them out of the way, and who only wanted to see somebody getting clobbered and who kept talking and screeching and shouting inane comments at the actors – especially at the walk-ons – all through my carefully constructed pieces. Thus I learned early in my career how my fellow-dramatist, Shakespeare, could feel so frustrated at having to please the groundlings. My works, too, were 'caviare to the general'. And speaking of caviare reminds me that, as with the bonefire fund, we also had a party on the Sunday after our Saturday one-and-only performance. Even at what should have been a pleasant function where author and cast would relax after their artistic endeavours, there was trouble after my first play when some of the minor players, probably disgruntled anyway, accused me of giving the nicest sweets and biscuits and more of the lemonade to my brother and myself and one or two of our special pals. They were right too, but surely the author/director and the principals were entitled to more of the goodies? Anyway, they announced that they would refuse to take part in any future works of mine. That didn't knock a feather out of me or my supporters – after all, minor players could be found on the street at any time!

Like the poems of my early period, and like those works of illustrated history and gospel that my loving mother unwittingly caused me to destroy, none of the plays of my Woodrow's backyard period have survived. I probably tore up the pages of each script after the performance, already thinking forward to the next one.

26

THE SCHOOL AROUND THE CORNER

The Convent of Mercy schools were just around the corner of Halpin's pub from our street but the boys considered that those schools were really for girls who went on as far as seventh class in the primary school. Secondary education for girls was not available there until a Secondary Top was opened in 1943. The boys' infant school was regarded as a place where we had life easy for a while before we went on to the real school, that of the Monks (the original name by which the Irish Christian Brothers were colloquially known and which was still in use).

In our day, the Brothers had four parish primary schools: St Mary's in our Parish, St Munchin's in Thomondgate, St John's in the Irishtown and St Michael's in Sexton Street. There was only one secondary school to which pupils from all four primary schools could graduate. This also was in Sexton Street, in the same grounds as St Michael's primary school and the central residence of the Brothers. Among the thousands of workers walking to their jobs every morning, the Brothers who taught in the outlying parish schools could be seen as they hurried off in pairs to their own daily labour in the cause of the Christian education of the youth of Ireland.

The Brothers' primary school in our Island Parish was around another corner from our street, in Quay Lane, directly across the road from the gate of St Mary's Cathedral. This historic edifice, like the two cathedrals in Dublin, Christ Church and St Patrick's, was built in the thirteenth century but was confiscated by the Protestant state religion in the sixteenth century. Our school was originally the courthouse, built in 1764 and taken over for use as a school by the brothers in 1845. The most famous trial held in the old courthouse was that of an ex-lieutenant in the Royal Marines, John Scanlan, a member of a wealthy county family, for the seduction and murder of the fifteen-year-old Ellen Hanly, the beautiful girl who was to be immortalised as the 'Colleen Bawn' (*cailín bán*, 'fair-haired girl'). And it was a young Limerickman named Gerald Griffin, sitting in the court-house to report the trial for the local paper (counsel for the defence was none other than Daniel O'Connell), who, as we have noted, was to make her tragedy into the novel, *The Collegians*. From Griffin's novel the prolific and patriotic actor-manager-playwright Dion Boucicault (1820–90) derived *The Colleen Bawn*, one of the most successful of his 150 plays. A third version of the tragedy of Ellen Hanly was the opera, *The Lily of Killarney*, by the anglicised German composer, Julius Benedict (1804–85). He transferred the action of the story to Killarney, with the result that the Killarney jarveys driving tourists around the Lakes now point out the 'Colleen Bawn Rock where the famous Colleen Bawn was drowned'. How anyone could be drowned on a rock only a Kerryman could explain.

After some success in London where he had gone in the hope of achieving fame in the literary world, Gerald Griffin, like St Augustine, St Alphonsus and many another, became disillusioned with all worldly glory. He burnt his manuscripts and returned to Ireland, where he joined the Christian Brothers in 1838. Just two years later he died in Cork, where he is buried beside the Lee rather than near his beloved Shannon, about which he had written some beautiful verses.

In 1904, when the centenary of Gerald Griffin's birth was being celebrated in Limerick, the citizens decided that the reconstruction of the old courthouse school in Quay Lane would be a fitting memorial to him. And so the renovated school was named the Gerald Griffin Memorial School and a bust of the writer was placed in a niche high up in the façade under the title. In the Parish, however, although everyone knew the story of the Colleen Bawn and the history of our school, it was still called, as it had been before the reconstruction, Quay Lane School ('quay' had the old pronunciation, *kay*).

All through our years at the nuns' infant school, where the cane and the stick were used mostly to maintain discipline or to punish misdemeanour, we had been warned by our older brothers of the dreadful daily horrors in the 'Monks', where, they assured us, every Christian Brother and lay teacher was armed with a leather strap and/or a cane, with which we would be beaten on even the slightest pretext, and especially for 'missing' our Catechism. But just as my sisters had brought me to concerts and processions in their school and in the convent grounds, where I had met some nuns, so my brothers had taken me to the Sunday 'class', as it was called, when the Monks trotted all the way down from their residence in Sexton Street to give a half-hour's religious instruction in the school. (Attendance at this was not compulsory.) In that way I had already met Brother O'Callaghan, the headmaster, who was known as 'Monkey' because of his somewhat crimped features, and Brother O'Reilly, a black-haired, stocky, lively young brother from County Cavan who presented me, at one of the Sunday classes, with a three-inch 'nail' fashioned from silver paper. I put that piece of magic along with my other treasures in my special box and it helped to alleviate whatever apprehension I might have felt at the thought of moving from the mother-hen care of Sister Felicitas for her flock to the no-nonsense milieu of the Brothers' primary school.

Nevertheless, on my first day as a pupil in that historic Gerald Griffin Memorial School in 1935, I got a disconcerting shock and was reminded again that answering too many questions in school can sometimes have unpleasant repercussions. The final class in the nuns' school was the equivalent of first standard in the primary, and so the Brothers' school began with second standard. On our first day in the school, the headmaster, Brother O'Callaghan, told me that I was being put in *third* class because Sister Felicitas had advised him to let me skip second. Apart from separating me from my classmates of the convent school, this was the cause of one of the extracurricular problems I was to have for some years after, that of being the smallest in my class and therefore prone to unwelcome attention in the school yard from the more aggressive of the boolums. Fortunately, I had two brothers in the classes above me and in the school yard this proved the truth of the Irish proverb, *Is maol guala gan bhráthair*, best translated as 'A brotherless shoulder is vulnerable.'

Unlike the convent school where each class had a room of its own, in Quay Lane the building was divided into four large rooms, two on each floor. An architectural peculiarity of the building was that there was no internal staircase leading from the ground floor to the upper storey. In the middle of the school yard, an incongruous red-painted iron stairs, with a right-angle bend at the halfway landing, led to a door in the centre of the upper storey. In spite of frequent stern admonitions, the rush down that stairs when the pupils were released can be imagined, and the lower part of the structure, especially the four iron pillars supporting the landing, were a constant source of business for the nearby Barrington's Hospital. Pupils chasing or fighting in the yard regularly crashed into pillars or stairs and were duly dispatched with a minder to have their split forehead or poll bandaged by the nurses in Barrington's.

There were two classes, seated in long benches at right angles to each other, in each room except the headmaster's, making seven in all, some classes being doubled (two fourths, two fifths). Although it was a Christian Brothers school, the staff, as was usual in all the schools owned by religious orders at that time, had more lay teachers than Brothers, three of the latter as opposed to four lay teachers (whose names I record, as I did with the Sarsfield Band: Teddy Kavanagh, John Liddy, Mícheál Ó Tuathaigh, Bob Crean). My first teacher, in third class, was one of the Brothers, a tall, curly-haired, bespectacled man named Murphy, but he was transferred to Belfast shortly after and replaced by a substitute lay teacher, Jack Danaher, a small, dark-haired and very friendly young man. By a strange twist of Fate, nearly twenty years later, when I was myself doing a six-month stint as a substitute teacher in the primary school in Sexton Street in 1952, Jack Danaher was teaching in the room next to mine, and his son Brian was in my class – and one of the stars in an Irish musical play I wrote for performance along with the secondary school's production of Wallace's ever-popular *Maritana* (in my own schooldays I had figured as one of the courtiers in another production of the same opera).

How those teachers in Quay Lane School taught us in those crowded classrooms is a mystery to me, but teach they did and with great dedication and professional skill. They were under constant harassment not only from the inspectors of the Department of Education, who could grade teachers as efficient, non-efficient, or highly efficient, gradings which had a serious effect on their already meagre salaries, but also from the diocesan examiner in religious knowledge, a priest appointed by the bishop in each diocese to carry out an annual examination of prayers and Catechism in every school.

In this annual inquisition, every child in a class was asked a question from the prescribed book – the most non-educational compilation of theological conundrums and verbal jaw-breakers ever imposed on children anywhere. Even the dullest pupil in a class might be asked something like – I use as an example the question I was asked when the bishop himself examined us in St Mary's Church to judge if we were fit to receive the Holy Spirit and his seven gifts in the sacrament of Confirmation – 'What is hope?' and he was expected to chant out, without hesitation: 'Hope is a divine virtue by which we firmly trust that God will give us eternal life and the means to obtain it.' That was bad enough, especially for a poor slow-witted pupil who might not be able to memorise the basic tables in arithmetic or four lines of a poem. He could have fared even worse by being asked to define the sins against hope: despair and presumption. The answer to the latter was: 'Presumption is the foolish expectation of salvation without making proper use of the necessary means to obtain it.' Incidentally, I quote these answers from memory, as I learned them off by heart in our little room in Old Church Street, asking my mother or one of my sisters to 'examine me in my Kadiksum, will you?' Imagine the unfortunate children struggling to memorise, not only the Our Father – a prayer which was composed by Our Divine Lord for his adult disciples – but a separate theological definition for each phrase in that prayer. (e.g. 'What do we mean when we say "hallowed by thy name"?')

Any pupil who failed to answer was marked as a zero, and schools were graded according to percentages in answering. Is it any wonder that the daily half-hour devoted to the Catechism became one of the most dreaded in the school day, or that the teachers, fearful of the repercussions for themselves, had to use corporal punishment to frighten their pupils into trying to memorise the answers to the hundreds of questions. (There were over 400 pre-scribed for the sixth standard in the primary school.) That inquisitorial system of religious instruction must have caused many a pupil in later life mistakenly to confuse the Catholic

Church founded by our Divine Lord Jesus Christ with what some of the officials of that Church do, whether through mistaken zeal or human stupidity, and in consequence to give up their membership of the Church, thus adding self-inflicted spiritual punishment to the mental and physical punishment they suffered in school.

In third class, Jack Danaher carried on the Sister Felicitas practice of putting us in for the *feis*, but only in a play in Irish for a drama competition. My previous experience in school and street plays and concerts got me the leading role, and my parents, like those of the other lads in the cast, although knowing no Irish, still came to support us on the night when the plays were staged in St Michael's Temperance Hall, where we got no prize higher than the commendation *an-mhaith* (very good). Like Sister Felicitas also, Jack Danaher unwittingly caused me mental anguish and general perturbation of spirit at the end of my year in his class. On the first day back after the summer holidays, we moved upstairs to the room where the two fourth standards were located, one taught by John Liddy and the other by my genial magician of the silver nail, Brother Michael O'Reilly from Cavan. The group who had been in Mr Danaher's third class were now to be Mr Liddy's fourth class, but when he made the initial roll-call, one name was missing from his book – mine. After some consultation with Brother O'Reilly, he told me that I was in the wrong room. I had been put into fifth class by the headmaster on Mr Danaher's recommendation. My first impulse was to run out the door and away home. But the Granny Connolly in nearby Crosby Row shook out her black shawl and called to me in spirit, 'Enough is enough! Consplawkus to you, me boy, and remember: "A dumb priest loses his dues." Open your mouth now, *a stór*, and fight your corner! *Sinn Féin amháin!*'

Forthwith I opened the gob and appealed to be allowed to stay where I was. I told Mr Liddy and Brother O'Reilly that I had already skipped second class and I wanted now to stay with my pals from third class. They held a further little pow-wow, and then Mr Liddy, who had taught my eldest brother, Tom, looked sharply at me and asked: 'Are you anything to Tom Flynn that I had in my class a few years ago?'

'I'm his brother, sir!' I almost shouted, seeing that Tom's good performance was rubbing off on myself.

'And you'd rather stay here in Fourth Class, is that it?' (putting the words into my mouth!).

'Oh yessir, I want to stay here, please!' He went into the headmaster's room next door, where Brother O'Callaghan was probably trying to sort out, on this first day of the term, many more urgent problems than in which class the latest young Flynn from Old Church Street wanted to continue his education. When Mr Liddy returned with a benign smile on his lean countenance, I knew Granny Connolly was right: 'A dumb priest loses his dues' – although it will be remembered that on other occasions she was likely to warn me in spirit that 'A shut mouth catches no flies.'

I spent three years with John Liddy. (Among themselves, the Parish lads always called him Luke Liddy, a name he was given because, it was said, in the Liddy clan there were members named Mark, Matthew, and another John; so, some wag decided that the Liddys might as well have the complete evangelistic quartet, and the John who was our teacher became known as Luke!) He was undoubtedly one of the finest teachers I have ever known – he subsequently became principal of the Model School in Dublin, a prestigious position for which there would have been highly-qualified applicants from all over Ireland. Over the three years we spent under his tutelage we were given a solid grounding in all the academic subjects. In retrospect, I feel that he did not relish the statutory two half-hour sessions of drill and games in the school yard which were then the physical education component in the curriculum.

At that time there was a Primary Certificate Examination

at the end of sixth standard in the primary school, the curriculum for which comprised Irish, English, History, Geography and Mathematics, and this, added to the burden of drilling the prescribed Catechism programme into the pupils' heads, made the daily labour of a teacher more like the slavery of a Fenian convict in the English quarries than the noble task of an educator developing the mind and cultivating the aesthetic sense of the pupils. Even with that Gradgrind burden imposed on him, Mr Liddy, like many other teachers, added extra books in Irish and English to our standard readers each year. I remember especially the thrill of opening Maurice Walsh's great adventure story of the Elizabethan wars in Ireland, *Blackcock's Feather* (1932). And as with the Catechism answers and the *Séadna* story Sister Felicitas taught me for the *feis*, I can still quote the opening paragraph of that book (which, of course, I ruined for myself as a class text by reading the whole thing at home in one night – and it was subsequently read by all the others in the family). Here is the opening, and a fine piece of writing it is:

> This is the story of me, David Gordon, and I will begin it on that day in May when I walked down the quay-wall at Mouth of Avon below Bristol and held discourse with one Diggory, sailing-master of the *Speckled Hind* – I begin it on that day because it was on that day Life began for me.

For our extra texts in Irish, Mr Liddy introduced us in fifth class to European literature in the form of the brief extract from the Cervantes masterpiece, *Don Quixote*, rendered into fine Munster Irish by the man who wrote *Séadna*, An tAthair Peadar Ó Laoghaire. (The Irish title, *Don Cíochóte*, is phonetically more true to the original than the English *Don Quixote*.) In sixth class, our final year, he gave us another work from the same author, *An Cleasaí*, a retelling of an old

Irish tale and a much more formidable test for us. An indication of the level at which this bilingual literary study placed both teacher and pupil is the fact that, when I was working as a secondary school teacher in the 1970s, the texts prescribed for the Intermediate Certificate one year included *Blackcock's Feather* in English and *An Cleasaí* in Irish, the same books we had read as extras in the primary school. And when I realised that under the new system a pupil could be awarded an honours mark in English in the Leaving Certificate without knowing the difference between a noun and a verb, an adverb and an adjective, or how to define any part of speech, I could not but think back on the day when, in our weekly practice of 'parsing and analysis' in preparation for the English test in the primary certificate, Mr Liddy wrote on the blackboard, with the usual instruction: 'Analyse the following passage into its clauses, giving the nature and function of each clause, and parse the underlined words,' the following passage, the provenance of which, being the good teacher he was, he first explained:

> And as the hare whom hounds and horns pursue
> Pants to the place from whence at first she flew,
> I still had hopes, my long vexations past,
> Here to return, and die at home at last.

Loving our Island Parish, and our native city, as we did, we could feel for Oliver Goldsmith in his literary exile in London. How proud poor Noll would have been if he could see children in an Irish school wrestling with his lines so long after his death in 1774.

Our Mr Liddy was active in amateur drama and when he once sold us tickets (at threepence each) to go and see him in an Irish play at the Catholic Institute opposite the Franciscan Church, we forgot that we were not at a rugby match between Shannon and 'some other crowd'. The minute our 'Luke' appeared on stage we gave an almighty cheer and stamped on the floor as was the custom in the cinema when the 'boy' finally caught up with and knocked out the 'villain' and thus saved the 'girl' and her aged father. Mr Liddy thanked us next day for our enthusiastic support but he never again encouraged us to buy tickets for a play in which he was taking part! Like Mr Danaher in third class, Luke Liddy also added a play in Irish to our other lessons, a more elaborate one entitled *An Rí a Bhí Breoite* ('The King Who was Unwell'), the old fable about the overfed and lazy king whose imaginary illness, diagnosed as such by several doctors who are forthwith sent to be beheaded, is 'cured' when a more astute physician prescribes the wearing of the shirt of a happy man as the certain remedy – the problem being that the courtiers cannot find a truly happy man anywhere until they encounter a tramp, who has no shirt on his back! Once again, I was given the leading role, and when the inspector called on his annual visitation, we performed a scene from the play for him. That same inspector, a portly man whose smiling face struck us at once as so different from the grim puss which was the usual object we saw on such occasions, was also the source of my first professional payment as a writer. In discussing poetry, he mentioned the figure known as alliteration, which he illustrated by quoting the opening lines of a poem in which the entire alphabet is used, line by line. I remember only the beginning:

An Austrian army awfully array'd
Boldly by battery besieged Belgrade,
Cossacks commanding . . .

The nice man then produced a big brown penny, held it up before our goggling eyes, and stated that he would give it to the first boy who could compose a whole sentence in alliteration. Before he had the words out of his mouth, I was clambering out of the long bench over the bodies of my neighbours with the following in an almost illegible scribble:

Bill Boyd bought big buns.

The inspector was impressed, Luke Liddy winked at me and even the lads gave a cheer, feeling that we hadn't let the teacher down. I fondly remember that impromptu alliterative penny-earner even though I am unable to recite a single poem from the twelve books of poetry I have published in Irish and English. Along with the penny, I got what my mother called – the phrase came from buying milk – 'a tilly for the cat'. (I wonder is that 'tilly' the Irish *tuilleadh* – 'more'?) As he gave me the lolly, the inspector said to Mr Liddy, 'I think we have the makings of a poet here,' and Luke replied, 'I think so too.'

In addition to my first professional payment of one brown penny, that impromptu alliterative composition got me my first literary commission, but without emolument. The poor Irish version of the pre-Lenten Mardi Gras consisted in a feast of pancakes for supper. And on Shrove Tuesday, known to us as Pancake Night, it was the custom in many schools that an unsigned note would be surreptitiously placed on the teacher's desk requesting freedom from homework. The wording was traditional but the calligraphy had to be neat and the spelling faultless, otherwise the appeal might have the opposite effect. So, having been praised as a budding poet by the inspector himself, I was subsequently selected by the class mafia, a gang from Athlunkard Street – Lynch, Fitz, Clancy et al, all tough lads but fair and loyal – to be the class scribe and write the following ('on a clean page, mind!'):

Dear Mr Liddy, so faithful and kind,
Don't let the pancakes out of your mind.
When you were young, you liked them yourself,

So, cheer up, Mr Liddy –
And give us no exercise.

Those years being the period of the flowering of Evelyn
Waugh, Aldous Huxley and Graham Greene, our trendy
Luke Liddy, who was truly tall, dark and handsome, was
conspicuous as he cycled around Limerick dressed in a wide-
brimmed hat and brown plus-fours. (When he was at
a safe distance, the shout 'Oxford Bags!' often reached
his ears from behind.) Much as we admired him as a
teacher, his personality kept him somewhat aloof from
us; he always called us by our surnames – a style with
which I was familiar only in those library books about
English public schools. We actually felt more at ease with
the teacher of the other class in our room, the young
Cavanman, Brother O'Reilly. He took the combined classes
for a half-hour's religious instruction every Friday and also
supervised us whenever Mr Liddy was absent through illness.
He coached the school teams in Gaelic football and hurling,
and it was one of our proudest moments when we went
with him one day to play a hurling match in the GAA field
out on the Ennis Road – the same field where we had seen
Mick Mackey and our other Limerick heroes play! We were
almost inclined to genuflect in the primitive dressing-room
as we were told by Brother O'Reilly that we were actually
togging out on the same benches as *them*!

Our Mr Liddy gave us an excellent education in music,
teaching us to read the tonic solfa and to sing in two parts.
He also taught us more songs than the Department's rules
laid down as the annual minimum for each class (four in
Irish, two in English) but the headmaster, Brother O'Callaghan,
was renowned all over the Parish for his musical enthusiasm.
He formed a famous school choir in which my two brothers,
Tom and Joe, sang; and he cashed in (literally) on their
success in the *feis* by having a photo of the choir printed on
the back of the large tickets for a raffle in aid of school

funds. In those days when photos were not as common as they are now, those raffle tickets were treasured long after the raffle – some people even framed the photo! – and they were sent all over the world to exiles from the Parish who had been pupils at the old Quay Lane School. I had a personal reason for being grateful to Brother Thomas O'Callaghan from Tullamore: after the *feis*, he organised a great outing by bus to Tineranna near Lough Derg, provisions for which he solicited from shops and firms all over the Parish and farther afield, and besides the choir he took any pupil from the lower classes who had done anything in the *feis*; so, a few of us from third class were included because of our effort with the play.

I should record here that although our headmaster was always known as 'Monkey' Callaghan, this was not in any way an indication of disrespect. Although I was never in his class, I knew from those who were that he was a dedicated and excellent teacher, even if he did not spare the leather in his efforts to get knowledge into the heads of his pupils. We had a story in the folklore about the day when, despairing of getting a certain pleasant but very slow-witted pupil to understand some problem, Brother O'Callaghan lost his cool, dug in his pocket, produced a sixpenny bit, and shouted: 'Here, you *amadán*, go out to the butcher in Bridge Street and ask him for sixpenceworth of sheep's brains!' The lad takes the sixpence and ambles off, but turns back at the door and asks: 'Will I say they're for you, Brother?' (There was an economic aspect to this yarn; we were all familiar with the maternal injunction, when being sent to the shop, to let the shopkeeper know that the item in question was not for the child, who could be codded, but for the mother at home who would check on weight and quality, etc.)

Once when my bigger brothers were protecting me in the straggling queue waiting to get into the pictures at the 'Bughouse' (aka the Tivoli Cinema) on Charlotte's

Quay, I witnessed further evidence of the high regard in which our Brother O'Callaghan was held. In the pushing and dragging, an altercation arose between some customers from our side of the Abbey River and some 'knackers' (in our view!) from the Irishtown or Garryowen or some one of those uncivilised territories. One boolum from that lot shouted, 'Ah, yere on'y a crowd of eejits in the Parish, and yere headmaster is a monkey!' I have explained the origin of the word boolum (a shield-banger, a challenger) and it came to life there on the roadway at Charlotte's Quay as truly as it was used in the days of the heroic Cú Chulainn himself. From the Parish gang, a burly son of one of the Abbey fishermen (so my brothers told me afterwards) stood forward and challenged the knacker who had shouted that insult to the Parish, to us, and to our respected headmaster. 'We're not goin' to let any ignorant dirty knackers like ye call our headmaster names!' he said. Battle ensued, a much better contest than we were to see in the phony fisticuffs between the 'boy' and the 'villain' in the Jeyes-Fluid-cleaned cinema later on. Fair dues, the boolum put his fists where his mouth was, but he would have had more than the bloody nose he got if the stout woman from the cinema, hearing the randyboo outside, had not sallied forth to quell the row. When telling the story at home that evening, my brother Tom said to my mother that the funny thing about it all was that the champion who defended the name of our Brother O'Callaghan was a fellow who was walloped nearly every day by the same 'Monkey' for failure at his lessons or for minor misdemeanours like talking in class.

Like all the other teachers, our Luke Liddy was compelled by the uneducational circumstances of school life in those days to wield the stinging cane as an aid to learning, but he did so in moderation and without any hint of the sadistic tendencies that manifested themselves in some teachers of that era before corporal punishment began to be questioned by educational psychologists and finally abolished – at the same time as the industrial schools were closed down. Some social commentators are now beginning to wonder if we 'threw out the baby with the bathwater' as we see the increase in juvenile vandalism and crime, and a court system where a modern 'Artful Dodger' of fifteen can cheerfully admit to fifty-five offences (I quote a recent newspaper report) and then be released on to the streets because there is no suitable place of detention such as the industrial schools were for novices in crime. My own occasional slaps were incurred, as in my days in the infant school, for talking and inattention, but one heavier dose came in a context strangely similar to that day when Sister Felicitas had to push back her veil and hold back her strength while she walloped the outstretched palms of the little blaguards who had been involved in the pissing competition that resulted in an unholy baptism for poor Miss Bogue. What made the primary school version even worse was that I myself had been the purchaser of the cane that cut four times along my tender fingers.

One day when he noticed that his cane was getting a bit frayed at the edges, Mr Liddy took out sixpence and ordered me to go to Polly Carr's shop in Patrick Street and get him a new one. Polly Carr's was like the Old Curiosity Shop in Dickens's book, an old style shop packed from floor to ceiling with all sorts of toys and gadgets so that there was hardly room to walk around in it; it was like a magic cave to us when we were children, but old Polly herself seemed more like a cross old witch than a woman, and we did not approve of one item in her stock, that bundle of canes hanging up outside the door. We often wondered why the 'Crooley Man' – i.e. the inspector for the Society for the Prevention of Cruelty to Children – didn't summons old Polly Carr for encouraging teachers and parents to use the cane.

As I went off on my unwelcome mission, Luke called after me: 'And get me a good one – or you'll be the first to feel it!' Now that was hitting below the belt, especially with some of the boolums in the class making threatening grimaces and gestures at me when he turned back to the blackboard. So, talk about being on the horns of a dilemma! If I brought back a cane he didn't like, I'd be walloped with it and sent back for a better one; and if I brought back a real swisher, they'd mollafooster me in the yard or on the way home from school. I decided to take the bull by the horns – at least by the most dangerous horn! – and ask Polly for 'a good one'. At which she went for me! 'Whatch-you mean, a good one, you cheeky little pup you! All my stuff is the best that money can buy! You won't get a better cane in the whole of Limerick than them! Look at that – ' and she bends the cane until the ends meet – 'that's a cane that'll warm the backside of any brat that needs it!' And she looked as if she would like to prove it on my own posterior.

What probably saved me from the unjustified vengeance of my classmates was the fact that the next day the incident occurred that made me the first victim to prove the quality of Polly Carr's canes. Brother O'Reilly had come down from his end of the room to have a confab with Luke Liddy, and we were supposed to be doing sums or something to keep us quiet. We were in long benches, about six in each. On my right side I had one of my best pals, Gerry Murphy from the New Walk, but on my left there was a right gilly-gooly who was always footering and messing, the sort of a gobdaw who was always picking his nose and scratching himself and looking around to see what he could see. It was this loodramawn who got me into trouble. When I was having the usual whispered chat with my pal Gerry, this eejit nudges me in the ribs. 'Look, look!' says he. And when I look, thinking he has a comic or a few picture cards under the desk to show me, what has he but the buttons of his trousers open and his thing sticking out in his hand! 'Now show me yours!' says the gilly-gooley. 'Will you feck off!' I said. But being the eejit he was, he wouldn't. 'Fair is fair,' says he, 'I showed you mine, you have to show me yours.' He wasn't one of the big booiums and although he was bigger than me, he was a sort of a wishy-washy type that I knew I'd be able for in the yard. 'If you don't put that thing away,' I hissed at him, 'I'll stab it with me pen, as sure as God!' But still he went on, with a big grin on his stupid puss, 'Ah come on, give us just a look, I just want to see what – '

'You'll see my fist in your eye in a minute, if you don't shag off and stop your coddin'!'

It was then I noticed that my pal Gerry was nudging me and kicking me. And when I looked up, I saw to my horror that Brother O'Reilly had gone back to his own department and our Luke was standing there, staring straight down at myself and the yahoo beside me.

Anyone who ever got into trouble in school could tell what happened next.

'What are you two talking about?'

First, put on an innocent face, look at one another, point at yourself, and then, together: 'Nothin', sir.'

'Come up here, the two of you – and bring up whatever it is you have under the desk.' With that, myself and mickey-the-prick look at one another, and then – oh, my God! – we start giggling. Our elegant and erudite Mr Liddy was not at all the sort of man who liked to see two miscreants laughing at him.

'So, you think it's funny, do you?' We thought it was hilarious, in a desperate way, but we couldn't tell him so. I could see that new cane hanging beside his desk. Already I was squeezing my hands in preparation for the stinging swipes. While we clambered out, he came down and leaned in to have a look in the space under the desk where we kept our schoolbags. He took out the bags and examined them. Then he came up to where we were awaiting execution, the whole class watching in anticipation of meela murder.

'What were you looking at under the desk?'

'Nothin', sir.' The way we said it, definite, resigned, no humming and hawing, showed him, as an experienced teacher, that as King Lear said to his favourite daughter, Cordelia, 'Nothing will come of nothing.' He knew we were lying, but he knew also that we were involved in a situation where we had to stick to our guns. So, he produced his own gun and gave us four each. But the wallops were worth it for me – he decided that we were 'too pally altogether' and he shifted gilly-gooley far away from me; and in the yard, and going home from school, I got such mileage out of telling the truth to my pals that I didn't bother chasing poor mickey-the-prick when he ran away every time he saw me for the next few days. Even Mr Liddy let it pass, because soon after he sent me out on another mission, a nicer one this time, and one that held no danger for me. He sent me to the bank with a sealed envelope and warned me to take great care of what I would be given there. What I was given, after the official had opened the envelope and examined me as if I was a potential Jesse James going to produce a revolver and blow his head off, was Mr Liddy's salary in cash in a thick sealed envelope. Teachers were paid on the tenth of the month following the month for which they were being paid, with the result that they were often, towards the end of that period, much worse off for ready cash than the ordinary workers in the docks and factories who got their wage packet every Friday. Poor Mr Liddy must have been desperate to get his hands on a few quid that day. It was the first time I was ever in a bank, and I was never in one again until I cashed my own first salary as a teacher.

When two city firms, Spillane's tobacco factory and Bradshaw's 'Olo' mineral water factory, put up cups for a primary schools competition in Gaelic and Hurling res-pectively (the cups were called the Spillane and the Olo) our school won the football cup – and some staff member added a few new songs to our repertoire. One, to the air of Davis's rousing 'Clare's Dragoons', contained the following modest boast:

> Our backs are as safe as a ten-foot wall;
> Our goalie could stop a cannonball;
> Our midfield men are true and tall;
> All out to win are the Boys in Blue.

And, to the American Civil War air of 'Marching through Georgia', we roared (with some reservations, feeling that whoever wrote this did not really understand regional loyalties in Limerick!):

> Hurray, hurray, hurray for Garryowen!
> Hurray, hurray, hurray for the Treaty Stone!
> Let the forwards do their duty and the backs they
>   will play up,
> And down to St Mary's we will bring the Spillane
>   Cup!

We did, but when we paraded it through the city that night, we were ambushed out in Thomondgate by the hostile and envious Soda Cakes. We had judged it safe to parade the cup across Thomond Bridge, because in the final we had beaten St Michael's, the Sexton Street primary school, which was the common enemy of the three parochial schools. We even had a song to prove it, based on an old local ditty:

> Up the stairs and into bed, parley-pooh;
> Up the stairs and into bed, the same to you;
> Up the stairs and into bed,
> And don't forget to cover your head,
> Inky-pinky-parley-pooh!

('Parley-pooh', like 'randyboo', was a linguistic souvenir of

254

the Great War, being what the Limerick Munsters had made of *parlez-vous*.) Adapted as a victorious football chant, it went as follows:

Michael's thought they were goin' to win, parley-
    pooh;
Michael's thought they were goin' to win, the same
    to you!
Michael's thought they were goin' to win,
But Mary's gevum a great suck-in!
Inky-pinky-parley-pooh!

We crossed Thomond Bridge unarmed, waving our blue and white flags and holding the Spillane Cup on high, but when a hail of stones greeted us we retreated in as great a disorder as the Irish troops who were pushed across old Thomond Bridge by Ginkel's forces in 1691 on that fateful day when a French officer ordered the drawbridge to be pulled up, with the result that hundreds of Irish soldiers were pushed into the river by the enemy force. (The Bard of Thomond has a plangent digression on the incident in his most famous poem.)

A teacher in whose class I never sat, the Ireeshan, Mr Toohey, added to my education when he and Mr Liddy selected me along with some other pupils for an oral examination in Irish, organised by the Gaelic League for the purpose of sending the two best Irish speakers in each school for a month's stay in the West Cork Gaeltacht of Cúil Aodha near Macroom. Although I was selected as one of the two from our school, Mr Toohey was worried that at the age of nine and a half I was so much younger than the others, from city and county (they ranged from eleven to fifteen years), and he called to my house one evening to discuss with my parents whether they would consent to my going, which they gladly did – one out of the way, and in safe hands, for a month was probably a relief to my mother! She came up to the bus with me to see me off, and all the mothers were crying as if we were going to China. By a curious piece of timing on the part of Fate – no human agency could have managed it – as the bus came into Foynes where we were to pick up some students, one of the transatlantic seaplanes (perhaps the first from west to east) was just touching down on the Shannon.

In company with an older boy from Limerick, I stayed for the month with a family named Lucey in their farmhouse a few miles out from the village, and after our first embarrassment at not knowing what these native speakers of Irish were saying, we got on like a house on fire with the boys and girls of the family. We walked into the village every morning for classes. All I remember of them is that I enjoyed the songs, one of which, *An Capaillín Bán* ('The Little White Horse'), composed by a local poet, Seoirse Seártan of Béal Átha an Ghaorthaidh (1879–1957) when he was in exile in Liverpool, I still sing when circumstances are favourable (I included it, with my English version, in my *Irish Comic Poems*, Cló Iar-Chonnachta, 1995).

When Mr Toohey advised my father that I should take the piccolo with me to the Gaeltacht, he made a small wooden box for it, complete with strap and buckle, showing once again that an artistic nature does not preclude practical ability – after all, Michelangelo was a stonemason who made statues. At the interval in the *céilí* in the village hall, my valiant rendering of a few tunes was much appreciated, but one old man took me aside to warn me that blowing into that little yoke would severely damage my lungs. When I reported this to my father on my return home, he said very unkind things about old countrymen who talked through their hat. The opposite, he said, was true; playing the piccolo or the flute would strengthen and develop my lungs.

We were given some tuition in the *céilí* dances, our own

'Walls of Limerick' and the 'Siege of Ennis' but as I was so small I hated those team dances and preferred the leisurely rhythm of *An Staicín Eornan* ('The Stack of Barley'), in which you hold on to your own partner all through, and they found me a lovely partner of my own age in the dark-haired daughter of one of the local teachers. We must have looked like two leprechauns as we hopped and circled around the hall in among the adults and bigger students. When another old man asked me my name one night at the *céilí*, and I replied, in my best Limerick school Irish, '*Críostóir Ó Floinn is ainm dom,*' he let a blast out of him as follows: '*Ó Floinn, an ea? Mhuise, th'anam 'on diabhal, a gharsúin, is ag teacht abhaile atánn tú!*' I was familiar enough with the musical West Cork accent by now to know that he was telling me that I was coming home. I began to try to tell him that my home was in Limerick until the young local curate who was sitting beside him took pity on me and explained, in English, that what the old man meant was that I was coming back to my roots, because all that area of West Cork was called in Irish *Múscraí Uí Fhloinn* ('O'Flynn's Muskerry'). I told them then that my father had often told us at home in Limerick that our ancestors came from West Cork a long time ago. This caused the old man to go into another peroration, all lost on me. When I reported back to base in Limerick what he had said in his first pronouncement, my father was ready to accept that there were some very wise old countrymen in West Cork (as well as the other kind).

On my first day back in school in Quay Lane after that brief return to the hereditary lands of the West Cork branch of the clan, I encountered Brother Michael O'Reilly (his clan held on to their lands better than we did) as he bounded up the iron stairs in the yard three steps at a time. 'Weren't you away in the Gaeltacht?' he asked me. 'I was, Brother.'

'And did you learn much Irish?'

'I did, Brother.'

'Tell me something you learned.' I opened the gob and

all I could think of was '*N'fheadar!*' ('I don't know') which is at least a very distinctive West Cork way of putting it and sounds nice in the lilting Cork accent.

27

'INTROIBO AD ALTARE DEI'

Anyone who remembers the pre-Vatican Council times when Latin, the language of the ancient Roman Empire, was the liturgical language of the universal empire of the Holy Spirit, the Catholic Church, will recognise the above title as the first words the priest used to say when he bowed down at the foot of the altar, with his back to the congregation, to begin the ritual sacrifice of the Mass. Beside the priest, one or more altar boys responded to this opening with another mouthful in Latin: '*Ad Deum qui laetificat juventutem meam.*' Those in the congregation who could afford to buy a bilingual missal would be reading the beautiful words of the Psalmist in the vernacular:

I will go in unto the altar of God,
To God, who gives joy to my youth.

The rest of the congregation would be fingering their beads or just kneeling in silent participation in the ritual.

I have mentioned earlier that we used the more elegant liturgical word, 'acolyte', which the dictionary defines as 'one in minor orders, next below subdeacon' (from the Greek, *akolouthos*, an attendant or assistant) rather than the pedestrian *altar boy* (which will now have to become *altar person*, since girls have been admitted to the office). I don't think the acolytes in our day ever aspired to be 'in minor orders, next below subdeacon' but at least we had an important role to play in the ceremonial of the Mass, a role which has been reduced to such a minimal function now that the priest has no problem in celebrating without any server – as indeed, he often has to in these days when the young do not seem to have the loyalty and dedication to the job that was instilled in us as a necessary qualification.

The big problem for anyone aspiring to be an acolyte in our day was the Latin. Learning the *Confiteor* in English (the Latin title was used even in the infant school) was labour enough for children preparing for their First Communion, but in the Mass the acolyte had to recite it in Latin on behalf of the entire congregation, in reply to the priest's own formal acknowledgement of his sinfulness. Most of the other responses were short enough, but at the end of the Mass there was another linguistic Beecher's Brook to be faced in the form of Psalm 129, the solemn *De Profundis*.

Leaving aside the question of Latin versus vernacular in the Mass and other church services, and however much the 'Church' Latin might be denigrated by the classicist, there is no doubt that the repetitive exposure to it in the Mass constituted a good grounding for any acolyte in preparation for the study, not only of Latin as a school subject, but of the European languages derived from it. Not, of course, that these were on the curriculum in those days, apart from French for girls. In the same way, when my father taught us to read and pronounce the Italian musical terms, he was unwittingly extending our linguistic capabilities – anyone who had played a tune *allegro ma non troppo* would have less difficulty with the Italian title than with the English content of Milton's 'L'Allegro'. Add in our daily formal studies in Irish and English, two languages from very different families as regards grammar, syntax and vocabulary, and it will be seen that we managed to pick up quite a varied grounding in linguistics and phonetics. Unfortunately, most of the children of the working class had to leave school at fourteen years of age, and so got little chance to build on any such foundation they might have acquired.

In training acolytes for our local St Mary's Church, there was a liaison between the sacristan, Willie Bartlett, and the Brothers in Quay Lane. The Latin was taught in the school, with a rudimentary knowledge of the corresponding service on the altar, and the polish was applied by Mr Bartlett when the novice acolytes were assigned the most minor roles at first, both at Mass and at Benediction. Brother O'Reilly selected pupils he considered capable of learning the Latin and of moving around the altar without stumbling or knocking things over, and he drilled us slowly but surely in the responses. As I already had three brothers on the altar, I had been hearing them practising at home since the first day Tom, the eldest, began to learn the Latin. And it was one of our childhood indoor games on wet days to dress up as priest and server, in any white garment, even an old sheet, and to pretend to light imaginary candles on the wall of the stairs with a stick or the sweeping brush, and to intone the easier bits of Latin, like *Dominus vobiscum*, and the response, *Et cum spiritu tuo*. My mother or Mrs Sheehan used to laugh at us – even ask us to hear their Confession! – as they passed up or down the stairs.

When the day came for my entry to the sacred service of the altar in St Mary's beautiful new church I was again fortunate to have brothers who had gone the road before me (the two eldest, Tom and Joe, had by this time gone from St Mary's to serve in the Convent of Mercy, a path Dick and I would follow in due course). Kneeling on the altar step, I sometimes forgot where I was, and what I was to do, while gazing at the crescent of life-size mosaic figures of angel-musicians on a golden background which I could see above the altar. My brothers warned me not to accept the kind offer of the senior altar boys who would want to bring me outside the sacristy and lift me up so that I could see the goldfish swimming down there in the depths of the big barrel of holy water (from which the faithful filled their bottles for domestic use as in my mother's little font). Neophyte acolytes who had no big brother to warn them ended up with their heads in the holy water while the senior lads held their legs. What my brothers could not prepare me for was the irritation when some of the lads, even on our own street, called out 'Holy Boys!' in derision whenever they happened to see us going to or coming from the church with our rolled-up gear under our arm. (The mother of the acolyte supplied the soutane, surplice and dark sandshoes, making the clothes herself if she was a good seamstress, otherwise paying someone else to make them.) This mocking catcall was almost as bad as being called sissy, and what made it worse was that we were often passing by the mockers on a lovely summer's evening as they played games on the street, while we were on our way, perhaps to the May devotions, to spend almost an hour in the church, then back home to finish off the school homework. We could not very well attack our mockers and risk appearing in the sacristy with a bloody nose or a black eye. Our defence was psychological. We shouted back at them: 'Ye're jealous because ye're so thick ye could never learn the Latin!' And in that unChristian attitude, we took an intellectual refuge which was more a 'refuge of sinners' than of truly holy boys.

One of my most lasting memories of that period as an acolyte in St Mary's is not connected with the altar at all. We were in the sacristy one dark evening after the devotions when the sacristan called us out to see the night sky far off lit up by the *Aurora Borealis*, the Northern Lights. Popular superstition had always linked the appearance of that astronomical phenomenon with forthcoming disaster, and there were already indications enough in the political situation in Europe to make even the least superstitious fear that the Great War of 1914–18, the 'war to end wars', had been merely the preliminary to an even more devastating global conflict.

When my brother Tom left school at fourteen and could no longer serve in the convent, for which he was getting too big anyway, I was drafted in with Joe and Dick. When Joe in turn had to give up both school and altar service, Dick and I had alternate weeks serving Mass at seven in the morning, and serving together at Benediction on Sunday at two in the afternoon. (This was a big sacrifice in summer because it meant we could not go on picnics with the family or the street but had to dash out after them as soon as our duty in the convent was finished.) Serving in the convent was very different from St Mary's. The nuns knelt in two rows down along the sides of their oratory and they came up to two prie-dieus to receive Holy Communion, at which the altar boy held the paten under each nun's chin while the priest put the sacred host on her tongue. I was fascinated when I first began to do this job, because here came my old teacher, Sister Felicitas, and the other nuns I had known in the infant school, closing their eyes and sticking out their tongues just as she had instructed us to do when preparing us for First Holy Communion. I often claimed facetiously in after years that I was a leading authority on one subject – nuns' tongues! In even later years it began to occur to me that the Church authorities who had decreed that even nuns could not serve on the altar, with the concomitant hardship this imposed on young boys, and on mothers like mine who had to shake us out of bed to serve the seven o'clock Mass, winter and summer, must have had very little common sense.

While we did not go so far as to feel about our holy nuns like that barbaric general in the US who said that the only good Indian was a dead Indian, we were always delighted to hear that a good old nun had at last gone to her eternal reward, because we got a day off school to serve at the Requiem Mass and the funeral to the cemetery in the grounds of the convent. We were also needed for all the events in the life of a nun, from the reception of a young girl as a postulant, to her receiving the novice's white veil and finally the profession as a full sister, at which the bishop himself presided. After all such ceremonies we were given tea – not, of course, in the parlour with the bishop and the clergy. The nearest we got to that was when we marvelled at the silvery stuff on the table as we passed by the open door. We went across to another building called the House of Mercy, where there was a large bare dining-room with long tables and bench seats, and we were served by a motherly old sister and some of the grown-up girls who lived in that house. We never knew who these girls were – we called them the 'country girls' – or why they lived there or what exactly they did. When we asked my mother, she was very vague about them too. Two older women lived in the lodge at the gate and it was they who admitted us to serve Mass each morning. One of the benefits accruing from our being acolytes in the convent was that our family was among the privileged few allowed into the small side section of the nuns' oratory for the Christmas Midnight Mass; I had seen my older brothers serving at that Mass before I took on the duty myself.

The priests from St Mary's took it in turn to act as chaplain for the nuns, week by week; thus my brother Dick and I got to know them all more intimately than we did in our apprenticeship days on the altar in St Mary's. The parish priest, Canon Michael Hannan, we thought a bit aloof and cold and he was not popular in the fireside chat we overheard. Our favourite was Fr Dick McCarthy, a cheerful and very friendly man whose premature white hair was said to be the result of his experiences during the Black-and-Tan war. He had to emigrate to America in a hurry when, in a follow-up operation after an abortive ambush, the Tans found his hat, with his name inside the rim, in a country house where he had been giving the Last Sacraments to a Republican soldier who was fatally wounded in the ambush. Fr Dick was very popular with the Women's Sodality and my mother used to quote a prayer called 'the Irish *Te Deum*' which he sometimes recited as part of his sermon on the troubles of life. The bit I remember goes like this:

> Thanks be to God for the rain and the sunshine;
> Thanks be to God for the sleet and the snow;
> Thanks be to God when our pockets are empty;
> Thanks be to God when again they o'erflow!

We had two priests named Costello, Tom and Dan, but they were not related; one was rather dour, the other cranky (as I was to learn). Finally, there was the soft-spoken Fr John Kennedy, a gentle priest who, like Fr Dick McCarthy, would always say a few pleasant words to us when we were all disrobing in the sacristy.

It was from Fr Dick McCarthy and Fr Dan Costello that I learned a lesson that would stand me in good stead later on in life – that the Church is run by mere men, as mixed in their characters, personalities and temperaments as the assorted twelve selected by Divine Wisdom itself to teach us that lesson if only we would read the New Testament as diligently as we read the daily paper. One Sunday after Benediction, Father Dick called myself and my brother, another Dick, over to him in the sacristy and had a chat with us about the usual topics, school, games and so on. Then he asked if we ever went to the pictures. We did, to the 'Bughouse' on Charlotte's Quay or the new Thomond in nearby Nicholas Street – when and if we had the tuppence admission fee. Then he asked us if we had seen the lovely film in the Lyric, *Rose Marie*, with Nelson Eddy and Jeannette MacDonald. The Lyric was situated opposite the Dominican Church near Pery Square (of the

Carnegie Library). It was far removed from us, geographically and economically, admission being sixpence; but we had a story about the time when *King Kong* was drawing full houses to the Lyric and a Dominican preacher, looking at his sparse congregation, cried out from the pulpit the immortal words:

> Ding-Dong, the church is empty!
> King Kong, the Lyric is full!

Father Dick put his hand in his pocket, gave us each a shilling, and urged us to go and see *Rose Marie*. We did and thought it not half as good, with all that singing and mushy stuff interrupting the real action, as the cowboy and gangster and war films in the smelly old Bughouse where, if the 'boy' and the 'girl' started kissing, the mob began to pound the floor and shout, 'We want our money back!' until threatened with expulsion by the probing torch. Of course, when the genial Father Dick's turn as chaplain came round again, and he asked us the inevitable question, we lied with a grateful smile and told him that *Rose Marie* was definitely one of the best films we had ever seen in our lives.

It was towards the end of my service in the convent, when I was training in the Murphy brothers, Jerry (a classmate and close friend of mine in Quay Lane CBS) and Tom, who lived in the New Walk only a few doors from the gate of the convent, to take over from the O'Flynn brothers, that the cranky Father Dan Costello happened to be officiating at the Benediction one Sunday afternoon. I was in charge of the thurible and kneeling directly behind him with the hundred or so nuns in their two ranks stretched out behind me. I was swinging the open thurible to keep the charcoal glowing, in between the two ritual spoonings of incense on to it, and probably dreaming of swimming or hurling or cowboys, when suddenly the bottom of the thurible banged off the marble floor of the chapel, scattering bits of glowing charcoal around and rudely waking any of the poor old nuns who had been drowsing in her pew. Father Dan jerked and looked round – I think Jesus Christ himself present in the Sacred Host in the monstrance on the altar gave a bit of a jump – while I burned the tips of my fingers picking up the bits of charcoal and dropping them back where the liturgy said they should be.

We got to the end of the Benediction without further mishap, but in the sacristy, when he had taken off the vestments, Father Dan barked at me: 'You, come over here!' I put on my best Oliver Twist poorhouse face and went over to him. 'What do you think you were doing out there?' he snapped. As I opened the gob to tell him something he knew already, he gave me a slap across the face and told me that if the like of it ever happened again he would tell the nuns to get rid of me. Maybe if I had known the Gospels well enough, and if I was a real holy boy like Tarcisius that Sister Felicitas told us about, who got kicked to death by the pagan Roman rowdies, I might have turned the other cheek and asked Father Dan to give me another slap of his consecrated hand. But being only an ordinary little sinner, I just stood there and stared at him. The Granny Connolly would have approved of that. Of course, that was one incident she never heard about; neither did my father and mother. But I realised in later life that getting that slap in the face from a priest, and getting a shilling from another priest, was a special grace from the Holy Spirit to prepare me for things yet to come. And the Holy Spirit has whispered to me sometimes that maybe that was a bad day for poor Father Dan himself. For all I knew, he might have had, to quote the fireside philosophers, 'a pain where he never had a window', or some trouble with the canon, or even with his priesthood. All I knew at the time was that Father Dick McCarthy would have made a big joke out of my mishap with the thurible.

As far as our relations with the nuns themselves were concerned, we were always very well treated by Sister Conleth the sacristan and by any of the others who held us up for a chat now and again after Benediction – 'And tell me now, how is your dear mother?' and so on. My mother used to say that the nuns, by questioning anyone and everyone, knew more about what was going on in the Parish than Canon Hannan himself. After Benediction on Sundays, there was a brown paper bag of fruit and buns left out for us near the door at the end of the long waxed corridor leading to the sacristy. A more lasting reward than that material token has stayed with me all my life in the memory I have of the Mass and other ceremonies in the convent chapel, and I can still close my eyes and hear the angelic voices of the nuns – sounding all the more heavenly since the nuns were out of sight behind me – singing the *Ave Verum*, *Salve Regina*, *Te Deum* and the *Litany of the Saints*, and above all, the *Adeste Fideles* at the Christmas Midnight Mass.

28

'I AM A LITTLE CATHOLIC'

One of the hymns Sister Felicitas taught us for our First
Holy Communion went like this:

> I am a little Catholic, I love my holy faith
> And I will be true to the Holy Church
> And faithful until death.

If I replace the word 'little' with 'big', I can still sing
those lines (I'd have to say 'big, big' to be metrically
correct) while washing the dishes or sitting out in the
garden looking at the birds and the flowers and the
sky, and praising the Creator in whom I believe. There
was a saying in Limerick, attributed to some of the
hard chaws who, like my grandfather Connolly, had
taken the shilling and gone off to do England's work
by fighting the natives in India or South Africa or any
other part of the Empire. When they came back to the
Shannon shore they used to say: 'We robbed and we
raped and we plundered – but we kept the faith!' Since
the day the Granny Connolly took me to have the
sacramental waters of Baptism poured on my little
baldy head, I too have kept the faith – thanks to the
mercy of God, to the prayers of my mother and others,

and to the example of the many good Catholics, priests and religious and lay people, I have known from my childhood until the present day. As I compare the Ireland we grew up in to the Ireland of today, I am mystified by the fact that so many people nowadays give up the practice of the Catholic religion, while others want to pick and choose the doctrines they will accept or reject. People who regard the rules of their golf club as sacrosanct have no hesitation in discarding any of the Commandments and doctrines of the Church that disturb their comfort (which they call conscience) and every jackdaw commentator finds fault with the Pope personally and with the manner in which he guides the Church as the Vicar of Christ.

Religious and social commentators attribute these changes to many causes, principally to the more materialistic values by which moral choices are influenced nowadays. What concerns me more is that while people like myself who retain their belief in God and their orthodox allegiance to the Catholic Church are expected to view with silent tolerance and total acceptance the secularisation that is altering our society, our religious beliefs and our Catholic Church are constantly and increasingly being attacked and derided – 'made a feck of', in our Limerick expression – in the media, and this not only by atheists but by apostates, people who were reared as Catholics but who have abandoned the faith. That, of course, is precisely what the Divine Founder told his disciples would happen and he also told them – a point worth remembering in view of recent happenings in Ireland – that there would always be scandals.

That, however, in no way lessens the human reaction of annoyance when Catholics are treated by the atheists, pagans and apostates in the media as if we were conservative (meaning opposed to progress), naive (meaning simple), narrow-minded and even bigoted. What is even more irritating is that most of the smart-aleck journalists, puffed-up academics and yapping media mouths who engage in this denigration of the Pope and the Catholic Church (and of Irish Catholics in particular) clearly prove the truth of Alexander Pope's assertion in *An Essay on Criticism:*

A little learning is a dangerous thing;
Drink deep, or taste not the Pierian spring:
There shallow draughts intoxicate the brain,
And drinking largely sobers us again.

The first couplet in that quatrain was beaten into my head with a stick by Brother Murray during my first year in the Christian Brothers' secondary school. While I could have done without the stick, the longer I live and the more I read and hear of the type of anti-Catholic tripe and piffle in question, the deeper my debt of gratitude to that aggressively efficient teacher for having made me aware at an early age of one of the most serious handicaps from which pseudo-intellectuals suffer. It was a true intellectual, the French philosopher, Blaise Pascal (1623–62) – he was also a mathematician and an inventor – who said of such hostile critics of the Catholic religion: 'Let them first learn about this religion before they attack it.' That applies nowadays to people who write in the papers or come on television purporting to disparage the orthodox Catholic religion in which I was reared by good parents and teachers and priests in comparison with what they see as the more acceptable pick-and-choose version that allows each person to decide what to believe or practise. In this so-called liberal type of religion, most of the pick-and-choose has to do with the Church's teaching on sex and marriage; none of the liberal Catholics have problems with the mystery of the Trinity or with the Ten Commandments other than the sixth and ninth. The words *sin* and *hell* are taboo, and concepts like temptation and purity are mocked as outdated superstition.

Here it is relevant to quote from a sermon delivered, not by a Redemptorist priest in Limerick, but by John Henry Newman in 1834 when he was still an Anglican clergyman. (He became a Catholic in 1845, was ordained a priest in 1847 and created a cardinal in 1879. He died in 1890 and was declared Venerable in 1991.)

> What is the world's religion today? It has taken the brighter side of the Gospel – its tidings of comfort, its precepts of love – all darker, deeper views of man's condition and prospects being comparatively forgotten. This is the religion natural to a civilized age, and well has Satan dressed and completed it into an idol of the truth . . . Those fearful images of Divine wrath with which the Scriptures abound are explained away. Every thing is bright and cheerful. Religion is pleasant and easy; benevolence is the chief virtue . . . This form of doctrine, which I have called the religion of the day, is especially adapted to please people of sceptical minds . . . who have never been careful to obey their conscience, who cultivate the intellect without disciplining the heart and who allow themselves to speculate freely about what religion ought to be, without going to the Scriptures to discover what it really is. Some persons of this character almost consider religion itself to be an obstacle in the advance of our social and political well-being.

And what has all that blather about religion got to do with this chronicle of my boyhood in Limerick in that decade of the 1930s? Well, just as the sociologists tell me that, because we were poor, lived in large families and were badly housed, children like me must have been miserable and deprived – by now the reader will have enough evidence at least to question such academic deductions – there are other commentators who blame the misery and deprivation of the period of my childhood in Limerick in large measure on the Catholic Church, especially on the Christian Brothers and the Redemptorist priests who ran the Confraternity.

Much has already been written by hostile critics in denigration of the corporal punishment that was prevalent in the schools of the Christian Brothers (I myself have a few more unusual examples to narrate) but any social or educational historian will acknowledge that this system was not confined to the schools of the Irish Christian Brothers or indeed to Irish schools. As has been seen in this chronicle, even in the Brothers' schools the lay teachers were as active in using stick or strap as the Brothers themselves. And even in purely lay schools, urban or rural, the stick or cane was in constant use as a stimulus to learning and good behaviour. That there were sadists among the Christian Brothers cannot be denied – we got one ourselves in Quay Lane as a replacement for Brother O'Callaghan when he was transferred to St Munchin's CBS in Thomondgate – but that type of perverted human being occurs in every walk of life as well as in teaching. Those who are familiar with James Joyce's autobiographical work, *A Portrait of the Artist as a Young Man* (1916) may recall the scene in Clongowes Wood College when Father Dolan, the Prefect of Studies, comes into the classroom where the six-year-old James Joyce is one of the pupils.

'Any boys want flogging here, Father Arnall? Any lazy idle loafers that want flogging in this class?' he demands of his confrère. A boy who is kneeling because he failed his Latin grammar is given six slaps on each hand; then the Prefect notices that Joyce is not writing like the rest. The teacher explains that this boy is exempt, having broken his glasses. The terrified child is interrogated and explains how they were broken. 'Hoho! Lazy idle little loafer!' cries the Prefect of Studies. 'Broke my glasses! An old schoolboy trick! Out with your hand this moment!' The adult Joyce devotes a whole page to describing the pain and humiliation of receiving six slaps of the 'pandy-bat' on each hand. What we are not told in the book, but is revealed in the school records, is that the little Dubliner was punished on several other occasions for using vulgar language.

Even literary commentators sometimes quote Joyce as classifying the pupils of the Christian Brothers as 'Paddy Stink and Micky Mud' in *A Portrait*. Jesus Christ, who chose to be born in a stable and to live in a back-of-beyond village as the supposed son of a carpenter, might consider that a compliment to the Christian Brothers. The point I wish to make is that Joyce never said it. The derogatory remark was made by his conceited and snobbish father. It is of interest to note that the American critic, Richard Ellman, in what is regarded as the definitive biography of Joyce, mistakenly reads the remark as applying to the Brothers themselves rather than to their pupils. And in Joyce's own favour, it should be noted – Ellman strangely omits this from his massive tome – that towards the end of that book the author relates how, having resolved to turn his back on religion, nationality and even Ireland itself, he found himself 'on a day of dappled seaborne clouds' walking alone near the Bull Wall on the north side of Dublin Bay.

He turned seaward from the road at Dollymount and as he passed on to the thin wooden bridge he felt the planks shaking with the tramp of heavily shod feet. A squad of Christian Brothers was on its way back from the Bull and had begun to pass, two by two, across the bridge . . . The uncouth faces passed him by, two by two, stained yellow or red or livid by the sea, and, as he strove to look at them with ease and indifference, a faint stain of personal shame and commiseration rose to his face . . .

– Brother Hickey.
Brother Quaid.
Brother MacArdle.

Brother Keogh.–

Their piety would be like their names, like their faces, like their clothes, and it was idle for him to tell himself that their humble and contrite hearts, it might be, paid a far richer tribute of devotion than his had ever been, a gift tenfold more acceptable than his elaborate adoration. It was idle for him to move himself to be generous towards them, to tell himself that if ever he came to their gates, stripped of his pride, beaten and in beggar's weeds, that they would be generous towards him, loving him as themselves . . .

That, in my opinion, is one of the most remarkable and moving passages in all the works of Joyce – but one that I have never seen quoted or commented on. Joyce did, in fact, have occasion as a boy to 'come to their gates' when, between his spell in Clongowes as a child and his free admission to another Jesuit college, Belvedere, he and his brother spent some time in the Christian Brothers Schools at North Richmond Street in Dublin. Nowhere in his writings of any kind does he mention this. Like father, like son.

Before I replace Joyce's book on its shelf: any glib commentator who spouts the usual derogatory clichés about the so-called hellfire sermons of the Redemptorists in the Limerick of my youth would do well to read, or re-read slowly, the detailed report of a hellfire sermon which is recorded by Joyce in that same book. And it was not delivered by a Redemptorist to a congregation of working-class men or boys but by a Jesuit priest during the annual retreat for the students in Dublin's Belvedere College. It opens with the preacher's chosen text:

– Hell has enlarged its soul and opened its mouth without limits – words taken, my dear little brothers in Christ Jesus, from the book of Isaias, fifth chapter, fourteenth verse. In the name of the Father and of the Son and of the Holy Ghost. Amen.

The sermon extends to five pages of the book, it is given as if verbatim — either Joyce and his fellow-students wrote detailed notes of their retreat sermons, or he had a tape-recorder memory — and it is only one in a series of lurid eschatological discourses.

Before giving a brief account of my own experience as a member, boy and man, of the Redemptorist Confraternity, I offer the reader two quotations from professional historians which refute the general calumny that attributes our poverty and living conditions to the alleged malign influence of the Catholic Church on our society. In his comprehensive work, *Ireland Since the Famine* (1971), the Protestant historian, Professor F. S. L. Lyons, who became Provost of Trinity College, describes the miserable life shared by Catholic and Protestant children alike in Belfast in the 1930s:

> It is hardly surprising then that that very year saw a remarkable demonstration in the city's streets in which both Protestant and Catholic workers joined together — hunger and degradation obscuring for a brief moment the deeply etched lines of religious and political division. Nor was it surprising that the children of the Belfast unemployed in the 1930s were reported to be two or three inches shorter and ten pounds lighter than their middle-class contemporaries, or that a survey of working-class conditions in the city in 1938–9 showed that thirty-six per cent of those investigated were living in absolute poverty — unable to buy food, clothing or fuel to maintain health and working capacity.

In corroboration of that account by Professor Lyons, here is a passage from *The Irish Catholic Experience: A Historical Survey* by Rev Dr Patrick Corish, Professor of Modern History at St Patrick's College, Maynooth:

> In 1932 the hungry and humiliated poor rioted in the streets of Belfast, and for a brief period no man asked his neighbour if he were Catholic or Protestant. When the city suffered devastating air-raids in April and May 1941 it was found that among the refugees from the slums there were about 5,000 people who were described in a cabinet paper as 'unbilletable' because they were nearly 'sub-human'. These unfortunates came from both sides of the sectarian divide. Northern Ireland was a poor region of the United Kingdom, and life at the bottom of the heap was horrible for Protestants as well as for Catholics.

When the Redemptorist order was founded in Italy in 1732 by St Alphonsus Liguori, a disillusioned lawyer who became a priest, the Penal Laws were in force in Ireland, and it was to be more than a century before these zealous preachers arrived in Britain and Ireland at the invitation of bishops and parish priests. And speaking of 'zealous preachers' I quote from *A History of the Catholic Church* by Philip Hughes who describes the Redemptorists as 'an order founded for the single object of giving missions, that is of preaching organised courses of sermons to bring sinners back to the right way and to strengthen the faithful in their loyalty to it.' Which shows that the critics of the Redemptorists are blaming them for doing efficiently the very thing for which their order was founded.

The common people in Limerick could not remember their name (we already had the *Augusteenas* and even, in some cases, the *Franksextons*) but because they came to give the special Lenten missions, the people decided that these great preachers must be a cut above the other priests in holiness – a status previously enjoyed by the obviously poor Sons of St Francis. (An old man in our Parish who was on the way out, when asked by the family if they would get him a priest, replied, 'No, no, don't get me a priest, get me a Franciscan!') And so they became known as the 'holy fathers' (we never said we were going to the Confraternity, but to the 'fathers', the name by which the church is still commonly known). This, of course, did not go down well with the other orders in Limerick, especially with the Jesuits in their splendid new church and residence at the Crescent beside the O'Connell monument – and the 'Js' must have been even more chagrined when the humble 'holy fathers' got land on a nearby hill overlooking the Crescent and built a fine new church and monastery there, calling it 'Mount St Alphonsus'. A local builder named John Quin made a connecting side-street, with fine houses, from O'Connell Street to the new church, and also installed the magnificent peal of bells which was able to rival (ecumenically, no doubt) the bells in the ancient St Mary's Cathedral in our Island Parish. The generosity of John Quin gave rise to the legend that since they were installed the Redemptorist bells have rung out, 'God bless John Quin an' all his min!'

Hostile critics of the Catholic Church in Ireland have established the erroneous notion in the minds of ordinary people that the Archconfraternity of the Holy Family was actually founded in Limerick and was something unique to that city and that its real purpose was to keep the working classes in servile submission to the Church. In fact, the Confraternity had its origins in the Belgian city of Liège, and it was not founded by the Redemptorists at all. It developed from a small group of twelve lay Catholic men who came together in 1844 and whose leader was a young military officer named Henry Belletable (although Dutch by birth, he eventually joined the newly-formed Belgian army in 1831). Their object was to counter the nefarious influence on the working classes of the atheistic liberal movements generated by the French Revolution. Because of their connection with the Redemptorist Church in Liège, and as their numbers grew rapidly, the society transferred its meetings from an ordinary house to the church, and acquired one of the priests as its Spiritual Director. The bishop raised the association to the status of a confraternity in 1845 and two years later Pope Pius IX raised it to the dignity of an Archconfraternity. By that time, the Redemptorists had already established branches in thirty-two cities, including Metz in France and Philadelphia, Detroit and Buffalo in the United States.

After having given two missions in Limerick in 1851 and 1852, the Redemptorists set up a permanent presence in 1853, first in Bank Place and later in Upper Henry Street. The first four superiors, up to 1860, were Belgian or Dutch (I wonder what the men of Limerick made of *their* sermons!) and the first Irish superior was William Plunket, a son of the Earl of Fingal. The new church at Mount St Alphonsus was dedicated in 1862 and inevitably the Archconfraternity of the Holy Family became a part of the religious life of the city. However, so many men flocked to the church that three divisions had to be set up, corresponding to three areas of the city, each meeting separately on Monday, Tuesday and Wednesday nights. A junior section for boys met on Friday nights. Eventually the Limerick branch of the Holy Family Confraternity achieved the status of being the biggest such sodality in the world – a distinction that inevitably singled it out for further hostile comment.

The Redemptorists and their founder, St Alphonsus, were also responsible for adding a new baptismal name to the family and traditional names in common use in Limerick, although inevitably every new little Alphonsus soon became Al, Ala, Alfie, Fons or Fonsie. The Belletable Arts Centre in O'Connell Street commemorates the devout soldier who was the originator of what became the greatest working-men's religious association in the Church. In my boyhood, that building was the Coliseum Cinema, one of the 'up-the-town' cinemas that were too expensive for the likes of us. When it ceased to be a cinema in the 1960s it was bought by the Holy Family Confraternity as a social centre for the members and renamed in honour of Captain Henry Belletable.

The weekly meeting of the Confraternity, conducted by the special priest who had been appointed Spiritual Director – and remember, the poor man who got that job in Limerick had to do the business three nights in succession every week! – consisted of Rosary, Sermon and Benediction, lasting almost an hour. The sermons, far from being confined to hell and damnation, ranged over all aspects of Catholic doctrine and devotion, and were often illustrated by reference to figures or events in history. These sermons were a topic of discussion in pubs and homes later in the night, and even during the ensuing week. And if any proof were needed in rebuttal of the notion that the Confraternity was a means of keeping the working class in Limerick in a state of meek subservience, I recall a special four-week series in October 1951, on the occasion of the Diamond Jubilee of the great encyclical of Pope Leo XIII, *Rerum Novarum*, when four guest speakers delivered lectures on 'The Rights and Duties of the State, the Employer, and the Worker' (I quote the title from a pamphlet containing the text of the four lectures published by the *Limerick Leader*).

An impressive aspect of the Confraternity meeting was the singing of hymns, reminiscent of those splendid Welsh male choirs, except that it was in unison – but imagine about two thousand men belting out those hymns that have recently been revived, under the comprehensive and significant title of one of them, 'Faith of Our Fathers', to astonish the commercial world with their success on tape and disc. But I must confess that when we sang those hymns in the Boys' Confraternity, we sometimes amused ourselves by altering a word here and there. Thus, in that innocent little hymn which gave me the title for this chapter, we sang the final line as 'And faith*less* until death.' And instead of being 'lost in wond'ring contemplation,' we were lost 'in wandering constipation'. There was, of course, an old story about a poor *amadán* named Jim Mack who was rushing along late to the church when he heard the massed voices inside singing, as he thought: 'Jim Mack you're late, Jim Mack you're late.' (What they were actually singing was 'Immaculate, Im-ma-cu-late.') And there were a few of Father Faber's Victorian hymns that were a puzzle to the youth of Limerick, like 'Hail, Queen of Heaven', which was fair enough until we got to the second verse and sang, 'O gentle chaste (pause) and spotless maid'. We had some idea what a 'spotless maid' meant, but a 'gentle chaste' was a bit of a mystery.

Each street formed a 'section' and had a few seats in the church allocated to it (a few small streets would be put together) with a coloured 'shield' bearing a saint's name, and a young man as prefect who marked a book of attendance. In our section, we relished the singing of the hymn, 'Daily, daily, sing to Mary' because of the presence among us of Seán Daly, who lived in the house opposite ours, and whose father and older brothers were house-painters by trade. (Seán joined them later.) He was very popular with all of us, and a reliable fighter if we clashed with hostiles from another street, but as all house-painters were colloquially known as *dabbers*, we could not resist taking a rise out of our own comrade whenever the organist struck up that hymn. We all roared, 'Dabber Daly, sing to Mary' and were threatened by fist and grimace with meela murder by Seán. After the meeting, all was forgotten – we had to stick together as we made our way home, in danger of being accosted or ambushed by all those 'knackers' who had not been privileged to be born and reared in our Island Parish!

The Director of the Confraternity in my boyhood was Father Gorey, a zealous and forthright man who, like many another priest or bishop, has been foully caricatured as some sort of tyrannical religious policeman. The only time we saw Father Gorey outside of the pulpit was when he made his regular tour of the schools on a bicycle. He reminded us about attendance at the Confraternity and urged us to be loyal and diligent; but we regarded that as a man doing his job, just as we considered Guard White, the school attendance officer, to be doing his when he appeared in classrooms. I have related how a priest from St Mary's gave me a slap in the face in the sacristy of the Convent of Mercy. One night in the Redemptorist Church I saw Father Gorey do the same thing to a young fellow from the section next to ours. Apparently he had been messing and had been called out from the seat and reprimanded by the orderly. These were men who volunteered to patrol the aisles of the pillared church during our meetings. They just stood at intervals of about thirty yards and kept an eye on us, ensuring that we didn't start chatting, playing cards (I once saw two scamps at it in our own section) or engage in other such non-religious activity. Father Gorey happened to be on his way to the pulpit and came on the altercation. We could see the brazen snout on the miscreant – we knew him well as a blaguard of the dirty rotten knacker class (very serious!) and in a recent randyboo over cheating in a street card game a few of us had chased him to his own house in a street near ours. When he dashed in home his mother rushed out and threw a basin of dirty water at us! He must have given Father Gorey some fierce cheek to cause the priest to give him that slap in the face. But, blaguard or not, we all felt that it was wrong of the priest to lose his temper to the extent of hitting anyone – although again, as in my own case with grumpy Father Costello, we knew Father Gorey was not an angel but a man, and St Peter himself would lose his temper with the likes of that knacker.

We had a good giggle during the annual mission one year when the Director told us from the pulpit that some shopkeepers had complained to him that the boys going up to the seven o'clock Mass were kicking over their dustbins. It was a regular game with us to jump over the bins outside shops but because of what the Catechism told us was 'the inclination to evil in human nature' consequent upon the Original Sin of our First Parents, some fellows took to giving the bin a hefty side-kick as they went over. 'Now,' said our Director, 'boys will be boys, but they mustn't be – ?' The rhetorical question is fatal at times. Together, two thousand Limerick lads roared: 'Gerrels!' After he overcame his confusion, the good priest told us that *blaguards* was what boys should not be!

For men and boys both, the Confraternity was a kind of religious social club, and in a world without television or cars – also without drugs, rock music and the lounge bars of today – it was a good way to spend at least one evening a week. We also felt a loyalty to the Confraternity and we had a great love and admiration for the Redemptorist priests. In the changed conditions of the last third of this century, the Confraternity, like all such religious sodalities everywhere, has become a shadow of what it was in our time. On the other hand, the Redemptorist Church is packed nowadays with people doing the devotions to Our Lady of Perpetual Help, the title under which the Redemptorist order tradition-ally promoted devotion to Mary, and this devotion has spread from that church in Limerick to many churches even in other cities and towns.

Two of the priests who served as Directors of the Confraternity achieved a place in the folklore of Limerick – one of them far beyond that. It was a Limerick-born priest, Father John Creagh, who was Director of the Confraternity in 1904 when the event occurred which made the name of Limerick and its Redemptorist Holy Family Confraternity notorious. 'What about the pogrom, eh?' is the question I am inevitably asked after someone has learned that I am a native of Limerick and a Catholic and then brought up the name of the Confraternity. I answered the most recent inquirer, in a pub in Dublin, in the Kerry style by asking him a question. 'When was that?'

'Some time about 1935, wasn't it?' he said.

'And what happened exactly?'

'A mob in Limerick killed a whole lot of Jews.'

'How many?'

'I think it was a few hundred, was it?'

If only Father John Creagh knew what we still have to suffer because he lost his cool one night and launched into a tirade about Jewish moneylenders and the misery they were causing in Limerick! Unfortunately, most of the Jewish community – there were not many more than a hundred in Limerick in 1904 (in 1871 there were only two) – were living just a short distance from the Redemptorist Church, in Colooney Street, now Wolfe Tone Street, where their synagogue was also situated, and when the men were dispersing from the Confraternity meeting, some of them, probably fired more with porter than with any religious zeal, began to attack the houses of the Jews. It has been aptly suggested also that some of the attackers might have been heavily in debt to Jewish moneylenders and saw a way out of their problems by burning the Jews out. Some houses were burned and some Jews injured but, contrary to what my recent pub interlocutor believed, no one was killed – and of course it did not happen in 1935 but in 1904.

The real pogroms that happened in Ireland were carried out in the north of Ireland when Protestant mobs burned Catholics out of their homes and killed hundreds in the process, as they did in 1886 and regularly thereafter up to the pogrom of 1935. On the latter occasion, some persons unknown decided to break a few windows in Protestant shops in Limerick, and one evening a group of us sat on the pavement wondering if we should do likewise with some Protestant houses. We were saved from such youthful but innocent bigotry by the fact that we didn't know any

Protestant houses! As far as we knew, all Protestants were rich people who lived out in the Ennis Road area or somewhere 'up the town'. Of the really barbaric pogroms that took place in Ireland we hear hardly a word from our revisionist historians and anti-Catholic media pundits who regularly trot out the terrible affair of the Limerick 'pogrom'. But in a comprehensive study of the Jews in the modern world by an eminent Jewish writer, Chaim Bermant, *The Jews* (1977) there is not so much as a mention of Limerick or its 'pogrom'.

Some of the Limerick Jewish families fled to Cork, where they would seem to have done very well for themselves, becoming solicitors and doctors and merchants, but others remained on in Limerick and became highly respected members of the business community there. Regrettably, even some Irish Jews, then and since, have contributed by their selective comments to the making of a mountain of intolerance and anti-semitism out of the molehill of a very minor incident in comparison with what was happening to the Jews in Poland, Russia and the Baltic states in those years. (It was refugees from those countries who came to Limerick, where they were able to set up in business and make a good living for themselves.) Anyone opening the mouth or taking up the pen to discuss those regrettable happenings in Limerick in 1904, might first consider that the small Jewish community in Killaloe, County Clare, was attacked in 1896 after some priest had given a dramatic sermon on the Crucifixion.

It is of interest also to note that only six years before the 1904 outburst by Father Creagh, the British Chief Rabbi, Dr Adler, came to Ireland on a pastoral visit, during which he issued a circular condemning involvement by Jews in moneylending and appealing to the Jews of Ireland to be 'of scrupulous honesty and integrity' in business dealings. (All of this, and more, is available in the files of the local papers for the period.) He also had to intervene in disputes between the Jews themselves in Limerick.

In 1884, when some men attacked a Jew's house in Limerick after they mistakenly thought he had shown disrespect to Good Friday, some of them got a month in jail from the magistrate, the historian and newspaper-owner, Maurice Lenihan, who said: 'The Irish should be the last persons on earth to persecute anyone. For centuries they had suffered for their religion and those who had suffered so much should feel for others.' In 1902, only two years before the incident resulting from Father Creagh's harangue, the Jewish community bought some land outside the city for use as a cemetery. In the following year at a reception in a hotel in Limerick in honour of one of the Jews, an active Zionist, who was emigrating to South Africa, the old Fenian and current Alderman, John Daly (who had spent many years as a convict in English jails), was invited by the Jewish community to preside on the occasion. He did, and he proposed a toast: 'To Israel, a nation.' To which a prominent member of the Jewish community, Mr Goldberg, replied with the toast: 'To Ireland, a nation.'

One of our fireside stories concerned another Director of the Confraternity, Father Mangan, who entered the folklore of Limerick on Whit Sunday in 1915. On that day, trains arrived in Limerick from Dublin, Cork and Tipperary bringing contingents of the Irish Volunteers to take part in a parade and review. Another special train from Dublin brought a battalion of British soldiers to reinforce the garrison in Limerick for the day. Over one thousand Volunteers marched in the parade, fully armed, although it is recorded that some of them 'wore broken boots and shabby attire, because their scanty earnings were devoted to paying for the guns they carried'. Among the officers that day were Pádraig Pearse, Tom Clarke, Terence MacSwiney, George Clancy, Tomás MacCurtain, Willie Pearse, Liam Mellows, Seán MacDermott, and Limerick's own Ned Daly.

The parade was led by the band of the Limerick Volunteer Regiment, in which my father played, and it was jeered, firstly by British soldiers from the windows of the New Barracks ('in typical filthy language,' says one account) and later in Mungret Street and the Irishtown by thousands of women whose husbands or sons were fighting with the Munster Fusiliers in France – and one of those women was my father's mother, Bríd Bhán ('She hated the Volunteers,' my mother told us). After parading across Thomond Bridge and around by Sarsfield Bridge back up to Pery Square, the Volunteers were unable to hold their review as planned in the People's Park (where the Carnegie Library stood), the mayor having rescinded permission and caused the gates to be locked.

After having disbanded for refreshments and an afternoon of sightseeing (there were many members of Cumann na mBan, as well as female relations who came for the outing, along with the Volunteers) the parade reassembled in the evening to march to the railway station and it was then that a serious attack was mounted on them by drunken hooligans in Parnell Street – not now with jeers and taunts but with stones and bottles (from some mysterious source, money, it was said, had been made available to selected publicans along the route to supply free drink for the day to all and sundry). When a young boy was hit by a bottle and taken away to hospital bleeding from a split head, the rumour spread that the Volunteers had opened fire and attacked people with fixed bayonets. This brought even sober men running to take part in the attack on the Volunteers. (It is recorded that Eamon de Valera got some women who were in danger into a pub, where he and some other men held the fort until the Limerick Volunteers rescued them.) It was then that Father Mangan, one of the most respected figures in Limerick, got up on a jaunting car and called on any Confraternity men in the crowd to come forward and form a protective cordon around the parade, and many hundreds obeyed his call at once. The Volunteers, with their distressed female supporters, were able to get to the nearby station without having to retaliate with the weapons they could so easily have used. It has been suggested that the British authorities allowed the Volunteers to parade fully armed in the hope that such a retaliation would take place. A few dead Limerick civilians would nicely balance the four civilians killed by British soldiers at Bachelor's Walk in Dublin on the day of the Howth gun-running just a year before, and it would also blacken the name of the Volunteers and of their leaders.

The Dublin papers next day reported that over a thousand Irish Volunteers had run away in disorder from a few hundred women in Limerick and were saved only by the intervention of the Royal Irish Constabulary! The same papers were to call for the execution of at least one hundred of the rebels a year later when it was the turn of a Dublin mob to jeer and taunt the Volunteers and Citizen Army as they were being brutally herded at the Rotunda and other centres after the Easter Week Rising.

So, the 'little Catholic' that I was in Limerick in the 1930s grew into the 'old Catholic' that I am as I write these words. And while I believe the promise of Christ that his Church will last till the end of time, when I consider the neo-paganism that is prevalent in Ireland today, in contrast with the too rigid subservience to authoritarian bishops that was the norm in society in my boyhood, I wonder if Saint Patrick might not be asking God to let him 'come and walk once more among us' as he heard the Irish people calling to him in a dream before he returned to bring the Good News of Christ to those civilised Celtic pagans in their green island on the edge of Europe. I must confess that as I endure the waffling inanities of the homily at Mass nowadays, I find myself wishing for a fine, solid, well-prepared sermon from a Redemptorist priest that would put the fear of God into me – that being merely the beginning of wisdom, according to the Bible, and I, like Socrates, being still anxious to acquire even a modicum of sense. But I might as well wish for a feed of Nana Ledane's crubeens or my mother's potato cakes and bread pudding.

29

PARADISE LOST

When the Corporation of Limerick decided in the mid-1930s to make a drastic clearance of some of the worst slum areas in the city, they looked around for a site where they could build about five hundred houses and they decided on the Island Field. This low-lying part of our Island Parish was hemmed in on one side by the Shannon and part of the Abbey River. It had been a training ground for the British garrison in King John's Castle for centuries, and when the castle was abandoned in 1922 it became a natural playground for the children of the area, especially in summer. In winter, much of it became a swamp because of the overflow from the trench below the Island Bank, a high grassy causeway which separated the Island Field from the river. In the summer evenings, apart from other activities, we used to ride the donkeys left by traders to graze in the extensive field, but if any of the owners came on the scene, we had to wade through the trench and clamber up on to the Island Bank to escape.

I should mention that we had a resident donkey in our own street, an animal which my father said was surely the best-fed donkey in Ireland! It belonged to two poor women named Weldon, an elderly silver-haired mother and her middle-aged daughter, who lived in one of the old cottered houses and who made a meagre living by purchasing 'seconds' or slightly damaged kitchenware and other items at the city's stores and then hawking them around the countryside with their donkey and cart to sell to the farmers' wives in County Clare. The boys on our street provided the Weldons' donkey with the finest of hay by blatant robbery which in our innocence we considered an act of great charity. While playing in Castle Street, if we saw a hayfloat coming in across Thomond Bridge, we hid behind the corner house of our own street. As soon as the hayfloat passed by, we ran out and pulled fistfuls of hay from the back of the load. The Weldon ladies showered blessings from God and his Blessed Mother on us, but many a farmer must have scratched his head on arrival at Cantrell's store on Charlotte's Quay – where my father had to pay hard-earned cash for the hay and straw and oats for his own horse – and found that some thieving horse or donkey, as it seemed, had made a large cavity in the back of his load of hay. In their trips around the villages and farms the Weldons were able to supplement our hay donations with other food; but how the donkey survived the winter I don't know. It was hard enough on the poor women to feed themselves.

Like many another mother of a large family, mine would have been glad to be allocated one of the houses that were to be built in the Island Field, but my father and many of our neighbours were convinced that building houses there at all was madness. Not only was the land swampy but the winter fog from the river, they said, would cause the people to die like flies from consumption and pneumonia. We listened in wonder at the stupidity of the Corporation, not yet realising the cataclysmic change that was about to disrupt our own lives. When the preparatory work began, we were chased out of the Island Field one day by a foreman, and ordered to crouch down behind the wall beside the entrance – the old firing ranges of the soldiers were being blasted. We heard the bang and imagined ourselves to be under shellfire in France with the Munster Fusiliers. And when they began to dig miles of trenches to lay the foundations of the houses, we had even more stimulation for our imagination in wide-ranging war-games every evening when the workers had knocked off, with tons of mud available to make 'hand-grenades' as we charged the enemy trenches or defended our own.

But already our street was resounding to the clatter of the builders' lorries, and our street games of hurling and rugby, as well as the girls' games, were being interrupted with increasing frequency every day, not only by the trundling lorries but by the hundreds of men walking or cycling to and from the building work. Even the wider Castle Street, leading from the corner of our Old Church Street down to Thomond Bridge, became less safe. When opening the new Thomond Bridge in 1840, Daniel O'Connell recalled having seen, after the rebellion of 1798, the gruesome sight of corpses hanging from the lamp-posts on the previous centuries-old structure; but for us – apart from the night-terror of the Bishop's Lady's ghost – the bridge and Castle Street had always been an extension of our own street, the more open and sunny part of our tranquil playing area. Rolling hoops, spinning or pegging tops, playing conkers or dobbers (marbles) or taws in season (certain pastimes mysteriously came into seasonal fashion), throwing our slang-bangs (a small metal object into which a 'cap' was inserted to explode when the 'slang-bang' hit the ground), sometimes having rides in a homemade go-cart, the children were always under the watchful eye of mothers from the open doorways of the houses or of the men who used to gather in the evening for a chat at the corner of the castellated little tollhouse near the bridge.

As soon as the first section of the Island Field houses was ready, we knew that not only was our playground in the field itself gone forever, but our street games – and eventually even our annual bonefire – would become impossible to continue. And it was not just traffic that brought disruption; after our ball had been snatched on several occasions by young ruffians passing by, we realised that only by building high walls at each end of our street could we ever again hope to use it as a playground. The completion of the nearly five hundred houses was a long-drawn-out process but from the time when the new residents began to move in, our street was like something out of the war films showing the refugees streaming along the roads in France. The people from the tenements and other areas had to transport their goods and chattels by any and every means – horse, donkey and cart, handcart, box-car, pram and human shoulders – and this traffic went on from early morning to late at night. Even when all the houses were eventually occupied, there were now some thousands of new residents packed into that small area between our street and the river, and the great majority of these, going to work or shopping in the city, had to pass along our street that had hitherto been practically a cul-de-sac (except for a further short street beyond the bend in the road and leading to the Island Field itself).

A further interesting light on the way planners plan is the fact that for what was, in effect, the equivalent of a small town, there were only six small shops provided, all in one row at the very entrance to the estate. This gave rise to the story about 'Gurky' MacMahon – one of the new residents who was to become well known as a much-loved 'character' in our Parish – on the first occasion that his wife sent him off to the new shops with a jug to buy milk. On the way back he was unable to locate his own house in the maze of identical yellow-washed and red-roofed streets of houses with their little gardens. After wandering around for a while, he asked one of the girls skipping in a street, 'Tell me, little girl, did you happen to see e'er a man comin' out of a house with a jug in his hand?' Such yarns did nothing to lessen the hardship imposed on the residents in the new estate, not only by the lopsided location of their few shops but by the failure to provide a church, school, medical centre or even a pub in such a comparatively huge centre of population packed into an area that was in effect isolated in a dead-end from the rest of the city. Their problems became our problems when the two schools in our Island Parish, the Sisters of Mercy school and the Christian Brothers' school at Quay Lane, were being asked to add the children from five hundred new houses to their already full classes. The Brothers divided the four big classrooms in the old school with partitions and packed as many pupils as they could into the school. Teachers in those days just had to accept that the size of a class was the number of pupils that could be fitted into the available space. The nuns also took in as many as they could but most of the children of schoolgoing age in the new estate had to continue at their old schools, with the consequent hardship of a very long walk twice a day. In the churches, too, St Mary's in the Parish, St Munchin's across Thomond Bridge, there were soon almost as many people standing and outside the door as there were seated, especially at the later Masses on Sunday. (There was no evening Mass on Saturday or Sunday then.)

Our summer playground on the riverside Island Bank was also doomed. In the old days, when we enjoyed 'Home Rule' in the Island, as my mother would put it (by extension, she would call a big sandwich or any other such item 'a real Home-Ruler'), there would be only the children from a few families paddling at the Fairy Steps under the watchful eyes of our mothers; but as the houses mushroomed in the Island Field beside our Island Bank, there suddenly came swarming across from the new estate hordes of children who had every bit as much right as we, the Island natives, to enjoy the pleasures of the Shannon with its sandy coves and grassy bank. We couldn't even swim now there was such a crowd jumping and splashing and pushing. And what about our clothes that we used to just throw there on the grassy bank? We were all from the same few streets, and even if we had not been raised with very strict standards of honesty we could hardly have appeared in public wearing clothes stolen from a neighbour. Not only were our clothes unsafe now but even our swimming togs could no longer be left on the grass to dry. And when winter came, we found that our traditional slide in the New Walk, which led down to the big double gates of the convent grounds, was also invaded by strangers. Our cry as we ran to commence our slide, 'Offa dee ice, Mag-gie!' must often have penetrated the conventual silence. That too was silenced when we natives realised that there was no point in pouring water on the road on a frosty night and then not being able to enjoy ourselves with some semblance of order and control.

Here it must be firmly stated that the knackers and robbers among the thousands of people who came to live in the Island Field (officially renamed St Mary's Park) were only in the same proportion as in any other area of Limerick or Dublin or any other town or city. Just as happened in Dublin when the people in the city tenements were moved to estates similar to St Mary's Park, the few vandals and blaguards soon earned a bad name for the entire estate, with the consequent unfortunate discrimination in employment and social life. My father and mother were vehement in their opinions on this kind of snobbery. Some of the men who had played with my father in the Sarsfield Band and had lived near his own family in the Mungret Street and Watergate areas, were among the new residents in the Island Field, as were some of my mother's friends, both from her childhood days in Arthur's Quay and her teenage working years in the caramel factory. She went to visit them and admire enviously their lovely new homes, and they sometimes stopped for a chat when going up the town or on their way home. And in our class in school we had new pupils who were the same mixture as ourselves, 'good, bad, and middling', whether academically or at games or in general behaviour. But after my father had repaired our window three times – at least we learned how to do it by watching him – and the midnight rowdiness of rolling-home drunkards (the small pub at the corner of our street, Halpin's, was the nearest pub for the five hundred new houses) had often made us children think the Bishop's Lady was on the rampage again, even he began to add his prayers to my mother's that the promised new house on the site of the old distillery out in Thomondgate would soon become a reality.

Whether coincidentally or as a result of the traffic and population problems in our streets, we noticed also that the casual traders and characters whom we had known for years gradually disappeared. Even 'Annie the Cabbage-Woman' from Park came no more. The call of 'rags, bones and bottles' from the tall foreign-looking man who gave a balloon or a plastic windmill in exchange, was heard no more. The street-singer who cupped his hand to his ear would not have been able to hear himself even with that natural echo-chamber. And most of all we missed the man who used to come along pushing an old bicycle which was loaded down with coils of wire and old batteries. He was dressed in the dirtiest clothes we ever saw, with a big cap of the same quality around which there were more wires, and his face was greased with vaseline and dirt, causing his eyes to gleam like little blue stars (an appropriate image, as will be seen). He used to park his bicycle and stand on a tin box, doing strange movements with the wires. He never spoke to us except to answer our greeting in a gentle voice and he even responded with a polite shake of the head when we inquired if there was any news from Mars today. We had seen the film serial (or 'follin'-up one' in our dialect) *Flash Gordon's Trip to Mars,* and so when we gathered to watch this poor man 'communicating with Mars' we were able to suspend our disbelief and even the cruel mockery with which we, like all children, sometimes added to the misery of other such afflicted people.

The only recompense the new estate afforded us for the loss of all these old characters was the arrival of one new character, the aforementioned 'Gurky' MacMahon, about whom there were soon many stories to add to the incident of the jug of milk. He too became a patron of Halpin's pub, but he was no rowdy, rather a genial and convivial man, and a man my father had known long before he came to be one of our new neighbours in the Island Field. 'Gurky' won his way into the hearts of us children the very first time he came strolling along the street from Halpin's, with his cap on his ear and his benign smile taking in the scene where we were playing. He stopped up and called us to gather round him. Then he produced a penny and offered it to anyone who could sing 'The Legion of the Rearguard', a rallying song of the Republican side during the civil war. Money, like death, is a great leveller, and there was a serious fight in our street after the benevolent 'Gurky' had ambled on down to his new house – because (would you believe!) didn't some of the Free Staters join in with us genuine Republicans as we sang:

Soldiers of the Rearguard, answering Ireland's call,
Hark, the martial tramp is heard from Cork to
            Donegal;
Tone and Emmet guide you, though your task be
            hard;
De Valera lead you, Soldiers of the Legion of the
            Rearguard.

Our subsequent fight had as much to do with the money as with that Treaty: Gurky had only three coppers in his pocket, and faced with the impossible task of selecting three from about ten, he decided to throw the pennies 'up for a rawk'. The civil war after the signing of the Treaty was only a bigger and more violent version of the hostilities on our street for a week after that night. A lot of Shannon water has flowed along by the Island Bank and under

Thomond Bridge since then, and in the three score years that have gone by since it was developed, St Mary's Park has become an integral part of the Island Parish in Limerick. And what we considered to be its isolated position is now nearer to the centre and amenities of the city than many of the big housing estates that were built in subsequent years far beyond what were the urban boundaries in the 1930s.

30

'OH, TO HAVE A LITTLE HOUSE!'

In an early chapter of this chronicle I told how, shortly after their marriage in 1918, my parents moved from their one-room home in Rutland Street to share with another couple, the Sheehans, the 'house-and-a-half' beside the Bishop's Palace in the Island. I surmised that, while both couples considered themselves fortunate to have such accommodation at the time, each of them probably hoped that the other couple would soon find some other place and move out. Unfortunately for all concerned, it was to be nearly twenty years before that happened. When the move finally happened, it was the O'Flynns who moved out.

Growing ever more desperate as the years passed by and the patter of tiny feet crescendoed to the clatter of boots and shoes, my mother stormed heaven and earth, as the saying is, to get 'a little house, a house of my own', anywhere. Since we, the boys in the family, having been trained to perfection as altar boys in St Mary's by Liam Bartlett, had subsequently been engaged by the nuns in the nearby Convent of Mercy, where we had all gone to school as infants, to serve as altar boys in the convent, my mother hoped for many years that the nuns would give her one of the houses they owned in the area. Unfortunately, none became vacant during those years, or if it did, perhaps – who knows? God knows – the nuns might have considered a family like ours too large for the tenancy of one of their properties.

Like all troubled mothers in those times, my mother, without neglecting to appeal regularly to that ever-sympathetic Mother who gave birth to her Divine Son in a stable, also enlisted the special assistance of the universally popular Franciscan saint, Anthony of Padua, and every Tuesday morning she went to the seven o'clock Mass in the Franciscan Church in Henry Street, passing by her first room in Rutland Street and near her childhood home in Arthur's Quay on the way. Although St Anthony obliged by finding my mother's lost wedding-ring on one occasion, after we went under the bed every night to say a special prayer to him – this was thought to make the prayer more sincere and efficacious – he let her down badly in the matter of the house. Or perhaps the good Anthony did his best in the celestial court but was overruled by a higher authority who decided to shorten my mother's Purgatory by having her suffer more on earth.

In fact, it was a very decent man named Eamon de Valera who eventually provided my mother with a lovely new house. He has, of course, some other claims to fame. One of the more ridiculous calumnies perpetrated against his reputation was that he was a naïve agrarian idealist who, while neglecting to clear the slums or develop Ireland as an industrial nation, concentrated the resources of the state on trying to restore the Irish language and develop an idyllic Emerald Isle that would be symbolised by 'comely maidens dancing at the crossroads' – words often mockingly quoted by Dev's political opponents and by journalists or shallow commentators but words which Dev himself never actually said.

Anyone who has been duped by such *ráiméis* would do well to study the following brief extract from the newspaper reports of a lecture given at the Merriman School in August 1997 by Professor Tom Garvin of University College Dublin:

De Valera abandoned a party plan to settle as many people as possible back on the land. He realised that such an undertaking would wreck the country's already feeble economy during a time of great world crisis. Most of our semi-state bodies, which have been the nation's pride for many years, originated in his era. *Under de Valera, a determined effort was also made to rehouse poor and working class people, using public money* [my italics]. Although the elimination of TB and other infectious diseases was carried out by other governments, plans were first initiated by de Valera's government. Later governments also cancelled progressive moves such as a transatlantic air service and a roads modernisation scheme. The introduction of rural electrification during de Valera's time in office was a large step in the emancipation of rural women, reducing the weight of physical labour.

Anyone with the slightest knowledge of Irish social history in the twentieth century will confirm that it was only when De Valera and his Fianna Fáil party came to power in 1932 that the first steps were taken to solve the problem of clearing the slums left as a legacy of the British occupation of Ireland, slums that had deteriorated even further under the Cosgrave government during the first ten years of the Free State from 1922, and also to set up Irish factories that would stem the tide both of emigration and of imports from Britain and elsewhere. Soon after Fianna Fáil came to power, along with the new factories being built by the pragmatic policies of Seán Lemass, and benefiting by the supply of electricity from the new Shannon Scheme at Ardnacrusha – a project which some Fianna Fáil politicians in opposition had mockingly dubbed a white elephant – new housing schemes to replace the slums in cities and towns got under way everywhere. In Limerick, the Corporation's first housing scheme was unpretentious and cautious, consisting of a small number of dwellings in the actual courtyard of King John's Castle or the 'Castle Barracks' as it was still known locally, although without a garrison now since 1922. The New Barracks, built in 1798 but renamed in 1922 for Sarsfield, the hero of the Limerick sieges, was now the centre of military affairs in Limerick. The next scheme was the more ambitious Island Field one already mentioned: here a major project was undertaken, with the building of hundreds of houses in order to clear out and demolish the worst tenements in several parts of the city. Before the outbreak of the Second World War, further extensive building schemes had been completed in various parts of the city: one in Thomondgate (in which my mother's dream came true), another just beyond that in Kileely at the edge of Limerick City's encroachment on County Clare, and others in Kilallee near St John's Cathedral and in Janesboro.

In 1934 when I made my First Holy Communion my poor mother was watching with envious eyes the building of those first few dozen houses in the courtyard of King John's Castle, just at the corner of our street. Then came the big scheme in the Island Field, a few hundred yards to the other side of us. She would have been glad to be listed among the fortunate citizens who were given new houses in either of those schemes but an old-time friend of hers, a city councillor whose more mundane help she invoked along with that of Saint Anthony, although he was of the Fine Gael persuasion, advised her to be patient a little longer, to wait for another scheme that was in the pipeline and about which he would give her the tip-off when Town Hall talk was about to be replaced by the sound of concrete mixers. My father was a philosophical man whose main interest in life was music, but he was also of an independent spirit, disdainful of all political machination in any area of life, too proud to ask a favour of anyone or even to apply for the dole when his livelihood was wiped out by the war of 1939–45. My mother, on the other hand, was a firm believer in the pragmatic approach to any situation, although her forthright and colourful manner of expressing her opinions – in this she was truly our Granny Connolly's daughter! – was not always likely to 'win friends and influence people'. She herself used to admit that fault, if fault it be, when, commenting on some controversial incident, she would add the dictum, 'We were always very straight, but that doesn't go down well with some people.'

When the word finally came from the benevolent Blueshirt, my mother could hardly wait for my father to arrive home that evening. When he did, the poor man was hardly in the door when a little drama of great significance took place, a drama that has played over and over again in my memory and which is as vivid at this moment as on the night when, along with my siblings, I watched and listened to the protagonists. I record it as it happened:

Mother: I was up the Irishtown today and I met Mossy Reidy, and he told me they're going to build about a hundred houses out in Thomondgate where the old distillery is. And he said you should go up first thing tomorrow to the Town Hall and put down your name for one.

Father: (frowning) Where did you say they're going to build houses?

Mother: Out in Thomondgate; they're going to knock down the old distillery and build new houses there along by the river.

Father: (gaping, pointing vaguely) D'you mean, out across the bridge?

Mother: Amn't I after tellin' you? Out in Thomondgate.

Father: (horrified) But – but you couldn't go out *there*.

Mother: Why couldn't you? Sure it's only across Thomond Bridge to the other side of the river from

303

where we are now.

Father: I know, I know, but – but, my God, you'd die out there!

Mother: (losing patience) For the love and honour of God, will you rise outa me! What are you blatherin' about? A lovely new house out beside the River Shannon, how could we die out there?

Father: Well, I know it looks nice but there's a breeze comes down from the Windy Gap up there in the Clare Hills and it freezes all before it out there on the Thomondgate side of the river. You wouldn't last a winter out there.

Mother: And how is it the wind from the Clare Hills don't freeze us all to death on *this* side of the river?

Father: Because we have protection here from the castle and the other buildings, and the bend of the river directs the wind more to the other side anyway.

Mother: But how is it the Soda Cakes in Thomondgate are able to live out there in the winter? Aren't their seed, breed and generation living out there since the time of Saint Patrick or longer?

Father: Ah but sure that's the very point, d'you see! They're used to it for generations; all their people before them lived out there; so, they're hardened to it, but the likes of us that were born and reared inside here in the city –

Mother: Oh wisha God and his Holy Mother give me patience! If you don't go up to the Town Hall tomorrow morning and sign on for one of them new houses in the distillery, I'll do it myself, and when we get the new house you can stay on here if you're afraid of the breeze from the Windy Gap!

(Curtain)

So, to make a long story short, the old distillery on the Clare bank of the Shannon was duly demolished and the new houses were built, nearly a hundred of them, in the standard model favoured by municipal authorities everywhere at that time; they were in terraces of four or six, with all modern amenities, gardens front and rear, and a reasonable weekly rent, but unfortunately still with only two bedrooms, so that large families had to convert the front parlour into a bedroom or divide the upstairs bedrooms with partitions. The houses were in a horseshoe loop, one row facing the River Shannon, the other facing away from it. We were fortunate in the draw, being allocated number thirty-six, an end house in a terrace in the riverside section. By coincidence, the area fire-hydrant was located in the footpath outside our front garden, so that the Corporation affixed a plate bearing the letters FH to the front wall of the house. This we interpreted joyfully as standing for 'Flynns' House', so that in our settling-in days we never needed to remember or look out for the number.

We made the fateful exodus from the ancient Island to the territory of the Soda Cakes in Thomondgate in 1938, a year before Hitler's invasion of Poland plunged Europe and the world into war. The emotional wrench of our move was lessened by the fact that our next-door neighbours in Old Church Street, the Nealons, were also allocated a house in the new development; unfortunately, the draw did not make our two families next-door neighbours again, although happily we were only a few houses apart.

My father's horror at the thought of crossing Thomond Bridge to live on the Clare side of the Shannon was surely an echo of the mentality of the citizens of any walled city looking out at the potentially hostile countryside, the most notorious example of which is the inscription said to have been placed on the walls of Galway City by the Anglo-Irish citizens: 'From the ferocious O'Flahertys, O Lord, deliver us.' And his Cassandra prediction of the fate that awaited us on that hostile Clare bank of our beloved Shannon River proved not altogether mistaken. Within a few years, he saw the coffins of a son and a daughter carried from our new house. It was not, however, the chilling winter breeze from the Windy Gap in the Clare Hills that brought his prediction to fulfilment, but the more insidious and malevolent plague of tuberculosis that was in those years sweeping through Ireland and Europe like a veritable scythe of Death. Less than four years after our move to what was apparently a more salubrious house and situation, my brother Joe died at the age of nineteen, to be followed in 1944 by my sister Lily, aged twenty-four. My father survived that dreaded Windy Gap breeze for almost twenty years, and my mother was to live to within a year of her century, having asserted all her life, in her already noticed forthright fashion, that the farther you keep away from doctors the longer you'll live. Granny Connolly's assessment of the medical profession in general was equally forthright and even more cryptic: 'Them oul' doctors, they want to know everything!'

31

Into the Murder Machine

It was the poet-patriot Pádraig Pearse, being also an idealistic and innovative pedagogue, who published in 1916, only a few months before the Rising, a pamphlet entitled 'The Murder Machine', based on a lecture delivered in the Mansion House in Dublin in 1912 and on a later article. His thesis is stated bluntly early on: 'There is no education system in Ireland.' He compares the examination system in secondary schools to a machine that murders the mind, whereas a true system of education ought to develop the talents of the individual pupil. Even George Bernard Shaw, born twenty-three years earlier, recognised this when he said that he began his education when he left school and credited music, his visits to the National Gallery in Merrion Square and his ramblings on Dalkey Hill with being important factors in it.

On the Monday morning when I entered the 'murder machine' of secondary school in September 1939, a more realistic and universally destructive one had just been switched on in Europe. A few days before, on Friday 1, Hitler's *Blitzkrieg* had been unleashed against Poland, and England and France had declared war on Germany on the Sunday. In those pre-television days, it was all still very far away from us, but as we sat around getting to know one another on that first day in our secondary school career – we had graduated from different primary schools – the main topic of discussion was naturally the war. Some fellow said, 'Warsaw saw war' and we thought that was funny. As the war dragged on year by year with increasing horror and intensity, we would realise that if De Valera had not asserted and maintained Irish neutrality in spite of British and American pressure – just as Franco did for Spain, under similar pressure from Hitler and Mussolini – we would have been laughing on the other side of our face before the war ended.

We had moved into our new house in Thomondgate the year before, when I was starting my final year in the primary school in Quay Lane. It was decided that I should finish my course there, even though it meant having to run even farther to get a bite to eat during the half-hour we were allowed for lunch; previously I had to run only the length of Nicholas Street, from St Mary's Cathedral to the castle, but now I had to pass by our old street and run on down by the castle, across Thomond Bridge, turn right at the Treaty Stone (then in its old position at the end of the bridge) and run along by the river as far as 36 O'Dwyer Villas, the resplendent new home of the O'Flynns, formerly of 2 Old Church Street, off Castle Street.

When we were still in the old house I had been the envy of my pals on a few occasions when I got a 'bar' from Seán Nealon, the eldest boy in the Nealon family who were our next-door neighbours. Seán had been a classmate of our eldest boy, Tom, and he had gone into his father's trade as a house-painter. When some job he was on at the time meant that he was cycling past our school at dinner-time (all shops and factories closed for dinner from 1 p.m. to 2 p.m. and the city streets and bridges were like anthills with the rush of pedestrians and cyclists) Seán stopped up and put me on the bar of his bike, and for a 'big fellow' who was actually working to take such notice of a 'small fellow' was a feather in my cap in the eyes of the gang. With the longer run to Thomondgate, I hardly had time to sit down and eat whatever was going before I had to dash off again. Being late for school, morning or afternoon, was a criminal offence, punishable without appeal by a few wallops of leather or cane. My mother used to take pity on me, especially, she often said afterwards, when it was my favourite, bread pudding, for dinner; so, while I polished off one lump, she put another in a paper bag. I brought this back to school, where, with some assistance from the pals on either side, it was consumed surreptitiously, growing colder as the inevitable delays between snatches occurred. We were, of course, risking summary execution if caught – men have got medals for less daring – but we boasted that we never were. Our brilliant and dedicated 'Luke' Liddy was too engrossed in his blackboard demonstrations to know that a large portion of Mrs O'Flynn's succulent bread pudding was being enjoyed by three brats in the fourth bench.

People who have gone to school under the new regime will hardly be able to appreciate that I, like my classmates, had no desire whatsoever to go 'next nor near' a secondary school. We hated school, of any kind or level, and our ambition was to reach the age of fourteen and get a job, any sort of a job. The boys who were assured of being apprenticed to their fathers' trades – painter, carpenter, plumber, tailor, butcher (all of them closed trades in those days) – or who hoped to get into a shop or factory through the influence of parents or relatives already working there, were envied by the others who had to be satisfied with becoming delivery boys for some shop or store, in the hope of something better to come as we grew older.

My sailor grandfather's grandiose scheme to ensure the commercial independence of his four sons having been scuppered by a combination of war, emigration and music, we, the children of his son Richie, were now in the 'free-for-all' category. As has been seen, Mr Liddy was anxious to retain me in his class because my eldest brother, Tom, had been his star pupil. All of the family preceding me through the school system, my two sisters, Mary and Lily, and my brothers, Tom, Joe and Dick, were, as the formidable Sister Felicitas often told my mother and ourselves, 'bursting with brains' – the nuns in St Mary's had urged my parents to let Mary and Lily do the exam for a scholarship to the Preparatory College for Teachers in Dingle, County Kerry, which was run by the Mercy nuns, and where the normal secondary course was followed, guaranteeing successful students entry to the training college in Limerick. But having had experience of the student teachers from that same training college, our girls were horrified at the idea of spending four years locked up in a college in Kerry where the vast majority of the students would be from the Gaeltacht areas of Kerry and Cork. Anyway, they, like the boys and like all their friends, had the firm belief that the best thing in life was to be finished with school and get a job. So, when I began in the secondary school – I was aged eleven and a half, and the law stated that I could not put an end to my academic career until I reached fourteen – Mary was working as a machinist in a tailoring firm, Lily was in the new shoe factory in Mulgrave Street, Tom was a messenger boy for the bus company in Sarsfield Street, Joe, the potential writer, had just stepped up from being messenger boy in a confectioner's to being a counter-hand in a drapery firm, and he had got Dick a job there as messenger boy. Part of Tom's job was to deliver the films to the new Savoy Cinema, where he was given two complimentary tickets every week; so, we all got the breathtaking experience of going to what seemed more like a palace from the *Arabian Nights* than a cinema.

On the one hand, the fact that five of the family were now earning a weekly wage of some kind might indicate that our standard of living would improve; against that, however, must be put the fact that children have a habit of growing bigger, needing more food and new clothes and footwear. Also, as they grew older, my older sisters and brothers could hardly survive socially on the one penny pocket money my father used to give them every Sunday when they were children. (It might be of interest to note that in those times everyone was proud to bring home the weekly wage packet and hand it over to the grateful mother, who decided what sum to bestow on the dutiful son or daughter.) I don't know how things might have developed if the war had not broken out. When it did, it put the kibosh on everything. My father's two sources of income were gone – whatever coal got through in our few Irish ships was assigned to essential uses, and the rationing of petrol meant that he could only hope for casual one-night stands at dances in the city. He talked of going to England, as many men were doing, but in the end it was the eldest girl, Mary, who went, recruited along with other girls by an agent from Britain. And as happened with so many other families in Ireland, it was her money, earned making bullets in what had previously been a chocolate factory in Worcester, that was to be the main factor in keeping the family during the war.

It was simply impossible for working-class parents with a large family to keep their children at school longer than the law ordered. Even the handful of scholarships for secondary education provided by local authorities – there were only six each year in Limerick for the whole city – were more an example of bureaucratic ineptitude than a really effective remedy. For instance, anyone who won a scholarship in Limerick was guaranteed a total sum of £75, spread over the five years of secondary school at the fixed rate of £15 per annum, out of which the school fees were paid. The annual fee in the Christian Brothers' school then was £12 – but let it be noted that the Brothers never turned away anyone who could not pay – provided he wanted to learn and that there was a place available in the two first year classes. They were housed in one large classroom, that had to cater in the first place for all the applicants from the Brothers' own four primary schools in the city. The fees paid, the parents had the princely sum of three pounds to feed and clothe their bright little scholarship winner for a year – this at the age of twelve or thirteen. If he survived to Leaving Cert level he would be a young adult of seventeen or eighteen, in long trousers, with feet the size of his father's, and they would still receive the same sum, £15. And if he had the talent and the application to gain one of the even rarer scholarships to university, he would have to go to Galway or Cork and survive for three or four years, again on a doled-out pittance.

Apart from that mirage of university, there were three careers for which the working-class pupil might compete – if his parents could keep him at school until Leaving Certificate. These were national teacher, army cadet and civil servant. There were also ESB clerkships and the local Post Office clerkships. The Brothers also had contact with many firms in the city and were able to recommend pupils for office or other jobs. From what I have said about the older members of our family, it will be understood that the three youngest, who all of us, by one route or another, became teachers, were not in any way more gifted than the others. It was because they, like their friends, left school at the statutory age of fourteen and went to work that we were able to prolong our education. It will be appreciated also that I find it hard to contain my anger with the politicians and the bishops of that era, all of them from the middle and upper classes, who were quite content to let that system carry on forever – until Donagh O'Malley, himself one of that class, took the first step in the 1960s to make a reality of the words of the 1916 Proclamation:

> The Irish Republic ... guarantees equal rights and
> equal opportunities to all its citizens, and declares its
> resolve to pursue the happiness and prosperity of the
> whole nation and of all its parts, cherishing all the
> children of the nation equally ...

My brothers had prepared me for the respective terrors of the infant school and of the 'Monks' in Quay Lane but their advice for the secondary school was concise: get out of it as fast as you can. In addition to the normal disruption felt by a pupil who has to leave the primary school where he has been a senior and go to a completely new academic system where he suddenly reverts to being the lowest of the low, in Limerick at that time, as I have explained earlier, the four primary schools of the Christian Brothers all sent their finished products – those who wanted to go (some would go to the Vocational School to learn their fathers' trades) – to the single secondary school. But because one of the primary schools, St Michael's, was actually part of the same complex as the secondary school and the residence where all the Brothers lived, the few pupils who came from the three outlying schools were outnumbered by those from St Michael's. They also felt, rightly or wrongly, that the Brothers in the secondary school looked with more favour on the graduates of St Michael's, many of whom were of a somewhat higher social status, sons of shopkeepers, teachers, civil servants, and so on. In fact, some parents of that class, although domiciled in one or other of the outlying parishes, sent their sons to St Michael's. I knew two or three who cycled past our Primary School in Quay Lane on their way up the town to what their parents considered (mistakenly, of course!) to be the Brothers' best school of the four.

On my first day, I was surprised to find that there were two classes in one large room, like the old arrangement in Quay Lane before the rooms were partitioned in my final year. The new pupils were divided into A and B, the A class being the pupils who were young enough, and reported by their primary school teachers as bright enough, to try for the Corporation scholarship (this exam was held at Easter). My brothers had prepared me for the fact that I would now have several teachers instead of the one. I had three: a layman, Jim Scallan, for Latin and History, Brother White for Irish and Brother Murray for everything else. In our room, Mr Scallan and Brother Murray moved to the A or B class for their respective subjects. For Irish, we transferred to Brother White's room. The Irish for white being *bán*, this red-faced, rough, balding, bespectacled pedagogue from County Cork was known by the unimaginative nickname, Bánaí (Bawnee). Brother Murray, our principal instructor and tormentor, had a square, sallow, wrinkled face topped with close dark curly hair. He also wore spectacles, and he was enthusiastic in his methods to the point of being the most hyperactive person I have ever met (*enthusiasm* is derived from the Greek *enthousiasmos*, 'a god-inspired zeal', but this 'ball-of-fire', as my mother called such people, seemed to me to be driven more by some malicious demon). More than the common run of teachers, he had a selection of cliché expressions, the most common being 'Bosh boy, bosh boy!' uttered almost as one word. He thus provided his own nickname, Bosh. The lay teacher, Jim Scallan, reminded me somewhat in his quiet manner of our 'Luke' Liddy. He was a member of a well known Limerick family of teachers and musicians (my father sometimes played with a brother of his in a danceband) and the Limerick lads must have judged that he suffered enough trying to teach in the same room with Bosh Murray and so he was known to us only by his own name.

On that first day also I had clear proof of the hypocrisy and futility of the Irish language revival policies of successive governments since the establishment of the Irish Free State in 1922. In the infant school and in the

314

primary school, we were taught Irish – and every other subject, except Religion – through the medium of Irish, even while we were struggling to learn Irish itself. No such law had been applied to the secondary school system or to the colleges, with the result that we now had Bosh Murray teaching us Mathematics and Geography through English, and Mr Scallan doing likewise with History and Latin (the latter a new subject). We had therefore to learn the terminology of these subjects all over again – first being mystified by Bosh shouting about things we had never heard of, like 'an isosceles triangle' and 'the square on the hypotenuse' etc. And after having daily, year after year, heard my name called out at roll-call each morning as *Críostóir Ó Floinn*, to which I answered, *'Anseo!'*, I was now to hear Bosh Murray calling out, *O'Flynn Christopher*, to which I must reply 'Here!' The Bosh inversion of our names resulted in two decent boys in the class hearing themselves called every day Long Thomas and Short Joseph but woe betide anyone who would emit so much as a giggle.

We were given a list of books by each teacher, with the injunction that we were to have them by the following Monday. When I saw that one of the five books on my Irish list was *Séadna*, I was thrilled at the prospect of reading the whole story of my old *feis* friend, the cobbler who sold his soul to the devil for a purse of gold. Little did I know that on the following Monday, Bánaí White would give me my first two slaps of his leather strap because I had not succeeded in buying, begging or borrowing that book. As I went home with that list of books in my bag, I knew that showing it to my father that night would be only a waste of time: man of many talents he might be, but he did not have the Midas touch that would turn lumps of coal into gold nuggets.

Some of the books on my list were in the press at home, having been used by others in the family – and they had got them second- or third-hand, so that now the books were

315

battered and patched up, bearing several owners' names. The atlas especially was more like a world that had been bombarded by Martians, but I still treasure a very battered copy of *The Merchant of Venice* that was used by three of the family before it came to me. Any pence my mother could spare had to go on exercise copies and other minor articles but the older ones in the family promised to ask friends and people with whom they worked. Eventually, I had all the books, but not before I had learned my first lesson in the secondary school, which was to hate one of my teachers.

Bánaí White's system was simple: he called out the name of each book on the list and if you didn't have the book you got 'out to the line' (he shouted it in Irish: '*Amach go dtí an líne!*'). No explanations were asked for, you just collected your two slaps of the leather and sat down – only to get out to the line again for the next book you didn't have. I had found only two of the five Irish books at home, and so the first week I was given six slaps; this was reduced to four the next week and the minimum two for the next two weeks. It had taken the combined efforts of our family four weeks of foraging all over Limerick among their friends before my brother Tom bought a secondhand copy of *Séadna* from the son of one of the bus conductors at the bus depot. By that time, my fond memories of learning two pages of the book with Sister Felicitas had been blotted out by the evil wish that the *Fear Dubh* who made that Faustian deal with the poor cobbler would come some night and carry off the this rawmouth savage who was belting me because my father could not give me the money to buy schoolbooks.

While Mr Scallan used the leather in moderation to initiate us into the rules of Longman's *Latin Grammar* and place our neophyte feet firmly on the first rung of *Scalae Primae*, Bosh Murray supplemented the machine-gun leather with a broken blue window-pole (modern students will never have seen the old sash-windows that opened from top or bottom, with a clasp in the top into which a hook on the window-pole was inserted to open the window down). The leather was used vigorously for anything and everything, but the broken pole could reach us even when we were seated in the long benches, thus saving the time that would be wasted in hauling us out to be slapped with the leather. A crack of a timber pole on the skull or shoulders is a powerful incentive to concentration. Even at singing class, for which we had a visiting teacher, an elderly, silver-haired, courteous musician named Brae or Bray – whichever version the poor man used, he was inevitably known as 'Donkey' – who wore a faded black suit and an upturned collar (I always saw him as some character out of a Dickens novel), Bosh Murray would pace around the sides of the class keeping discipline with his stick. A blow on the head, with the snapped command: 'Open your mouth, boy!' always served to add volume if not melody to the results of old Mr Brae's professional efforts.

In view of the fact that modern psychology has decided, contrary to the opinion of philosophers and educationists for thousands of years, that corporal punishment has no place in schools, it is of interest to record that Dr Johnson, when asked his opinion on 'whether there should be flogging in schools', came down on the side of corporal punishment, with the comment that 'What the scholars lose at one end, they gain at the other.' And when he was once asked how he had acquired so accurate a knowledge of Latin, he said: 'My master whipped me very well; without that, Sir, I should have done nothing.' In the days when I was myself being beaten with leather strap or stick, it was some comparative consolation to remember an illustration in my favourite volume of our *Newnes Pictorial Knowledge*, which showed the artist's conception of a school room in ancient Rome. Behind each pupil sat an older person with a long stick in his hand. The text informed us that when the sons of the Patricians went to school a slave accompanied each youth and sat behind him in the classroom. His duty was to beat the noble youth, his master's son, if he did not pay attention, and subsequently to report to the *pater* on how the son had behaved that day. This classical example, of course, did nothing to alleviate the pain and the puzzlement on the day when Bosh Murray gave me and others two of his best with the leather because we could not recite the passage from *The Merchant of Venice* prescribed as part of our homework (I can recite it now, but, alas, many years too late!). It goes like this:

The quality of mercy is not strain'd,
It droppeth as the gentle rain from heaven
Upon the place beneath: it is twice blessed;
It blesseth him that gives and him that takes:
'Tis mightiest in the mightiest: it becomes
The throned monarch better than his crown . . .

Apart from the daily slapping that was accepted as part of the system everywhere in those times, the memory of two unusual punishments has remained with me all my life as if the slaps had cut grooves in my brain as well as raised welts on my hands. We now had three-quarters of an hour for lunch, but there was no way I could run from Sexton Street to our new home in the Distillery (it was still so called, in spite of the houses having been named O'Dwyer Villas in memory of a Bishop of Limerick). My mother bought me a flask, and along with some other lads I stayed in school for lunch, which we ate in the classroom and then (weather permitting) went out to play in the yard. After lunch one day, Bosh soon had occasion to slap one or more of his pupils; he went to the press where he had left the leather before lunch, but could not find it. Like Bánaí White with regard to our acquiring the new books, Bosh had a simple solution to this problem – he decided that one of the boys who had stayed in the classroom for lunch had taken the leather, and he announced that until that boy returned it, he would punish all those boys every quarter of an hour. (If only we had a few judges like that in this country, crime would soon be eliminated − all the criminals, actual or potential, would be flogged to death.) He dished out the first dose with his broken window-pole, then told us to sit down while he went on with his enthusiastic teaching; as the clock ticked on towards the next quarter, I − and my lunch-time companions − felt something of the sentiment Dr Johnson had in mind when he said to Boswell: 'Depend upon it, Sir, when a man knows he is to be hanged in a fortnight, it concentrates his mind wonderfully.' The minute hand had only a few ticks to travel when a fellow sitting in the centre of the class 'found' the leather on the floor.

For lessons in geometry, we were often ordered out of our desks and gathered in a huddle between the front bench and the blackboard. After one such lesson, when we returned to our seats, Bosh was leaning his blue stick on the front bench with his hands clasped on it and his chin on his hands when he noticed that there was an inkwell missing from the bench; further investigation revealed that all four inkwells were gone. A general threat of blue murder stimulated a frantic search under benches, with no result − until one unlucky boy found an inkwell in his pocket! Three more were found in pockets − and why was I selected by the Fates to be among the victims of this prank by some blaguards who had been leaning their backsides against that front bench and, instead of con-centrating on the geometrical demonstration on the black-board, had deposited the inkwells from the front bench, with mathematical precision, in the pockets that happened to be nearest to them. Any ordinary teacher would deduce (QED) that even desperate characters like young Limerick Catholics would not form a plot to steal four inkwells half-full of ink; but Bosh Murray was no ordinary teacher; his mind was still so full of Euclidean logic that he put two and two together and got four − the four of us, who were forthwith accused of stealing and got six of the leather each.

An incident which hurt me more than any slaps did not involve me at all, but a big lad from our neighbourhood. He and his brothers, well-built, but taciturn and lethargic by nature, were good friends of ours. He was being interrogated by Bosh Murray one day; they were standing literally face to face since he was as tall as his inquisitor, and when his answers were not forthcoming, Bosh slapped him across the face four times, left, right, left, right, and then used the leather on his hands. He could have knocked his tormentor down with one blow but he just stood there, his head jerking from side to side. Then the tears he could not hold back began to flow, tears not of pain but of humiliation. He never came to school again.

The lesson I had learned from a sacerdotal slap in the face and a sacerdotal shilling in the sacristy of St Mary's Convent, 'Don't tar them all with the same brush,' was being reinforced by the contrast between the Christian Brothers I had known in Quay Lane and the two under whose draconian tutelage I now found myself. Categories and groups are made up of individuals, and whether it be priests or plumbers, politicians or businessmen, beggars or popes, it is illogical to evaluate any human being by a generalisation based on the good or bad behaviour of someone else in the same category. And in spite of their use of such severe corporal punishment, religious teachers like the two men I suffered under were dedicated and hard-working, labouring day in, day out, year after year, not for any personal reward or emolument but for the spiritual and material benefit of the youth of Ireland. 'The evil that men do lives after them; the good is oft interred with their bones,' said Shakespeare. And it is grossly unjust, although it is often done, to denigrate what is now perceived to be the negative aspect in their methods and to overlook the self-sacrificing lives of all those religious teachers, nuns and brothers, who were the educators of the vast majority of the children of this country for nearly two hundred years. Who in Limerick now knows – or cares? – that when the first three Christian Brothers came to the city in 1816 their pupils were so poor and ragged that, in addition to teaching them, the brothers begged from door to door for clothes for the worst off among them. Later they began to make a weekly collection on payday from the men coming out of the factories, mills and docks. My Granda Flynn told us that his father used to see the Brother standing at the dock gate.

My brothers had added a rider to their warning that I should clear out of the secondary school as soon as possible: whatever else you do, they said, don't let them put you in the scholarship class; if they do, for a few months before the exam at Easter you'll have to stay back for an hour after school, and for the last month or so he brings them back to the school for two hours every evening. From my first day with Miss Mack (she who tumbled over the haystack) I had always hated school and loved learning (a love that is natural in every human being and one that had been developed in me, without forcing, before I ever went to school). I was not a month in the secondary school before I hated learning as well as school. Psychologists will tell me correctly that what I really hated was the strap and the stick and the shouting. When slapping us, Bosh would sometimes shout, 'Good luck to you, boy!' meaning, of course, the opposite, which is what we wished him. At other times his wrinkled face contorted even more into what he thought was a smile and he wagged his square curly head and said, 'This hurts me more than it hurts you.'

I began to consider the possibility of mooching but as I was still not even twelve years old, the spectre of Guard White and Glin Industrial School kept my mooching to days when, for example, there was a plainchant festival for schools, with Mass in the morning and competitions in the afternoon. I did my plainchanting up in the Clare Hills like the ancient druids, happy in the knowledge that there was no roll-call that day. I suffered a few moments of worry when Bosh prescribed the plainchant festival as the topic for the weekend composition in English. (It was his custom to ruin every such event by making us write an essay about it.) But I gathered sufficient information from trusted pals to write an essay, upon which Bosh inscribed in red pencil the one word: *Excellent*. By degrees, I lost all interest in school work – hence my failure with Portia's eulogy on mercy – and instead of doing the prescribed sums and Latin and anything else that could safely be cogged, I came to school early enough to benefit from the honest efforts of some of my pals, always, of course, with the precaution of not copying as faithfully as if I were Colmcille making his ill-fated copy of Finnian's Psalter.

The day came when Bosh announced that he had the application forms for the Corporation scholarship, that he was now about to give one each to the boys who were under the age limit, and that the forms were to be filled in and signed by a parent and returned before the closing date. Having no wish to die at such a tender age, I could not stand up and say, 'Excuse me, Brother Murray, but I don't want one because me brothers said . . . ' I put the big form in my bag and began to brood. I was still brooding on the way home from school. And whatever about Portia on mercy, I was well enough acquainted with Launcelot Gobbo's self-analysis when the devil told him to run away from his master, Shylock, and his conscience told him it was his duty to stay, to realise that I was in much the same position.

Having parted company with my pals, I was making my way alone past King John's Castle, with a nostalgic glance towards our old home, when one of the Granny Connolly's proverbs came into my mind, whispered, not by that good and honest woman, but by Gobbo's fiend, who said: 'What they don't know won't trouble them.' Instead of crossing Thomond Bridge, I went down the slip near the castle tower, took out my many-paged scholarship form, tore it, page by page, into very small pieces, and sent that monochrome confetti, white as the lilies of innocence, floating away on the waters of the Shannon River. A few inquisitive seagulls swooped to have a pick but they were of a mind with me and had no interest in forms for the Corporation scholarship. I then, as the old novelists used to say, resumed my journey, arrived home safe and sound, and told my mother that school had been just like any other day.

The days and the weeks passed; some forms were returned as if they were boomerangs thrown by Bosh, others came in by degrees; finally, only a few were outstanding; fierce threats brought all but one back, signed, sealed, delivered. To all queries, threats, and other inquisitorial ploys, even when they were accompanied with innuendo concerning my negligent and uninterested parents, my innocent face was my protection as I stuck to my story: 'My father didn't sign it yet, Brother.' My later gleanings in Moral Theology – and I do mean gleanings, more meagre than the pickings of Ruth in the cornfield of Boaz – tell me that I was not telling my teacher a lie; some scholars (as the Granny used to say about some 'head' of knowledge: 'He never went to school, but he met the scholars') would find me guilty of prevarication, while others would classify my statement as mental reservation, permissible, even commendable, in some situations. Myself, looking at the glaring and menacing wrinkled face of Bosh Murray, I considered it just a cast iron excuse.

And so, the Earth turned on its axis with delightful regularity until the closing date arrived. I heroically endured the terrible things Bosh said to me about myself, and to me about my parents – 'especially your father, he must have very little interest in your education, I don't know why he bothered to send you here taking up a place; you might be better off in the Tech.' (The Tech was the Vocational School, to which Bosh advised unsatisfactory pupils to go when he expelled them.) That day I almost danced my way down by the castle and across Thomond Bridge. I was still, of course, in the A class, but not now listed among *les misérables* doomed to have all those extra hours of school and learning imposed on them. I even began to take an interest – not too much, just a little now and then – in learning. And I put up philosophically with the fact that from now on I would be regarded by Bosh and Bánaí as the no-good offspring of no-good parents. They might even demote me to the B class. If things went on like this, I should be able to leave school altogether when I got to fourteen – even earlier. Guard White had enough on his hands without bothering to pursue messenger boys if they were over thirteen.

32

SHOULDER TO THE WHEEL

Even the greatest criminals sometimes make mistakes and that vitiating error usually consists in not noticing something that was under their noses all the time when they were planning the 'perfect' crime. That was a common factor in the detective stories I had read in so many comics, and it should have made me think more carefully before I offered my pagan sacrifice of a shredded scholarship form to the ghost of the Bishop's Lady and the god of the Shannon. If I had paid more attention to Sister Felicitas when she was telling us about that snake-in-the-grass who assured Adam and Eve they could be like gods if only they would disobey God, I might have realised that Launcelot Gobbo's demon, who gave me the brilliant solution to my problem and assured me that I would never be found out, has been called many things, and one of them is Father of Lies.

As with those criminals in the stories, what I overlooked was also a simple and obvious fact. I knew that neither Brother Murray nor Brother White away 'up the town' in Sexton Street had ever met my parents. But they happened to be living in the same residence, just across the yard of the secondary school, with all the other Brothers, including Brother O'Callaghan and Brother O'Reilly, both of whom knew my parents very well because I was the fourth boy in the family to pass through their school in our parish. Later, too late, when my tears were dried at last and I was chained to the galley oar, my fertile imagination often conjured up the little drama that was enacted in the Brothers' residence one evening when Bosh happened to be in casual conversation with one of our Quay Lane mentors. I could almost hear what Bosh was saying about 'that boy, Flynn, you sent up from St Mary's – and all the fine things you said about him! Do you know what his father did – or I should say, did not do?'

The sequence of events after that conversation proceeded like the steps in the proof of a Euclidean theorem. My mother got a note from Brother O'Callaghan, asking her to call on him. He asked her to ask my father to call to see Brother Murray. I came home from school one day to find my mother's face in the accusative case. 'Come here to me you!' (No *a stór* today!). 'Are *you* in trouble in school?' Open the eyes wide and say the most stupid thing you can say: 'Me! How could I be in trouble?'

'All right, wait till your father comes home tonight. You're goin' to meet your Waterloo!' And still, she fed me as if I was the Prodigal Son home from his spendthrift travels. That only made me feel worse. I knew from some of my pals what would happen to *them* if they were in my blaguard's boots.

Even when I confessed to them that night, there was no ranting and raving, no kicks or thumps or threats. They didn't even call me a liar or a blaguard. They asked me one question: 'Why?' And they listened to my reasons. Then my father told me quietly what Brother Murray had told him, and if ever you saw a film about the old times where the judge puts on the black cap and says: 'You are to be taken from hence to a place of execution and there you will be hanged, drawn and quartered – and may the Lord have mercy on your soul!' you will know how I felt. I could still point out the spot on the kitchen floor where I was standing in front of my patient parents when my father said: 'Brother Murray looked up your age,' – I was still some months under twelve – 'and he says you'll be young enough to do the scholarship next year; so, he's going to give you another chance.' (Later, I realised that this contretemps – nice word – was an indirect result of Sister Felicitas, with the best of intentions, having caused me to skip second class when I went up to the primary school.)

It was at that point in the proceedings that I began to cry. I told them that Bosh Murray and Bánaí White were two savages, not at all like our teachers in Quay Lane. I even told them – something none of us would dream of doing in normal circumstances – about the frequent slaps, justified and otherwise, including all I had got at the beginning of the year because I did not have the books. But when I ran out of steam and tears, my father pointed out to me something that was obvious and inevitable – I had no option but to stay on in school, being still under twelve years of age, let alone fourteen! So, I might as well be in with the best as the worst, and if I got the scholarship I might find that the Brothers would be nicer to me after that. My mother's line was what you would expect from the daughter of old Granny Connolly: 'You'll have to put your shoulder to the wheel now and don't be makin' a holy show of your father and myself and the whole family. God gave you the brains and you have to use them or you'll have to answer for it. And Rome wasn't built in a day.' I don't know what that architectural phenomenon had to do with our lives but the Granny and everybody else seemed to be very fond of telling us about it. Our ancestors had an indigenous version that would have suited better, with King John's Castle towering over us from the day we were born: *I ndiaidh a chéile a thógtar na caisleáin* ('It's by degrees that the castles are built').

My final ploy, and plea, was that after what I had done, Bosh Murray would cut me into giblets if I went back to school the next day or any day. My mother countered that by saying that now that he had met my father and discussed the whole business, he would not lay a finger on me (I was not worried about the Bosh finger but about that broken window-pole and that heavy leather strap). And to make sure that I was not kicked around, she said, she would bring me to school herself the next morning and have a chat with himself. My brothers and sisters were sympathetic when they heard the story but they had their own troubles in life. That night I lay awake when my brothers in the big bed with me (three of us, heads and toes) were in dreamland. I was thinking about David Copperfield and how he ran away from his cruel stepfather and eventually got to his fussy but loving aunt, Betsey Trotwood, and the eccentric Mr Dick. The aunt used to go into a fit if she saw donkeys on the grassy patch in front of her house, and shout for the maid – 'Janet! Donkeys!' – and then charge out to wallop the donkeys and the boys riding them. It was those donkeys that put me thinking. I wouldn't dream of stealing our pet donkey from poor old Mrs Weldon and her daughter inside in Old Church Street but if only the Corporation hadn't built those houses in the Island Field, where we used to ride the donkeys in summer – I could see the lights of the houses across the river from our new house – I could steal out (with a bag full of bread) and – and – where the hell would I go, even if I could steal a donkey? And when they caught me, as they inevitably would – I knew now that crime does not pay – it would be off to the Industrial School in Glin until I was sixteen, learning a trade and being walloped even worse by the special Brothers who were probably put working in Glin because they were even more savage than you-know-who.

I woke up next morning resigned to my fate like Robert Emmet and Kevin Barry and all the rest of them. 'What can't be cured must be endured,' was in some old song. And one thing my mother said during the trial scene the night before was beginning to twist a knife in me – that I had let them down, disgraced them, let the Brothers in Sexton Street think they were negligent parents who didn't give a damn what happened to their children. I was too troubled in my mind yet to tell them how sorry I was for that part of my antics; but I made up my mind while trying to swallow my porridge that I would suffer the worst those twin monsters, Bosh and Bánaí, could inflict on me during the rest of this year and the extra year I would have to spend in the scholarship class. I would study so hard that some day, when/if my name was in the *Limerick Leader* for winning one of the six scholarships, the Granny Connolly might be thumping me on the shoulder and saying, 'Consplawkus to you, *a stór*! You're a chip off the oul' block! *Sinn Féin amháin!*'

My mother decided it would be better if we arrived at the school after the mob had gone in; so, we set out from our new house by the river, down to the Treaty Stone, in across Thomond Bridge to the castle – I gave a guilty look at that slipway where I had gone down the steps, coaxed by that supreme artist in deceit, who whispered: *What they don't know won't trouble them* – past our old street, along Nicholas Street and Mary Street to Baal's Bridge; up the Irishtown and past the bandroom of the Sarsfield Band in John Street (if it sounds like the *Via Dolorosa*, you didn't expect it to sound like the 'Campdown Races', did you?); in by the waste ground where the tenements used to be whose occupants were now in the new houses in the Island Field, into Gerald Griffin Street, past the Dispensary and Griffin's Undertakers (even if I felt like a walking corpse, I didn't feel like running in now and asking had they any *empty boxes*); then up by the stinking tanyard, where we sometimes tried to sneak in, if the men had their backs turned, to dip our hands in the pits and harden them for the slaps in school; into Sexton Street and to the door of the classroom of First Year A and B, where we stood for a moment listening to 'noises within'.

My mother knocked at the door, a boy came out, she told him her business, he went in, Bosh came out, grim-faced, and closed the door behind him.

'Good morning, Brother Murray, I'm Mrs O'Flynn and this is – '

That's as far as she got.

'Thank you, Mrs O'Flynn,' said he, and to me, with a finger pointing like a gun, 'In!'

My mother was gawking at him with her mouth still open and I was not feeling at all like poor brave Kevin Barry – she used to sigh and have tears in her eyes when she sang:

Proudly standing to attention, as he bade his last
　　　farewell
To his broken-hearted mother, whose sad grief no
　　　one can tell.

I went in with my tail between my legs, Bosh following on my heels; he closed the door behind us, pointed to my place, went up to his own place at the top of the class and resumed his day's work for God and Ireland (and don't think I say that in any way except with all due respect). Maybe, like St Alphonsus, he had made a vow never to waste time; he certainly wasted none with my poor mother.

That night at home she recounted all the *exploits* to my father. She was still in a state of mild confusion but, fair dues to her, she concluded her account by saying, 'God forgive me, but he looked like the divil himself! And when he wagged his finger like this at poor Christy the way you would at a dog – ' (here I put on my poor little doggy face, lapping it up) 'and ordered him into the room, I declare to God I felt like goin' in after him and takin' him back home with me!' *O mother dear, why didn't you!*

And to give the devil his due: after the door closed behind us that morning, and in spite of all my father's promises and reassurances, I thought Bosh would order me up before the class, read the riot act, telling the whole class of my terrible crimes (dodging out of scholarship class, destruction of form, defamation of parents, etc.) and then belt hell out of me with the leather. The man didn't say a word to me about my misdeeds, not a word, then or ever after, only the usual 'Bosh, boy, bosh!' when I got the statutory wallops (I got a few the next day in the science lab, along with some other unscientific specimens, our crime being that the Bunsen burners had caused the water in the little white dishes to evaporate and then cracked the dishes). When I began to breathe easy after a few days, realising that he wasn't going to say anything about my crimes, I thought of the rhyme we had learned at the Confraternity one night from a gentle delicate sort of a priest who was our Director for a while (Father Gorey was probably gone off to give a mission somewhere): 'There's so much good in the worst of us and so much bad in the best of us, that it little becometh any of us to talk about the rest of us.' And, an even greater puzzle, I began to think that maybe I would yet find some good points in that red-faced roundhead rawmouth, Bánaí White, who was day by day causing me to hate the Irish language and everything connected with it.

There was one thing more to be done to make restitution, as the Catechism said we must do if there were evil effects of our sin that we could do something to remedy. I knew that all the class still thought they knew why I had not brought back my form. To clear my parents' name and let the world know that they were good and decent people, I told my pals the true story, knowing that they would spread it round. At first they thought what I had cooked up to get out of the 'schol' class was brilliant, but when I told them the consequences, that I had to finish out the year with them, and then say goodbye as they went into second year to start the course for the Intermediate Certificate while I, a marked man, stayed back in first year with a whole new crowd coming in from the primary schools, they agreed with me that maybe it hadn't been such a good idea after all.

While Fate, using the combination of good parents and dedicated teachers, thus decreed that a young lad in Limerick should be pushed still more firmly into the Murder Machine, what was happening in our family? And what was happening in the big, bad world outside of our house? When we became 'run-in' Soda Cakes by moving from Old Church Street out to Thomondgate, the splendour of the new house, all to ourselves, with electricity, hot and cold water in the kitchen, a bathroom and gardens, made it seem as though, if the development in the Island Field had signified 'Paradise Lost' for us, this new life was to be 'Paradise Regained'. Our old next-door neighbours, the Nealons, were only a few doors away from us and our new neighbours on both sides, the O'Hallorans and the Mulcahys, were the kind of decent and civilised people anyone would choose as neighbours if given the choice. My mother's sister, Cissie Connolly, and her husband Joe O'Connor, whose Republican record – as in the case of my mother's brother, Joe Connolly – had limited his hope of employment after the civil war, had returned from New York some years earlier with their small family. Now they too had been fortunate enough to get one of the new houses, not near us but far up on the inland line. Cissie's husband was a baker, and he had come back to a job in the bakery in Sarsfield Street, owned by the famous Republican family, the Dalys.

We soon got to know all the families along our riverside line, much the same kind of people as we had lived with in Old Church Street, and we made plenty of new friends. At first there was very little traffic along our road, so that we could play as freely as we used to before the 'invasion'. The only hazard was the river itself; the wall was only waist-high, and in spite of our firm resolve to 'keep it on the ground', a vigorous swipe or kick often sent the ball over the wall and into the river. If the tide happened to be on a strong ebb, it was goodbye ball! But when the tide was filling or full, we often succeeded in retrieving the ball by an ingenious two-stage method: firstly, we threw stones outside the floating ball to drift it in near the wall, then, with the operator standing precariously on the curved top of the wall, a bucket weighted with a few stones was let down on a string and sunk gently under the ball, just enough to let it float into the bucket; up she comes, and on with the game – until the next eejit kicks or hits the ball too hard!

A further excellent advantage of playing games on the road beside the river was that, when the tide was coming or full, before the game began we fixed up handlines baited with worms on three or four hooks, and when my mother called us in for our tea we often had the finest of eels to give her for the meal. Fried on the pan or boiled in milk, they were on the same level of succulence as those delicious crubeens we used to buy from Nana Ledane in the New Walk. At low tide we had a different method for catching eels, which we called 'forking': we climbed down the wall to the river's edge armed with ordinary kitchen forks. The eels sometimes stayed in the water and mud under stones when the tide ebbed; we lifted a stone and any eel under it was jabbed with the fork. These were usually much smaller than the ones caught on the handlines, sometimes so small that we didn't even try to jab them, just let them slither away to the river. Because an eel is a fast and wriggly mover, even when we jabbed at a sizeable one we sometimes missed him and jabbed a stone instead. This, of course, did nothing to improve the symmetry of my mother's forks, and in spite of her delight when we brought in a good catch for supper, and in spite of our best efforts to straighten bent prongs with another stone, sometimes when she was laying the table she would examine a fork and moan a ritual complaint, 'Oh, Mother of God! Were ye forkin' eels again? I won't have a fork left in the house with ye!'

In our early days in the new house we were delighted to find a replacement for the Island Field in an area just at the end of Thomondgate, a green expanse that we had often passed by in the old days when strolling out on our street picnics. We hurled and played soccer on that grassy area, and it was there that I learned to cycle, at eleven years of age, on the bicycle of one of our new friends. Like the first time we swam without the support of a bundle of green rushes, the sensation of speeding along on that bike remains one of the greatest thrills of my life. Little did I know that at that very moment, inside in the Town Hall, the planners were plotting to deprive us of that new playground just as they had done with the Island Field. Before very long, hundreds of houses began to sprout like mushrooms in the new Killeely estate, and we were once again confined to the road between our houses and the river.

There was no hope of transposing our old bonefire ceremony to that road; even if the increase of traffic consequent upon the beginning of the new housing estate in Killeely had not happened, the attitudes of people seemed to be changing, and the outbreak of war put an end forever to the old ways. Even when Christmas came, none of my new pals wanted to 'folly the wran from block to block'.

Whatever about paradise lost or the same regained, the situation of our new house was heavenly. From our front bedroom we could see the bend of the Shannon upriver and the chequered pattern of fields and woods on the nearby Clare Hills. From our little side-window in the front bedroom we could see the perspective-diminished white structure of the power station at Ardnacrusha, where our Uncle Joe had earned his fare to America as a muck-shifter. (When the war brought air-raid precautions, we could see the searchlights at the station beaming into the sky in practice for the defence against German bombers.) Only a stone's throw upriver there was a small jetty which was famous in our folklore. It had been built over a period of seven years by Michael Hogan, the Bard of Thomond, when he owned a pub on the New Road, as it is still called, and decided to make a little riverside garden where he could sit and enjoy the idyllic view of the river and hills while he composed his poems. Speaking of the Bard: when we went to live in the new house the old wall along by the river was being repaired. One day when the men were working on the section just across from our house, my mother got into chat with one of them, an old acquaintance, as we came home from shopping in town. And as we went in the door, she said to us, 'Did ye see that man I was talking to? That man is a son of the Bard of Thomond.' We thought it ironic that he should be working at repairing the river wall so near to the point where the Bard had reclaimed a piece of land from the river and built his poetic jetty.

When we looked across the river from our bedroom at night, it was nice to see all the lights of the houses in St Mary's Park, as our old playground was now called. And as if in recompense for the few blaguards who broke our window and ran off with our ball in the old street, when we lay in bed in our new house on a summer's night we could hear, coming across the water from the new estate over there, songs from light opera and from musical films sung by the finest of voices as some fellows made their way home from the cinema or the pub or a dance. One fellow we loved to hear singing 'You Are My Heart's Delight', and some other fellow who fancied himself as Nelson Eddy used to give a powerful rendering of 'The Indian Love Call'. Limerick being the most musical city in Ireland, there were singers of both sexes in every parish in the city who could have graced the professional operatic stage if life had given them the opportunity.

My sisters had bought bicycles and joined a new cycling club in St Munchin's Parish. The elder, Mary, was staid and motherly in her manner but the blonde Lily was vivacious and mad about dancing and singing. She was soon very popular with the lads in the local Treaty-Sarsfields GAA Club and I think she would have married one of them if the plague of tuberculosis had not marked her out for destruction in her early twenties. So that, a few years later, those hurling lads were destined to walk with our family behind her hearse two days before Christmas Day. My brother Joe, whose juvenile efforts in verse had prompted me to emulate him, was the first to be singled out by the gods to die young; he was already in and out of St John's Hospital for brief periods, where the doctors came up with various explanations for his increasing tiredness and lethargy, but none seemed to know anything at that stage about the enemy within that was going to rot away the lungs in what had been his vigorous young body. When the summer came he was unable to go to work at all, and my brother Dick, who had been employed as messenger boy by the firm, was promoted to Joe's job behind the counter. I got a summer job as messenger boy, an experience which was to be a further step in my real education and cause me to weigh more maturely the pros and cons of going back to school for my second year in the first year scholarship class.

When it became obvious that the war was going to drag on and get worse, and that food and fuel would be rationed, my father decided that he would store a whole ton of coal in the stables in Watergate for our own use. Joe was in hospital again and we heard Dad saying to mother that, with the winter coming on, he wanted to be sure Joe would have a fire to sit in to. (We wondered afterwards if the doctors had told him that Joe would not recover.) He bought the ton of coal as usual in Sutton's yard and put it into the covered shed in the stables where the old jaunting-car was mouldering away. He arranged with the boys who were working that on their weekly half-holiday, he and they would dig up the cobbled floor of the shed, bury the coal and cover it over again. He agreed that I could come in to help on my way home from school in Sexton Street. We had often helped him before to clean out the stables, a job that gave us more education and an insight into the less glamorous side of the relationship between man and horse (Dad used to sell the manure to a farmer in Park). We never got to bury that ton of coal, because the next morning after he had put it into the shed, Dad found the double wooden gates of the stable yard hanging open, and the twenty bags of coal had vanished.

I can only remember seeing my father crying twice, apart from when we buried Joe and Lily, and both occasions were connected with coal. That night at home, when he was talking to my mother about the robbery, Joe was sitting there with the rest of us, home that day from another session in St John's, and I think it was the sight of his thin pale face that caused Dad to break down. The supplies of coal soon petered out, and my father eventually sold his horse to a farmer, and that was the end of the black-faced father who used to puzzle me in my baby days. After the war, he concentrated on the saxophone and he was a very happy man when he became a member of a small new danceband called The Sylvians, organised by Earl Connolly (same clan, but no relation of my mother or the Granny Connolly) who was advertising manager with the *Limerick Leader* and a talented performer on the drums. The other members of the band were Gretta Tucker, piano, Marie O'Farrell, vocals, Sammy Prendergast, trumpet, and Christy Fallahee, piano accordion.

The other time my father had cried was when we were still living in the old house near the castle. He came home late one very bad winter's night and he was so upset he could hardly eat the dinner Mam had kept hot for him. We all listened to his story while she tried to get him to change his wet and dirty clothes. He had been told by one of the men at Sutton's coal-yard that a mutual friend of theirs, a man who used to play with them in the Sarsfield Band, was very ill. This man lived in a tenement near Arthur's Quay and Dad decided to make a detour on his way home, after stabling the horse in Watergate, in order to see his old friend. When he got there, he found the poor man lying on a heap of dirty straw – 'I wouldn't put it under the horse,' Da said – in a corner of the one-room apartment in the tenement, coughing his heart out. The man's wife and children were sitting shivering around a fireplace where a few bits of wet wood were filling the room with smoke. There wasn't a stick of furniture in the room apart from an old table. The wife told our Dad that her husband hadn't been able to work for months and that the doctor said he hadn't long to live. They had no food and no fuel – whatever they had been given by the St Vincent de Paul men for the week was gone. Dad went back to the stables in Watergate, tackled up the horse again, and brought two bags of coal to the family; he also gave her a few shillings and probably was short of his Woodbines the next day. 'If you saw him lying there . . . !' he said, and that was when he started to cry. And of course my mother joined in.

When the priest asked us all at the Confraternity to play our part in defending Ireland by volunteering as bicycle couriers in the ARP (Air-Raid Precautions), my brother Dick and I went on the night appointed to the small park at the old Custom House where the Abbey River rejoins the Shannon. We thought we were going to be given a free bicycle but of course we were also willing to do our bit for Ireland against all comers, Germans, British, Yanks or Russians. A small man who seemed to think he was Napoleon lined up the crowd of boys who had come along and gave us a big talk about the war, the likelihood that the Germans would bomb our cities – he seemed to have a poor opinion of the German bomb-aimers, saying that some of the bombs intended for the power house up at Ardnacrusha were likely to fall on Limerick – and that the air-raid wardens would need messengers to cycle here, there and everywhere during the air-raids. Then he said that unless you had a bicycle of your own, you could go home. (Some fellow must have asked him about the free bikes.) He said the government would have to spend money on air-raid shelters and guns, and there would be no money for free bikes for the ARP boy couriers. Sadly for the efficiency of Limerick's ARP services, that announcement at once diminished the force of boy couriers by more than half. My brother Dick had bought a secondhand bike, so he was all right; but he said that when I started work as a messenger boy in the shop in the summer, as had been arranged, I could use the shop bike. It was not the big heavy bike used in grocery shops and other places; it was really only an ordinary bike with a small iron grill, like a tray, fixed in front of the handlebars, and leather straps to tie on the parcels of clothes and shoes that had to be delivered to customers. So, not for the first time, or the last, I thanked God for providing me with big brothers before he decided to put me on this planet. Napoleon ordered us to go over to where another man was sitting at a table, ready to take our names and allocate us to specific areas of the city. And when my turn came to sign on, ready to brave the bombs and die for Ireland if necessary, the man at the table asked me my age. He told me I was both too young and too small – and to come back next year! (That man was no optimist.) On the way home, Dick tried to console me, saying that I was lucky in a way, because when he and the other lads would be cycling around with urgent messages and the bombs falling all around them, I'd be safe in the air-raid shelter with all the women and children. Mind you, the more I thought about it that night in bed, especially when we looked out the little side-window and saw the yellow beams of the searchlights above at Ardnacrusha, the more I began to agree with my sensible and protective brother.

The war also brought a great recruitment drive and Radio Éireann began a new Sunday night programme called *Barrack Variety* for the army, a concert staged in the barracks around the country. When Limerick's turn came, our school choir, organised and drilled by Bosh Murray, a sergeant-major more draconian than any in the Irish army, gave a fine performance, ranging from patriotic songs like 'God Save Ireland' to a choral version of Strauss's 'Beautiful Blue Danube'. Early in the year he had announced that we were going to do an opera, and Mr Brae began to teach us the 'Anvil Chorus' and 'Home to Our Mountains' from *Il Trovatore*. When he heard this, my father's considered opinion was that Verdi's opera would be far too difficult for schoolboys. And Mr Scallan must have so advised Bosh, who wouldn't know the *Tantum Ergo* from 'Show Me the Way to Go Home' – the man hadn't a note in his head – because soon we were told that the chosen opera was Balfe's *The Bohemian Girl*. Among the music my father had at home there was a band selection of airs from that opera, and both my parents knew it inside out from the days when they used to see the touring opera companies in the old Theatre Royal in Henry Street.

I had often played the selection on the flute and I could sing several of the arias. And because I had always been given the leading role in the school plays in the primary and infant schools, I hoped – against hope, surely – that Bosh might give me a role as one of the principals in *The Bohemian Girl*. I even practised some of the songs at home, expecting that he would get Mr Scallan or Mr Brae to test us all. One day he announced that a double list of principals had been selected (if there had been tests, they must have been held at midnight). Like our Brother O'Callaghan in Quay Lane with those famous raffle tickets that each bore a photo of the school choir, Bosh had a very good sense of business. Having two sets of principals, not just as leads and understudies, but singing on alternate nights, would ensure that there would now be two sets of parents, friends and many relations all over Limerick eager and willing to buy lots of tickets for the opera. And he carried this profit-making duplication even to the several chorus groups, so that costumes were swapped for alternate nights, with the uncostumed still obliged to sing while hidden in the wings.

It may have been through chagrin and sour grapes but, eschewing false modesty, I was convinced that I had a better voice than some at least of the chosen ones, and I considered that his allocation of the principal roles, two sets of them, proved what my brothers and their pals used to tell us – that the pupils from Sexton Street, many of whom were more or less better off than those from the three outlying schools, were more favoured by the Brothers in the secondary school; none of the principal roles went to a pupil from those parish schools, and the role I fancied went to the son of a publican. To add insult to injury, even when he put the common mob into groups as the back-up chorus – courtiers, soldiers, gipsy men and gipsy girls – he put me among the gipsy girls, and then announced that he was ordering beautiful costumes from Ging's in Dublin for the principals and the courtiers and the gipsy men, but the gipsy girls could easily get colourful clothes from their sisters and thus spare him some expense. I don't know how his close dark curly hair didn't burn off his square head with all the silent curses I heaped on him then and for long after. My machinist sister Mary, who was soon to leave for the profitable war-work in England, made a skirt and blouse for me. (If I had appeared on stage in clothes belonging to either of my grown-up sisters, I would have been taken for a comic intrusion by the audience.) Herself and Lily provided me with a headscarf and earrings. Bosh certainly took me down a peg – gave me a great 'suck-in', in our parlance – but after a while the music of Balfe soothed my spirit enough to have me dancing around the kitchen floor banging a tambourine, while my mother joined with me in singing, '*Oh, a gipsy's life is free-ee-ee, and full of spirit-stirring glee-ee-ee . . .*'

Mr Scallan took over the job of teaching the music for the opera. If it had been left to the combined efforts of the refined old Mr Brae and the stick-wielding Bosh, the opera would never have got to the stage. When it did, for a week in St Michael's Temperance Hall, it was a resounding success, with the bishop making a speech at the first night and being honoured with a spirited rendering of another of those ludicrous Victorian chants (if Father Faber did this one too, he has a lot to answer for) entitled 'God Bless the Pope'. (The opening line, '*Full in the panting heart of Rome,*' gives a taste of the rest.) It was house full every night, of course, as a result of the sales tactics of the Bosh-man himself. During the performance each night, he stood in the wings, switching from side to side backstage, and ensured with fist in the back and knuckles on the head that even when we were not on stage we were adding volume to the members of the chorus who were.

Later we took the opera down to the Good Shepherd Convent for the nuns and the girls. We dressed in the big laundry under long lines of drying sheets and other items hanging above us, but little did we know, as people do now, the slavery those unfortunate girls had to endure because of the social injustice that left the care of orphans and unmarried mothers to nuns who were themselves overworked and unassisted by any professional staff. To my mind an injustice of another kind is being perpetrated nowadays by commentators who condemn those dedicated nuns as if only they, and not also the politicians and the hierarchy, were responsible for that unChristian system. I can only hope that our performance of *The Bohemian Girl* gave those poor girls and their overseers a little respite from their common imprisonment and hard labour, and that they enjoyed the show as much as we enjoyed the tea and buns they gave us afterwards. Back at school the following week, the Man himself, elated with the success of his initial venture, announced that the opera for next year would be Wallace's *Maritana*.

I finished out that year as a non-scholarship contender in the scholarship class, but knowing even more now about the extra lessons and study that would be my lot in the coming year. In between those two years of grinding in the Bosh Murray version of the Murder Machine, the summer I spent as a messenger boy, delivering parcels of clothes and footwear to addresses all over the city, was, as I have said, a further instalment in my real education. The firm, Fulham and Murphy, was, as the name implies, a partnership, owning three shops: two on opposite sides near the top of William Street – one of them sold only clothes, the other only footwear – and a third, which sold both clothes and footwear, around the corner in Wickham Street. I was based in the clothes shop in William Street, the manager of which, Mr Mullins, had lived near the Sarsfield Bandroom in John Street and so knew my father and Uncle Danny well; he was now also a neighbour of ours in O'Dwyer Villas, on the inland side of the estate. He was a philosophic and sagacious man, while his silver-haired assistant, Mr Malone, was a joker and fond of his pint. Both of them were very kind to me all through my brief career as a messenger boy. When business was slack I used to sit in the far dark corner of the shop, reading the paper they gave me, and also enjoying their comments on the customers, and their discussions about current affairs, especially the war. I remember one day when I was reading the latest news on the war and I heard Mr Mullins say: 'Hitler's goose is cooked now.' Although it was still early in the war, I had such respect for Mr Mullins that

I believed the Germans might as well give in that day; in the event, he was proved a prophet.

For the tea-break at eleven in the morning, they used to take turns sending me across the street to buy a few buns at a bakery shop that, like Daly's Bakery in Sarsfield Street, had the name in Irish over the front: *Éamonn de hÓir*. And that was not the only connection between those two premises. Eamonn T. Dore was married to one of the six sisters of Commandant Ned Daly, executed in Kilmainham Jail on 4 May 1916 (another sister was married to Tom Clarke), and he had fought beside his brother-in-law in the Four Courts garrison during the Rising. Both my father and Mr Mullins had impressed on me the fact that this quiet, pleasant man who was giving me a few buns and taking the money from my hand was just as much a patriotic Irish hero as Pádraig Pearse, James Connolly and our own Ned Daly, and anyone else who had died in the cause of Irish freedom from England down through the centuries.

My duties included sweeping the two shops in William Street every morning, washing the rubber mats, the windows and shopfronts, and the pavements in front of the shops. My brother Dick was now assistant in the Wickham Street shop, where one of the partners, Mr Murphy, acted as manager, but he also did those morning chores for that establishment. My wages were fixed at ten shillings a week – and 'my chances', as my mother used to say about any job where tips might add to the official salary. It was part of my education in life to learn to divide the human race into two kinds: not the lenders and borrowers of Lamb's essay, *The Two Races of Men*, but those who tip and those who don't. In the latter hateful category, I gave pride of place to the wives of the two partners who owned the three shops; at the Fulham house in Ballinacurra and at the Murphy house near the City Home, all I ever got was a curt *thank you* and the closed door. An old lady in a big house off the Ennis Road was my clear leader in the tipping category; even when I

brought parcels 'on appro' (our trade term for the arrangement whereby customers could have a selection of garments
or shoes delivered on approval, so that they could make a
leisurely choice at home) she looked at me as if I were Oliver
Twist – remember, even the ARP had rejected me as too
small! – and said, 'Ah, you poor child! You must be very
tired pushing that big heavy bicycle around the city!' I sighed
and let the manly shoulders droop and said heroically, 'Ah,
it's all right, ma'am, I don't mind it.'

She was as bad as the nuns for the questions: name, age,
address, how many brothers and sisters? But she always ended
up by getting the little black purse and producing a lovely
shiny sixpence (twenty of which made up my week's wages!).
'Now, my dear, here's a sixpence for you; you're to get yourself
an ice-cream in Mullany's; you're a good little boy and you're
a credit to your parents.' I don't know why she used to get
so much stuff 'on appro' from our small shops which only
sold men's clothes and shoes. Her husband or her sons must
have been shy of shopping and hard to please; or maybe she
was buying stuff for some poor people; anyway, she didn't
seem to like the big stores like Cannocks and Todds, which
was lucky for me.

On the first Friday night when I got paid I nearly broke
my neck cycling home to give my mother my first week's
wage – and 'chances'! The latter amounted to one shilling
and ten pence. (How we remember amounts like that when
every penny was so hard earned!) I knew things were bad
now on account of Joe being sick and the coal business gone,
and I felt also that the trouble and disappointment I had
given my parents in the matter of the scholarship form would
be still heavy on my mother's heart even though she said no
more about it. She gave me back a half-crown! Two shillings
and sixpence! I had never seen such wealth since I made my
collections for First Communion and later Confirmation.
And one of the lessons I learned in those months was 'easy
come, easy go'. I didn't need the advice of that benevolent

old lady to pop into Mullany's in Bedford Row now and again and buy a wafer of their delicious ice cream. And for the first time in my life, I could buy a bar of chocolate if I felt like it. In fact, it was in Mullany's shop that I got one of the lessons that formed part of the education process.

I was buying an ice-cream one day when another customer doing the same thing spoke to me. He was an old schoolmate of mine from Quay Lane who was now apprenticed to his father's trade and also attending night classes at the Vocational School. He was on some message for his father but the two of us adjourned to the nearby grass-covered jetty known as 'the Poor Man's Kilkee' where we sat on a seat and enjoyed our wafers at leisure, watching the swans on the Shannon and having a chat. I nearly fell into the river when he said to me, 'Ah, but you're lucky! You're goin' back to school in September. I wish to God I was back in school. God, wouldn't I learn! I was such a friggin' eejit; all I wanted was to get out of the shaggin' place!' And he went on with more of the same. When we first met, I was about to tell him how much I envied him – free at last and sure of a job in his father's trade. But by the time he was finished telling me his troubles – he even wished he was old enough to go to England and join the RAF – my mind was *rí-rá* and also *trína chéile*; in short, I was perplexed.

The general lesson I was learning day by day was what the biblical 'curse of Adam' means for the human race – at least for that great majority who are not born to wealth. After the novelty of cycling around Limerick wore off – and the rainy days, when I had to put on a heavy cape and a sou'wester rain-hat, made cycling into hard labour – the morning chores and the repetitive deliveries became boring and wearisome. That had the effect of making me think of how my father, a talented musician, had spent year after year of his life, and how my mother worked seven days a week from dawn to well after dusk, and then of all the other good parents in our street, and the decent people everywhere in the city, in factories, shops, mills, docks, who had no choice but to spend most of their lives at repetitive and often very hard and boring labour of one kind or another.

Add to these philosophic musings the fact that I had two bosses, the frenetic Fulham (his face was as wrinkled as that of Bosh Murray, but at least he carried no leather strap or stick) and the smooth but more menacing Murphy, either of whom would suddenly ask me if I had done the windows that morning or why had I been so long on some delivery, not that they ever timed me. (Fulham brought me out one day and, showing me a mark on one of the windows, ordered me to clean them all over again.) My brother Dick had warned me that this was only one of their nasty little ways of letting you know that there are bosses and workers. One day Murphy came into our shop and saw me reading the paper in my little nook. First he berated me and then he turned on Mr Mullins and told him that there must be something he could find for me to do, not have me getting my wages for sitting there reading the paper! Mr Mullins answered him fair enough but, of course, he had his own job to think of, and he couldn't let fly as I could see he would have liked to.

Murphy then took me over to the boot shop across the road, and told Mr Young, the manager, to put me cleaning shoes in the storeroom, which was the old cellar below street level. There were lots of shelves down there full of white cardboard boxes with a pair of shoes in each, and when Mr Young brought me down, having provided me with shoe brushes and a cloth, I discovered that the damp in the cellars caused a green mould to grow on the leather of the shoes. Murphy told me to continue cleaning the shoes, box by box, every day when I had nothing else to do. I spent many an hour in that airless dungeon trying not to inhale the horrible green fog that came off the shoes when I brushed them, trying not to worry about the rats I could hear scurrying around behind the shelves. They were in the other shop too, even in the rooms upstairs where empty boxes and other stuff were stacked and where I could hear them fighting when I was sent up to get some boxes or wrapping paper.

Maybe it was seeing the contrast between employers and workers, even in a small firm, that made me realise even more the differences between the classes in society, between the rich business people in their big houses, the ordinary people in houses like our own and the very poor people in tenements. And from that I got to thinking in a different way about the nuns and the Brothers and the priests; they were people who had given up everything for the love of God so that they could help others. And even though some of them were too fond of belting us with leather or stick, like the man I was going back to at the end of the summer, they all worked very hard, not to get anything for themselves, like the people in business or the politicians, but to help the likes of us to get on in life and to live in a way that would help us to get to heaven when we died.

There were people too like the St Vincent de Paul Society who gave up a lot of their free time to go around to the tenements helping the poorest people, because they had the faith and believed God wanted us to love our neighbour as ourselves. That's the sort of stuff we were hearing, week in, week out, from the priest at the Confraternity and now I was beginning to see it in life. So, cycling around the city, or taking a break down by the river, I began to change my attitudes to a lot of things, even to school. And I made up my mind even more that when I went back to that prison at the end of the summer holidays I would – put my shoulder to the wheel!

These thoughts might have been stimulated also by the developments in our own family circle. Granny Connolly, who used to say so often, 'Well, thanks be to God, we never died o' winter yet!' fell down the narrow steep stairs in her house in Crosby Row and so we had her funeral before we had to kneel around my brother Joe's bed and watch him dying. Then there was trouble in the house in Watergate. For a few years now, my father had not brought us to visit there, because on our last visit his sister, our Aunt Brigid, began to tell us that she knew all the people passing by the door were talking about her, saying she'd never get married, and about the man who wanted to marry her when she was young and so on. My mother told us that Aunt Brigid was going a bit strange. She had been the pet of the family, being the youngest, and she still had boxes of lovely clothes stacked away in a room, all out of fashion now. There had been several young men courting her but she couldn't settle on any of them. Our Uncle Danny, mother said, also had lots of girls crazy about him but he was so taken up with music and the Sarsfield Band that he didn't want to settle down.

The situation got worse when the old sailor, our Granda Flynn, who used to sit at the fire and tell us stories when we were small, now surprised everyone by getting married again. Just as he had impulsively gone away to sea as a young man and left his wife and young family, he now upped and left our Uncle Danny and Aunt Brigid and went off to live in a small house in Ellen Street with some woman from Tipperary. But he wasn't the wild young sailor any more and within a year we were walking behind his hearse to Mount St Lawrence Cemetery. That made Aunt Brigid go even more strange, so much that eventually Uncle Danny also cleared out. (Like my father, he had sold his horse because of the collapse of the coal business.) He married a woman he should have married thirty years earlier and went to live in a room in Mungret Street, where he and my father had been born. Poor Aunt Brigid, with her lovely long hair going very grey now, was left telling her troubles to Robert Emmet and Daniel O'Connell in their posed pictures up on the wall. Mary went off to England with a lot of other girls to make bullets and Lily began to cough *the* cough, thinking it was just a cold from a wetting they got on some outing with the cycling club. My father was idle, except for a very rare call to play at a dance in the city (travelling to far-off towns or villages was at an end because of the petrol problem) and my mother wasn't singing as much these days in the lovely new house with all its amenities as she used to sing over the washing-tub in that cluttered kitchen in the old house.

In the last week of my career as a messenger boy we read in the papers that German bombs fell on a creamery in County Wexford and three girls were killed. That night we looked out the window at the searchlights up there at the power station and we were thinking that maybe the little Napoleon fellow at the ARP meeting wasn't just imagining things when he said bombs might fall on Limerick. On the following Monday, I went back to school, and found myself in the same room but with a whole new crowd. The fellow beside me was a big strong red-haired lad with a gentle voice, Jack South from Henry Street (the ballad-maker would put him into folklore as 'Seán South of Garryowen').

Our Guardian Angels could have told us that nearly twenty years later I would get into trouble with censors official and unofficial because of a poem about his death, along with a young man named Fergal O'Hanlon, in an attack by the IRA on a police barracks in Brookeborough, County Fermanagh. In the school yard on that first day, we were interested only in dragging one another off the flight of steps at the end of the yard when we formed two gangs to play King of the Castle just as I used to play it with my brothers and our pals on the steps of King John's Castle when we lived in Old Church Street.

That was the day my boyhood ended.